"Political correctness has a big mouth, and Nick Adams fills it with a well-deserved knuckle sandwich. . . . Retaking America an unvarnished lo-down from Down Under . . . Adams once again provides a terrific read that tells the Left in plain and simple Aussie where it can stick its tucker bag."

—NATIONAL REVIEW

"A must-read!"

—DICK MORRIS,
bestselling author of *Power Grab*,
former advisor to President Bill Clinton

"Nick Adams—the de Tocqueville traveller of our times—has captured the essence of why America is destined to remain great."

—EDWIN J. FEULNER, PH.D,
founder and former president of the Heritage Foudation

". . . an ode to individuality as well as a great game plan . . ."

—NRA NEWS

"Every times Adams says "God Bless America," we should think to ourselves: "God Bless Australia – for sending us Nick Adams."

—WORLD MAGAZINE

". . . a provocative and impassioned defense of the American idea, and a clarion call to abolish political correctness . . ."

—THE BLAZE

"Adams' conservative insight is invaluable and irresistible."

—BEN SHAPIRO,
Editor-at-Large, Breitbart.com

"Adams is an eloquent voice for conservatism, bringing intelligence and optimism about America's future."

—DARTMOUTH REVIEW

". . . a powerful pep talk for Team USA . . . the kind of bracing, snap-out-of-it, kick-in-the-pants that a great nation needs . . ."

—JACK FOWLER,
publisher of *National Review*

RETAKING AMERICA

NICK

NICK ADAMS

RETAKING AMERICA

CRUSHING POLITICAL CORRECTNESS

A POST HILL PRESS BOOK

ISBN: 978-1-61868-850-7
ISBN (eBook): 978-1-61868-851-4

Cover Design by Martin Kintanar
Interior design and typesetting by Neuwirth & Associates

Post Hill Press
275 Madison Avenue, 14th Floor
New York, NY 10016
http://posthillpress.com

In loving memory of Randy Nunn
who slipped from the surly bonds of Earth to touch the face of God.
Your inspiration, "sic'em" and generosity remain unparalleled.

CONTENTS

SECTION THREE

Tyranny is our foe, whatever trappings or disguise it wears, whatever language it speaks, be it external or internal, we must forever be on our guard, ever mobilized, ever vigilant, always ready to spring at its throat. In all this, we march together. Not only do we march and strive shoulder to shoulder at this moment under the fire of the enemy on the fields of war or in the air, but also in those realms of thought which are consecrated to the rights and the dignity of man.

—SIR WINSTON CHURCHILL

FOREWORD

Nick Adams is a young Australian defending the greatest country that has ever been created. And it isn't his beloved Australia he's defending. It is the United States of America.

Three questions will clarify why *Retaking America* needed to be written.

1. IS AMERICA REALLY THE GREATEST COUNTRY THAT HAS EVER BEEN CREATED?

Yes, it is.

It is great because it created the first large experiment in individual freedom. And it succeeded beyond anyone's wildest dreams. That is why such a large percentage of humanity from every racial, ethnic, religious, and national background yearns to live in America. That is why France presented only America with a Statue of Liberty.

It is great because it has given more people from more backgrounds more liberty, more affluence, and more opportunity to do in life whatever they wanted to do in life than any other country.

It is great because it has spent more treasure and spilled more blood for the liberty of strangers than any other country (though Australia should be honorably mentioned in this regard). America did not fight Nazism to gain an inch of European land, but solely to help Europeans shed the monstrous tyranny of Nazism. America did not fight Communism in Vietnam and Korea out of any colonialist impulse, or to gain any territory, or for raw materials (Korea in particular has none). Almost 100,000 Americans died on the other side of the world in the Korean and Vietnam Wars solely in order to preserve the liberty and independence of South Korea and South Vietnam against the successor to Nazi tyranny—Communist tyranny.

It is great because often alone or nearly alone, America so often stood by Israel when the tiny Jewish state was attacked militarily or politically by those many nations that seek to destroy it.

It is great because it was founded in the belief that the less powerful the government, the more powerful the individual. Therefore America challenged the whole world's belief in big government. And it succeeded.

It is great because it created a uniquely charitable society. Americans give more charity and devote more volunteer time to help others than any other national group of comparable income.

It is great because it showed the world that race and ethnicity mean nothing, that values are what matter.

2. WHY DOES AMERICA NEED DEFENDING?

America is being attacked—from within, no less—by those who wish to dismantle the American value system, what I have come to call the American Trinity. This trinity is composed of the three values that appear on all US coins and bills: "Liberty," "In God We Trust," "e pluribus unum" {"from many, one"). No other country lists those three as its core values.

3. WHO OR WHAT IS THREATENING AMERICA?

The Left seeks to replace those three values. It seeks to replace liberty with equality (material equality), to replace "In God We Trust"—a God-centered religious citizenry—with a godless secular society, and to replace "e pluribus unum" with "multiculturalism."

One of the major tools in undoing the American Revolution is Political Correctness, the focus of this book.

Nick Adams understands the threat that so-called Political Correctness poses to American values. It is, as he repeatedly points out, a war against truth. And to paraphrase the New Testament, "Lies are the root of all evil."

America is in deep trouble, and therefore the promise of producing a truly free, yet decent, society is deep trouble.

But when along comes a 31-year-old foreigner who understands this and has the courage and ability to fight it, at least one American sees rays of hope.

DENNIS PRAGER

AUTHOR'S NOTE

America is killing itself. Our civilization is being betrayed.

There is no polite way of saying it. No sophisticated collection of words can blunt the edge. And frankly, it's the last thing we need. It's the syrupy indulgence of cultural pathologies that got us here.

The worst of those pathologies, as I see it from half a world away, is political correctness—the cringing groupthink that forbids certain plain truths from being spoken or even thought, on pain of leftist disapproval and ostracism.

Nothing is more anti-American, anti-freedom, anti-truth, and anti-reality than political correctness. It is a noose around America's neck, growing tighter each day. From identity politics and secularism to the all-powerful welfare state and the war against national identity, every problem in America today is compounded by this suffocating regime of thought control.

Political correctness, when allowed to flourish, extinguishes confidence, impairs judgment, inculcates victimhood, and entrenches division. It makes a peaceful, cooperative society impossible. It is oppressive, discriminatory, unjust, and dangerous.

Unless plain speaking is allowed, clear thinking is denied. Political correctness parrots messages that are more myth than truth. It is more interested in sustaining a narrative than asserting facts. It dulls the moral sense, blurring good and evil. It is a communal tyranny, not dissimilar to the one America fought a revolution over. Its practitioners are every bit as condescending as the aristocracy America left in Britain.

Political correctness is one of the major reasons why Europe today is lifeless. The cancerous conformity has left it sickly, pale, and limp. Fortunately, America is not Europe; at least, not yet. Its proud, historic traditions of freedom, patriotism, and self-assertion make it Western civilization's last hope.

Thank goodness that beyond the smug commentators who monopolize academia, politics, and the media, the American frontier spirit remains strong. But even here, the loathing of our society by cultural elites is weakening our resistance to barbarity. Our country, my friends, is nonetheless on the wrong path. Admit it to yourself: even here in the home of the brave, Americans are being bullied by the anti-bullying mantra. Many who deplore it are still cowed by it.

Without free speech, creativity is dampened. We have lost so much already. Imagine the books we'll never read and the movies that were never made. Let's not lose any more. Our grudging equivocation with the thought police must be replaced by fearless repudiation of them.

After all, to fear an idea, any idea, is unworthy of a free society. America must stand up for freedom of choice, freedom of speech, plain speaking, and the free marketplace of ideas. These are the safeguards against tyranny. Their retreat is tyranny's advance. We must wrench the pendulum back toward free speech.

Political correctness is to freedom as tuberculosis is to life. The cough of disapproval from "them" when someone voices a moral or spiritual absolute is the death rattle of Western civilization. As Western civilization gasps with the fatal symptoms, America is the one nation that can reverse the prognosis. We have the vaccine: the American idea itself.

The targets of political correctness are many. Men, Christians, whites, and heterosexuals are all firmly in the crosshairs.

But make no mistake: America is at the top of the kill list. If the proponents of political correctness had "Most Wanted Playing Cards," the ace of spades would be America.

There is no clearer evidence of this than the myriad of politicians, teachers, artists, and journalists who deliberately and recklessly make America seem hateful to the young, old and everyone in between.

This is all because America is the major impediment to Leftist success. It is the last great holdout.

Re-assert the individual freedom of self-responsible citizens. Reclaim your confidence as the land of opportunity and open discourse where no one is silenced. Recognize that the unfettered American dream and the regimented politically correct mindset cannot co-exist. Expose its agenda, puncture its pretence, and make war on it. Believe you can win, despite the defeatists who despair you can't.

They snarl, sneer, hiss, spit, and finger wag. Usually, we run. We shouldn't.

It's time to hammer political correctness.

Only America can do it.

NICK ADAMS
"Highfield"
Australia
November 2015

WHY IT'S PERSONAL

I came to America for the American Dream—and to escape political correctness.

But the two are not mutually exclusive. They're one and the same.

While political correctness has gripped America's universities, schools, media, and large corporations, it has not yet reached most everyday Americans. This is why the American Dream remains alive—and why the United States is still the world's leading destination for immigrants.

One of the central themes of this book is that political correctness weakens the health and threatens the existence of the American Dream.

This is not simply because you can find yourself in hot water over something you may say, but because of the broader consequences it has on the cultural mindset.

Politically-correct ideology requires that success is resented. Ambition becomes suspicious. Mediocrity is preferred to excellence. The collective is elevated over the individual.

Unfortunately, even in countries similar to America where a version of the dream was once offered, it no longer exists. It is hidden by the symbols of political correctness: big government, gatekeepers, envy, an aversion to risk, and collectivism. When the focus is on the collective, individual dreams can never fully materialize.

The international perception of Australia and the domestic reality are worlds apart. It may surprise many of you, but Australia is one of the most politically correct countries in the world. It's not the U.K., but it's not far behind.

For as long as I can remember, the bureaucracy has insisted that people dealing with government departments (e.g. universities, hospitals, employment services etc.) be asked if they identify themselves as Aboriginal, or if English was their first language. Not surprisingly, more Australians are choosing to identify themselves as Aboriginal as ever before, as it is advantageous for affirmative action and victim status.

Generally speaking, Australians worship rules, dislike risk, and love structure. They have faith in government, and a reverence for bureaucrats. They are guarded, and there is a discernible lack of optimism in the culture. Given the choice between a leader who conforms to the consensus, and a leader who creates consensus to their own vision and goals, Australians will always choose the former.

In Australia, the control and power of the political and media establishment is far more influential than America's. 'Gatekeepers' exist at every turn in these fields, and if you judge the absence of any substantial objection in the community to their presence, one can only conclude that these establishment 'gatekeepers' enjoy the support of the Australian people.

This is not new.

All of you have probably heard of the Sydney Opera House. It is the international icon of Australia, instantly recognized worldwide. But the story of its construction is not so well-known. The masterpiece was the brainchild of award-winning Danish architect Jørn Utzon. He loved Sydney passionately, with visions of it becoming the international city it became. He worked on the Opera House for nine years, completing the concrete shells of the exterior, easily the most difficult part of the structure. But he was forced to leave the project before its completion, after repeated badgering from government officials over design, fees, materials, and costs. Such was his treatment (creativity stifled, boldness resented) and so underappreciated he felt, he left Australia in 1966, vowing never to return.

He kept his word. Until the day he died in 2008, he never returned, declining several invitations.

It shouldn't surprise Americans that the majority of the famous Australians they are familiar with choose to live in the United States, rather than in their own country.

All this is not to defame Australia.

It is a lucky country. It is a great country. I still love it. I'm proud of Australia's history, particularly its record as a longtime ally of America.

But I know that Australia is not America, and that my country has not achieved what America has achieved. No country in human history has.

How could it? America is much more than a country. It's an ideal, a value system. Put simply, it's the best idea the world has ever had. That's why American greatness and leadership is indispensable to civilization, as we know it.

It's why I have dedicated my life to ensuring America remains the different place it has always been. It's why I have sought to restore American confidence.

It's also why I set up the *Foundation for Liberty and American Greatness* (*FLAG*), a 501(c) (3) organization. It actively promotes American greatness, and boldly fights anti-Americanism. It does its work in America, and around the world. For too long, no one had America's back in the media, in classrooms or in popular culture.

Now *FLAG* does.

I have the same motivation for writing this book—to protect Americans from political correctness—an ideology that is already taking them down the same failed path of every other Western country.

I fervently want Americans to understand that America is still the exception, and because it is, it remains the only hope to crushing political correctness.

As an immigrant, I have a unique perspective from which to view America. Sometimes it takes someone on the outside to warn you what is coming.

I'll be blunt: I believe America is about ten years behind the U.K. in the political correctness stakes. That's scary. That's why we have urgent work to do.

America has been, and remains, the refuge for brilliant, creative, ambitious, and independent thinkers of other lands. Their dreams can only be accommodated in the land of the free and the home of the brave. America provides the most friendly, open, nurturing, free and optimistic environment for any individual to achieve their dream. This must be protected at all cost.

That's why it's personal.

INTRODUCTION

For as long as I can remember, I've had a compelling enthusiasm for people and things I like, tempered only by an equally fervent animus for those I don't like. Black and white colors tend to paint my world view, with only the occasional gray stroke.

I'm conservative in social tastes, appearance and politics, but that's where it ends. My approaches, manner and behavior are unconventional, eccentric and often amusing. I don't object to be called a "character".

Those who know me best say I love life. They're not wrong. In fact, if my perpetual struggle with my weight is anything to go by, they are probably more right than I'd care to admit! (I'd like to say any excess in every arena adds to my charm!). My hunger doesn't stop at food. It extends to freedom, success, and opportunity. I have always had an insatiable appetite for life's experiences. I've never needed recreational drugs, because I've always been high on life.

I like to say I am Australian by birth, Texan by appointment (thanks, Gov. Rick Perry) and American by choice. As far as I'm concerned, there's enough intoxication there to last several lifetimes.

My zest for life shapes my political outlook. It is one of the reasons why I have such animus for Islamists: it's not possible to find anyone who hates and devalues life as much as this group of people. And, I believe anyone who loves life will automatically hate political correctness, and its expectations. I suspect any passionate person feels this way. If you value life's endless possibilities and limitless opportunities, political correctness doesn't belong in our world. In fact, I would argue that political correctness interferes with the pursuit of happiness guaranteed by the founding fathers in the Declaration of Independence.

As well as possessing affection for life and passion, my identity happens to be quite politically incorrect.

I'm a straight, white, middle-class, well-educated Christian man who happens to be conservative and bold, and in my case from the *very, very deep* South. I'm sure you've heard of us . . . we had the biggest hand in establishing civilization, and now preserving it, but are regularly mocked as buffoons by the media. It's not even worth me to trying to complain that I have been discriminated against.

I'm a culturally conservative millennial. However, unlike virtually every other conservative millennial media figure in America, I don't support gay marriage, look hip off-camera or take selfies.

But there's more. I'm culturally confident, even though I'm now part of the counter-culture. Today's culture belongs to the hippies, meditators, and vegetarians, and that's definitely not me.

You'll never catch me eating kale, seaweed or tofu. When a waitress offers me a gluten-free menu, I decline almost immediately. My appetite may expedite my trip to the pearly white gates, but it will be ribs, brisket, chicken fried steak, mac 'n' cheese, fries, and onion rings, washed down with beer or soda, followed by pie, all the way.

I much prefer to pick up a telephone than send a text. I still write handwritten thank you notes, and post-Christmas cards. I refuse to use anything other than a plastic or paper bag when shopping. I still wear a wristwatch, and it's not of the *Apple* variety. For important occasions, I use my Canon SLR instead of taking low quality pictures with a smartphone. And, I must be the only person left, aside from the President and U.S. military, still using a *Blackberry*.

I like New York, Washington D.C., and Los Angeles, but would much prefer to be deep in the heart of Texas, or small town Mississippi, in my pick-up truck, at a *Chick-Fil-A* drive-thru (you wouldn't catch me dead in a *Smart Car, and if you do you'll know somebody moved the body*). Actually, I'd prefer to be pretty much anywhere in the Midwest, Southwest, and most of rural America. I'd choose to have a beer with a Southern conservative over a Northern liberal, six days a week, and then again on Sunday. Heck, I love everything about the American South: the drawl, the belles, God and guns, football, country music, and the swagger.

Early in 2013, following the University of Alabama's defeat of Notre Dame, the website *Real Southern Men* explained: "*Football matters here, because it is symbolic of the fight we all fight. Winning matters here, because it is symbolic of the victories we all seek. Trophies matter here, because they are symbolic of the respect we deserve but so rarely receive.*" That about sums it up for me.

I'm a Western civilization guy. I have little cultural interest in Asia and Africa. Except for Israel, I have no great impulse to visit the Middle East. I do have enormous affection for the Anglosphere—Australia, England, Canada, New Zealand, and the United States. I happen to think that the free world rests on these nations' shoulders.

When I see the America flag flying in the wind, I don't see oppression, exploitation, repression, inequality, bigotry, and warmongering. That's a load of baloney. I see freedom, bravery, progress, opportunity, and exceptionalism. The hair on the back of my neck stands up. It reminds me of the very best of humanity. You won't catch me sitting down having a beer with anyone who doesn't respect our military or calls servicemen and women "war-mongers" and refers to our "pointless wars".

I believe in a culture that is proud, brave, courteous and above all, loyal. I'm a family, flag, faith and neighborhood kind of guy. I can't stand liberals who don't like humanity, or even their country. The only thing worse than being a socialist—is being an international socialist. It's one thing to be misguided but still be patriotic; it's a completely different thing to use the ideology as a justification to deliberately weaken your country to strengthen others, out of some desire to "even" something up.

I'm the kind of a guy who'll flash his lights at oncoming traffic to indicate the drivers should slow down if they need to, because I've just passed hidden police. It's not because I want people to break the law, but because my anti-authority instincts prompt me to do so. I have little patience for people who honk their horn at me because it is clear I am about to break a road rule, even though it impacts nobody except me. I'm into minding my own business; in fact that's why I came to America.

Back in Australia, I regularly butted heads with teachers at high school and staff at university. I wasn't a bad kid, but I was bold and self-confident and I didn't mind challenging them.

I was raised by parents, within a nuclear family, with "old fashioned values." I was taught to stand up for myself, to speak directly, and not to be afraid to tell people what I thought of them, if it was warranted. That policy has got me in trouble a few times, but it always outweighs the alternative of shrinking the shoulders, bowing the head slightly, and slinking around with my tail between my legs.

I value my personal space. It irks me when I've just parked my car in a nearly empty parking lot, and someone comes and parks right next to me. Or when there are ten urinals, you're the only guy in there and someone comes in and takes the one right next to you.

I love working out, but you'll never catch me signing up for a yoga class. I enjoy swigging the odd stiff alcoholic beverage, but good luck finding me sipping an appletini. I hold doors open and pull chairs out for women. But I could never marry a girl not prepared, or eager to take on my last name. I've little appreciation for feminism. In fact, I think it's done far more harm than good. For the most part, it has created angry women and feminine men by declaring war on the concepts of masculinity and femininity. I happen to think men and women are distinct, and that civilization rests on preserving that distinction. Men do best when they are needed, and left-wing feminism has done everything possible to eradicate any need.

Observing the across-the-board feminization of men is the most tragic of all. It's politically correct to wear an earring as a man or sport a ponytail, but I can't think of anything less masculine.

In my world, traditional American masculinity, predicated on masculine toughness and stoicism with doing the right thing, has no peer. Its erosion is one of the most untold tragedies of the last half-century.

Unfortunately, this trend has extended to our national politics, too. Many of these people are afraid of their own shadow, incapable of leadership, dispensing tough love, and enacting painful reform, for fear of offending groups considered "victim groups" by politically correct elitists. Economic reform, for example, is almost impossible when one side of politics is all about unfunded empathy. I lament the ubiquity of vanilla politicians and the absence of political leaders who say what they mean, mean what they say, and do what they say that they will do. Every word has to be focus group tested; every message analyzed and every poll considered. Safety has become the status quo; great past political leaders like Churchill and Reagan would be unelectable today, guaranteeing weak leadership. As a result, America is no longer feared by the world's bullies who are jeopardizing civilization and making the world dangerous. I don't know about you, but taking action has never bothered me. It is inaction that keeps me up at night.

I'm not scared easily, but the reason that President Obama was elected twice frightens the hell out of me. If we elect another President determined to follow the political correctness dictates to the letter, we will be neck-deep in s@#*. I look for passion, pride of country, and concern for the health of the free world. I want a Commander-in-Chief who has the disposition of a lion, not a pussycat. I'm sick of UN lectures, and I'm tired of the multicultural, "feel the love," poppycock programs, and initiatives on which our governments waste millions of our money.

But it's not just politics. I'm disappointed at the disappearance of "characters" in our society, at the hands of collective conformity. Nothing can replace individuality. There is nothing more powerful than an individual with a dream, on a mission to fulfill that dream. Teamwork has its place in sports, the military, and patriotic unity but magic comes from individuals.

You may be wondering why I have revealed so much detailed information about my tastes, likes and instincts. Aside from wanting you to get to know me, I have chosen to share all these details because when you think about it, political correctness is the opposite of virtually every one of my tastes, likes and instincts. Political correctness creates the climate, if not actively demanding you honk the horn at someone executing an illegal U-turn, even though you're not being impacted. Political correctness says it is racist to have little cultural interest in a particular continent, and sexist to give up your seat on a train, or expect your bride to be eager to change her name on Facebook. Political correctness subconsciously suggests following the crowd, such as sitting down on the only other rowing machine at the gym, even though the entire gym is nearly empty.

It is often said that personal experience explains one's political leanings. Everything that has happened to me in my thirty-one years has led me to these sentiments and conclusions. I'm writing this book because I don't think I'm alone in drawing these conclusions. I believe there are millions of people out there—the silent majority—that, feels the way I do. All across America, and the world, there are people sitting around the dinner table, shaking their heads, saying, "The world's gone mad." They share despair for the world's—and their children's—future. Many people reading the newspaper over a breakfast of bacon and eggs mutter to themselves in frustration at their leaders dancing around issues, or what is being reported is even considered "news."

I intend to be the voice for those people. I believe in fearlessly and passionately standing up for conservatives and everyday Americans whose voices the mainstream press often tries to suppress, marginalize or silence.

These people are routinely caricatured as change-resenting, narrow-minded generational grumps, unwelcoming, and unpleasant.

But in my experience, these people are the ones who exhibit far more tolerance and charity when faced with things they dislike, compared to their accusers. The alleged victimizers are the real victims.

They're everyday people—like you and I—just wanting to go about their lives, eager to spend time with their family and friends, while pursuing their dreams. They have clear and open hearts.

But political correctness is stealing their confidence, marginalizing them, and weakening their country. That this is happening in America, a unique country that has long had the protection of the First Amendment, is particularly disappointing.

SECTION ONE

1

AMERICA AND PC—
HEAD TO HEAD

*"Good citizenship and defending democracy means living up
to the ideals and values that make this country great."*

—PRESIDENT RONALD REAGAN

This book is going to get me into trouble.

A *whole* lot of trouble.

But I am on a mission. That's why I'm writing it. Of course no book can, by itself, remove political correctness and restore the American Dream. But a movement, designed to re-invigorate American values as an alternative to political correctness, while harnessing the can-do spirit that defines the nation, has every chance. I want to help, guide, and inspire Americans to join that movement. I think my arguments are compelling, and long overdue.

Many people are going to hate this book. The handbag hit-squad, the lavender lobby, and the Islamist apologists are just a few of those will attack me. Social media will work itself into a rage spiral, blasting me for being a whiny white man. I'll be vilified, threatened, and abused, not because I'm saying things that are untrue, but because they are true. This always happens when someone puts political correctness ahead of truth.

I don't need to tell you that. You've probably experienced it yourself. If you haven't, you have certainly seen it happen to a public figure. Around the world, those who do not bow at the altar of political correctness are the object of persecution from the mob, and sometimes even prosecution by the state. It's ugly, and it's outrageous.

It's also why what you are about to read is rarely written about. But it needs to be *said*. It needs to be *heard*. We need to fight back and tell the truth, no matter how inconvenient. The truth hurts some people because they know their ideas are unlikely to look good when in the light. They are morally opposed to the facts. Symbolism, you see, always beats out fact. The last thing some people want is a debate of ideas; real public scrutiny is their mortal enemy. This is why they shut down debate as quickly as possible, using a number of tactics we'll explore later. But if we boldly challenge this agenda by making our case, the marketplace of ideas will spit out its progressivism right before their very eyes.

I am hopeful. I think you should be, too. I believe courage is contagious, and that tradition can be an effective new rebellion. We have no choice but to restore our broken world. Apart from speaking out fearlessly, many things need to happen to achieve this mission. We need to reclaim our classrooms, and restore integrity and impartiality to our universities. Objectivity must be returned to the mainstream media, and common sense once more taught to our children.

Among the changes we must preside over:

- School students should not be fluent in the weasel, attack words of the technocratic Left like "racist," "sexist," "misogynist," "bigot," "homophobic," "inappropriate," "harassment," and be prepared to throw them around at any time with some false sense of authority.
- Those purporting to argue white privilege should be exposed for what they are actually doing: perpetrating black manipulation.

- Those perpetuating their fetish for diversity with the fraud of multiculturalism ought to be revealed as the threats to social cohesion that they are.
- Those doling out faux, feel-good compassion with empty-headed hashtag media stunts must be met with thoughtful nuance and reason.
- Those apologizing for Islam, at all costs, need to be seen as complicit in the attack on civilization and as an equal danger to civilization as the Islamist jihadists who seek a Caliphate.

If asked to name the great triumph of the modern tolerance movement, I would say it is the happy suppression of freedom of speech while tolerating the most sinister aspects of Sharia Law. Even as the death cult of Islamic State continues to wreak barbarity on women, throw gay men off buildings, and take sledgehammers to museums with irreplaceable ancient artifacts, those of the Left have been SILENT. Gay rights crusaders have not said a word. Artists have been similarly mute. Some may suggest that this is out of fear for retribution. But this is not why. It is because most people on the Left care about the side, not the principle. Then there are those who aren't mute. Take prominent actor Ben Affleck who insinuated in a fiery debate with Bill Maher that those who claim a direct link between Islam and the violence are just "gross and racist."

For all the talk about minorities, the truth is that there is only one system of oppression in America that actively works to oppress and subjugate certain groups of people, and that's political correctness. I'm a straight, white, educated middle-class Christian male, and I am sick of being told I'm not allowed to have an opinion. It's a real test of my Christian charity when I am told that I wouldn't understand the issue and I should to check my white privilege. Yet, if I were a gay, disabled, vegan, feminist, Ecuadorian wind turbine engineer, I'd have the world at my feet. I could say whatever I wanted to say with cultural and legal impunity.

When I spent afternoons gazing out of my classroom window dreaming about and imagining America, I never thought it was a place where accomplished people lost jobs and opportunities simply because they held a certain opinion. It never occurred to me that good people would be dragged over the coals for no reason.

Yet here, as elsewhere, we are told what we can say, and what we can't say, and to be careful. The "victimhood" business and its crocodile tears run rampant in America. This is all while ponytailed grad students with so many gender studies seminars on their timetable struggle to distinguish a man from a woman and are able to set arbitrary standards for speech. If this isn't enough, social media technology unwittingly increased the scope of political correctness patrol and enforcement, and welcomed a generation of gutless cockroaches, doubling as keyboard Generals. They act no differently than a lynch mob, only with anonymity and unlimited access, and nothing better to do than dictate our culture and direct the news cycle from behind a computer.

The great irony in all this is that nothing could be further from the American way than the practice or consequences of political correctness. Consider these profound conflicts:

- America was founded on free speech, yet political correctness muzzles it.
- American culture and personality has always been about being bold, but political correctness fosters timidity.
- America has always emphasized unity, where political correctness concentrates on differences.
- Optimism is what people the world over identify as deeply American, yet political correctness is premised on bitterness, anger and retribution.
- America is the most religious nation; on the other hand, political correctness is proudly secular.
- America is concerned with equality of opportunity while political correctness is about ensuring equality of outcome.

- Where American life has been about achievement, political correctness insists on mediocrity.

I could go on, but you get the message.

On every level, political correctness is diametrically opposed to the American ideal. Yet it is political correctness with the momentum, not the American ideal. It is easy to love America for the enemies she makes, but it is tough to witness those very enemies outside, laugh at her turmoil inside, particularly when it assists them. There is no doubt in my mind that, if allowed to continue, political correctness will deliver America on its knees, and at the feet of its once vanquished enemies. Such a turn of events would mean that the American value system would be rendered extinct by the least desirable representatives of a deeply inferior value system.

But I won't let that happen in my lifetime. Not on my watch.

Europe and Australia determined long ago to become nations of bullies enforcing conformity among their own, while calling it tolerance. It is my opinion they are too far gone and might be beyond rescue.

Even conservative governments can only stem the tide, not arrest the slide, because culture trumps politics. Those governments' principles, no matter how conservative, will always be tempered by the reality that they must govern nations that aren't naturally conservative. America is not burdened with this reality. Its luxury is its silent majority, making it a center-right country, with a conservative cultural bent.

Many would counter, arguing America is changing, and that the demographics are shifting the culture. This is not wrong, but it still misses the point. Demography will only be an obstacle to the defeat of political correctness if those choosing to become American continue to support it. Our pleas to defy and destroy political correctness appeal to the hearts of people, not their color or ethnic heritage. The American experiment has shown that the American has a unique ability to transcend all else.

Some would also claim that new immigrants, by default a minority, would hardly be enthusiastic about shunning an ideology of which they are the supposed beneficiary. This is again, not incorrect, but presumes a dependency on the ideology that would blind them to change. I believe in the power of opportunity. Everyone has an innate desire to climb the economic and social ladder, a desire that trumps all else when given the chance to exist. Political correctness is the guy half-way up the ladder that keeps pushing you off. Once we bravely conceptualize and articulate our case with this single minded focus, the American experience will once again become too powerful.

The American ideal, the shot that was heard around the world, must be heard once more. If our country is to remain the place where so many can come with nothing and achieve anything, political correctness—one of the two great evils of our time (the other being radical Islam)—must be bludgeoned with the baseball bat of freedom. The effects will be felt in stadiums around the world.

It's our job to make this happen—and make sure the greatest country in the history of the world is not destroyed.

PART 1: AMERICA IN 2017?
TWO COMPETING VISIONS

When I was nine years old, I loved reading books in the *Choose Your Own Adventure* series.

Every book began with a warning and all-caps emphasis declaring "You and YOU ALONE are in charge of what happens in this story." The books were written in the second person, so "you the reader" had the feeling of being able to control your fate and you could choose from dozens of possible endings. In many ways, the American people are like those readers, able to control the future.

It is a cliché, but America truly is at a crossroads. The direction it takes will determine whether the country will continue its progression toward European culture and finances, and become the next Britain, or save the world. Fortunately for the world and for the British, when the sun set on the British Empire, America was there. None of us will be so lucky this time. No one can or will replace America. But plenty of far more unpalatable governments will try. Civilization and its centerpiece—the American Dream as we know it—are at stake.

The Obama administration's almost religious devotion to political correctness has caused virtually every single area of American life to be downgraded. America is poorer, weaker, less innovative, less confident, less family-oriented, and less free. We are more divided and more faithless. The result of this increasing divide in the American polity is that world perceptions of the American future are not favorable. The consensus is that this is unlikely to end anytime soon and that's why so much attention is directed at the election of a new President in 2016.

Imagine the difference it would make if the new President had nothing but contempt for political correctness. The prospect is almost too delicious to even contemplate. But before you get excited, envision a new President not only continuing the trend of political correctness, but intensifying it. These are the two possible trajectories. Of course, following this current President, almost anyone remotely straight-talking is going to be a refreshing change. So, how would an inaugural speech given by a President who has no time for political correctness sound? Well, if I were his speechwriter, this would be the transcript:

★

Transcript of the inaugural address by the next President of the United States:

MASTER OF CEREMONIES: *It is my great privilege and distinct honor to introduce the 45th President of the United States of America.*

INAUGURAL ADDRESS BY PRESIDENT

January 20, 2017
United States Capitol
11:55 A.M. EST

THE PRESIDENT:

Thank you. Thank you.

Mr. Vice President, Mr. Chief Justice, members of the United States Congress, distinguished guests, and fellow citizens:

It is with great humility that I stand before you. No thank you I can offer is adequate for your decision to allow me to serve as your President.

I thank President Obama for his service to our nation, as well as the generosity and cooperation he has shown throughout this transition.

This is the 58th time that we, the people, have celebrated this historic occasion. It continues to symbolize our ideals of renewal, continuity, and unity.

As we do, let us pause to remember the gallant men and women of our Armed Services, both past and present, home and abroad that allow us this opportunity. Those who have spilt blood, lost limbs and paid the ultimate price to defend and protect the greatest human virtue of them all: freedom. Let us join in a moment of silent prayer.

(Pause)

Eight years ago, my predecessor spoke of gathering clouds and raging storms.

Today the inclement weather has only intensified, with a moral fog worse than ever, and a forecast suggesting no let-up.

But while our hearts may hurt and our minds may be tempted to question; as ever, we look relentlessly forward. For the belief that tomorrow will be better than yesterday is part of who we are.

Many suggest only our past will reveal greatness and glory. We have heard these voices before. Each time they have been wrong. They can be wrong again. America is not a meteor that blazed across the heavens and is now exhausted; we are merely in a transient time of trial, in hours cold and dark before the ramparts new gleaming.

As we have had too many times in the past, we must re-calibrate our trajectory. Renew our hearts, revitalize our culture, refresh our memories and reaffirm our faith.

When our enemies threatened us in the moon race, we responded by changing our national curriculum to have greater focus on mathematics and science. When we were attacked in Pearl Harbor, we responded by leading the world to crush tyranny. When evil men cowardly plunged airplanes into our buildings in the hope of destroying our resolve, we responded with patriotism.

The time to respond has come again. The time for new vision is here. The next four years cannot be a continuation of the last eight: our glorious Republic cannot afford it. An American renaissance is called for, but it will not simply roll in on the wheels of inevitability.

Our new vision must be a return to the America our parents and grandparents remember.

Let us begin by re-affirming our core premise: we are one people, under God.

Ours is the experiment of humanity. Our nation is exceptional. Our role is indispensable. There is nothing wrong with America that cannot be cured by what is right with America.

Our flaws are many; our errors are rich; our failings clear. But our land shines bright, even as it strives towards unrealized ideals. We remain the inspiration for the world. We continue to plant the seed of liberty in our fertile soil. Let us nurture it, and let it grow to bear fruit for the world to enjoy.

We make no apology for America.

Our country is a force for good in the world, a noble chapter in human history.

For those beyond our borders who would magnify our deficiencies and ignore our virtues to author a false narrative, we are resourceful and generous enough to deal with them.

The voices among us that would abandon perspective, disavow our fundamental goodness, and deny our worthiness to lead the world, will be drowned out by a chorus of patriots.

Where American achievement has been at the hands of responsible, self-governing adult citizens, American decline is at the feet of the mindset of the spoiled child.

It is the mindset that confuses imperfection with malice, resents what belongs to others and condemns as abuse any refusal to be indulged, while demanding avoidance of consequences and continued enjoyment of unearned benefits.

As we move forward this twenty-first century, casting our eye around the world, let us be abundantly clear about our vision for America.

Erased borders, stifled enterprise, fading liberty, censored faith and a dwindling birth rate may be the hallmarks of other lands, but they will never be American goals.

We are a nation of lifters, not leaners, but will continue to lean on our tradition of lifting. Hard work, discipline and freedom are the values of economic success.

Nowhere else can so many come with nothing and achieve everything.

Let us occupy the dreams of people everywhere, and remain the haven for talented people from elsewhere. The country that teaches and proves to all that no task is impossible. No challenge insurmountable. In America, there is neither virtue nor reason in stifling human achievement.

Let us apply this motivation, as we strive, arms outstretched, for a more perfect Union.

As we do, we must turn and once more face God, resisting those that might rail against our religious character. Our rights come not from our government, but from our God. Equal, natural and inherent, no one may arbitrarily remove them. Not even a government cloaked in good intentions and a democratic majority.

Government's hand has rested more lightly on our lives because of our preparedness to self-regulate by the sense of moral obligation before an eternal Judge.

A belief in limited government is who we are as a people. For we understand, freedom and incentives unleash the drive and entrepreneurial genius at the core of human progress.

If we are to meet our potential, the Government must stop doing things our Founding Fathers never intended, and a better job at those things it was established to do. Only then can we relegate our economic difficulties, cliffs, ceilings, danger and debts, to footnotes of history.

To conquer our challenges, we require an American engine, comprised of different parts with varying roles, but all burning fuel for America.

There are some in our politics invested in separatism, who preference cultural diversity to patriotic unity. But it's not our diversity that makes us exceptional; it's our ability to unify the diverse. America can lead only when we are in it together. We must be more than the mere sum of our parts.

In recent times, we have spent too much time protecting the culture of those who join our country, and far too little defending the culture they have chosen to join.

Those that would seek to test our tolerance, interpreting it as weakness and unlimited patience, make a grave misjudgment.

The only birth certificate we care about is our Declaration of Independence, but know that we are a Christian nation, that speaks English and whose law must be obeyed.

Those who seek to change, rather than strengthen, our values and way of life should consider another home.

It is moral to keep our nation safe, our homeland secure, and our allies protected. Our commitment to this is unfailing and unconditional. Tyranny and evil will be met with full force. We will freeze the sweat and chill the bones of their aspirants and perpetrators. In the future, there may be nations whose armies outnumber us, but none will have our resolve or fearlessness. Our soldiers are the type who will re-enlist after losing a limb, or throw themselves on unknowns to absorb the blast of a detonated suicide vest so their teammates can complete their mission.

Where our enemies may drink from the poisoned well of bitterness, we are sustained by the clear liquid of freedom in the calm pools of liberty. We will break the back of envy and rebuild optimism.

For those within Islam who insist on global dominance, and are prepared to use any means necessary to achieve it, the United States stands ready to fight.

As custodians of civilization, we will stop at nothing to ensure your demise. Wherever you take your conflict, we will follow you. Wherever you hide, we will seek you. Wherever you advance, we will turn you back. You began this conflict, but we will end it.

We will not abide the mass murder, systematic rape, bombings and beheadings of Muslims and non-Muslims. Every act of terror in our homelands will renew our purpose. In bitter cold and scorching heat, we will hunt you. You are the ambassadors of barbarity, and we will make sure you enter the earth's embassy of hell.

Our country is about life, liberty, and the pursuit of happiness, not death, slavery, and the pursuit of power.

To acknowledge this struggle is to claim the most important truth of our time. It is clear that change must come to Islam. The actions of jihadists are rooted in Islamic scripture and endorsed by many of Islam's influential scholars. We call on all Muslims to loudly condemn the evil conducted in the name of their religion, and to agitate for religious reform. We stand ready to offer any assistance to achieve this end.

To those who would seek to penetrate our computers and hardware to steal our secrets, know our plans and potentially wreak havoc on our lives, be warned. We created the computer, the software, the programs, and even the keyboard you use to conduct your cyber-attacks. Until now, you have operated with relative impunity. That stops today. Anything you can do, we can do better. Our retaliation will not be proportional. It will be devastating.

If ever we needed a unifying force to regain control of our southern border, the threat of terror offers it. Illegal immigration has reached a crisis point in our national history, and only tough love can solve it.

We will determine who comes into this country, and the circumstances under which they come.

If you come to America illegally, you will never get to stay. You have broken the law; therefore we do not want you. You will never be an American. We will send you home. Period. You will have risked everything for nothing.

But in the spirit of American positivity, let us recognize that the efforts of millions to come here is not only a policy problem, but an accolade. It is a tribute to our material abundance, opportunity, innovation, cultural creativity, and the most optimistic educational system on earth.

Where others offer an endless conveyer belt, these are the steps of the magic escalator that propel groups from marginal status to full participation.

In cafes and barbershops, in the hallways of schools and in the pews of churches, in the bleachers at Little League and peewee football games, and on the sidewalks around town squares across America, people who have taken advantage of the escalator can be found. They include minorities, women, immigrants, and the disabled.

Edmund Burke suggested that "Society is a contract between the past, the present and those yet unborn."

For all, we owe our best efforts to keep liberty, justice and democracy, the flames of the American fireplace, alight.

For our children and those not yet born, we must ensure they understand what makes our country exceptional, and that they are capable of continuing to manufacture and export our value system.

Civility, industry, and self-restraint are what we must teach them, for they will be faced with same choice that we have: be responsible and free, or irresponsible and enslaved.

School curriculums must portray our nation's history fairly, and our culture must prepare our youth for the realities of life and competition. Self-esteem in America is earned, not granted. Only one winner can accept a trophy and only one student should walk up to the school stage deliver the valedictory address.

In America, we recognize competition nurtures strong individual performance. Our continued triumph on the world stage will demand our native culture accommodate fierce internal competition.

This spirit of competition extends to our national economy.

Some would weaken our economy and enlarge our government by embracing the climate of evangelism that insists our environment is the greatest threat to our national security.

But not us, because we are clear-eyed about climate change. We understand it is a threat based on false fears and false guilt. No more will it blind our perspective and priorities, or make us deaf to reason and science. Economic action on climate change is an act of self-harm. Repressing human activity through the state has never been the American way.

Never again will climate change and U.S. overreach be considered major threats to national security.

We remain faithful to our Constitution. For the America we once more seek, we must once again claim its promise. Rather than transform our constitutional agenda, we must protect it.

Rather than looking at unconstitutional solutions to unspeakable shooting tragedies, we must acknowledge our failure to pursue a policy that treats the mentally ill, and keeps our country safe.

We must also protect our liberty from the intrusions of foreign bodies, irrespective of how well-meaning they purport to be, with principles foreign and possibly harmful to our traditions and liberties.

As we promise to renew our nation, we must pledge anew to restore the family as the fundamental unit of American life.

Family may transcend politics, but its strength and integrity determines the health of freedom, the rule of law, economic prosperity, and opportunity in our union.

History has shown that the traditional family is the ideal setting for our children. It is why we encourage old values in new times.

And our destiny as Americans cannot be fulfilled until we give voice to those who could not, cannot, and will not be able to vote or speak unless they are allowed to live. This is why we protect the unborn.

As we continue our journey, we remember those who traveled before us, and those who will travel after.

Three thousand miles of continental landmass may represent our wingspan, but our reach is infinite. For being an American is not captured by the front cover of a passport. At its best, it means flying on the wings of the American eagle, and pursuing an American journey of happiness, opportunity and risk.

We pray for an America inspired and dedicated to the cause of liberty, not only for ourselves, but for all. A liberty founded on virtue, sealed and perpetuated through wisdom and prudence that, all together, embody our national character.

Above all, we pray for guidance by Divine Providence. We need God in our homes, in our schools, on our battlefields and in our hearts.

Only then can we remain the land of the free, and the home of the brave.

Thank you. God bless you, and may He forever bless these United States of America.

END
12:10 P.M. EST

Hear that?

Yes, I do, too. It's the screaming and caterwauling of media and academic elites all around the world. Blood vessels are bursting everywhere. Chris Matthew's "thrill up his leg" has suddenly transitioned to gout. The Left has gone totally bananas. Editorialists for the *New York Times* don't know where to begin, convulsing every few seconds. Liberal pundits on television, still with eyes glazed, shriek about the unprecedented nature of the speech, and wax lyrical about the challenges of overcoming such deliberate diplomatic faux pas. Howard Dean is on hand, but cut off early, experiencing chest pains, screaming incoherently about the indispensability of a university education. A quick live feed is established to an ashen-faced former Presidential candidate,

Al Gore, who is, of course, deeply shocked and personally injured, profoundly concerned for America. The sensitivities of the Twittering class are so offended, they are over 140 characters, and Twitter goes down.

But spare a thought for President Obama. He's just a few feet away, listening to the speech in person. He sits there wishing for a hole to suddenly emerge and swallow him up (sorry, Mr. President, you didn't build that). After he forces the initial deer in headlights expression off his face, the former President starts thinking of the places he would rather be, preferably as far away as possible. Chicago? Too close. Maybe Hawaii or even Kenya? Heck, even barbecue with those folks clinging to their guns and religion sounds pretty good, right about now.

Chinese keyboard warriors targeting American business and government secrets, spill their bowl of rice, as they slump and slide back into their chair. Islamists tug hard at their beards, kick their goat, furrow their brows as their fingers nervously dance around their AK-47, before finally turning upward and squeaking, "Allah, I Don't Want a Bar of this!". Climate alarmists suddenly feel the cold, and wish the Armageddon they warn of would come early.

Meanwhile, you're yelling "'MERICA!!" (or "HOO-AH!!" if you're military), and finding yourself involuntarily engaged in several bouts of shadow boxing, throwing haymakers Mike Tyson in his prime would admire. You're high-fiving and fist-bumping, running outside to salute the American flag in your front yard. Talk radio hosts breathe a sigh of relief. Business bosses, large and small, across the country look for champagne. Israelis in every kibbutz of the nation hug each other. Pastors could only look happier if Jesus returned. Clint Eastwood just grins, saying quietly to himself: "Now, that made my day." Even Fox's O'Reilly manages a smile, while Megyn Kelly looks hotter than ever. Yee-ha! We're back in business, boys. America's back!

What a moment it would be.

If the inaugural speech in 2016 is anything like that, America will snap out of its lethargy, with renewed energy, cultural cohesion and national purpose. It would make an American renaissance not just a possibility, but a distinct likelihood.

But I know what you're thinking . . . would that speech truly be delivered? Wishful thinking! It would never happen.

First off, never say never. This is America. Anything is possible. But it is unlikely that we would ever hear a speech that was this honest. But it doesn't mean we shouldn't strive for it, demand it, or seek to elect a person with the necessary cojones to deliver it.

This is the speech that the American people need to hear. It is the message America's allies want to hear. They are the words America's enemies must hear. This is an inspirational, unifying and substantive address, in keeping with the values and sentiments that made, and continue to make, America exceptional. I believe an inaugural address like this would begin to heal hearts, dissolve doubt and help Americans start believing in themselves again.

We can only hope.

Alternatively, the speech could be a continuation of the last eight years, with every line a tribute to political correctness dogma. Of course, it will be cloaked in "pro-American" language and jazzed up to sound patriotic as the Office of President demands, but when undressed, it is nakedly anti-American.

How might it read? Well, probably something like this:

★

PART 2: AMERICA IN 2017?

A POLITICALLY CORRECT VISION

MASTER OF CEREMONIES: It is my great privilege and distinct honor to introduce the 45th President of the United States of America.

INAUGURAL ADDRESS BY PRESIDENT

January 20, 2017
United States Capitol
11:55 A.M. EST

THE PRESIDENT:

Thank you. Thank you. Thank you so much.

Mr. Vice President, Mr. Chief Justice, members of the United States Congress, distinguished guests, and fellow citizens:

It is with great humility that I stand before you. No thank you I can offer is adequate for your decision to allow me to serve as your President.

I thank President Obama for his wonderful service to our nation. He has earned his place in our history and in our hearts.

(Applause)

This is the 58th time that we, the people, have celebrated this historic occasion. It continues to symbolize our ideals of renewal, continuity, and unity.

Eight years ago, President Obama spoke of troubling times—two wars, an unprecedented financial crisis and a planet in peril.

Out troubles are far from over, but slowly, sunshine seeps through, offering to light our porches.

Wars have ended and our economy has recovered. Steadily, we have worked to not just improve our great nation, but to transform it.

For the true genius of America is not what it is today, or what it has been in the past, but what it can be in the future.

Culturally, economically and philosophically, our work continues. But our sleeves must remain rolled up, as we unroll and button the attitudes that threaten our promise.

In reshaping our nation, lethargy is our formidable foe. We must never sink into it.

For we must forever seek an America that is brighter and kinder, more sophisticated, more enlightened, and fairer.

As a nation, we have only made progress when we have been on the right side of justice and equality.

There are those who would cling to tired and tried patterns. They seek fresh faith in the old dream. But these voices fear change and discount hope. They appeal to our patriotism but ignore our potential. They embrace reluctance, but reject progress.

As we pursue life, liberty, and the pursuit of happiness, let us never forget equity, diversity, and inclusion.

As we surge forward, let us commit to a politics where indifference to the suffering of our most vulnerable is never in fashion.

In our America, as in our military, we leave nobody behind.

We care for the poor, the downtrodden, and the oppressed. The weak, the disabled, and those down on their luck. Blacks, Latinos, women, gays, and Muslims.

We carry those who cannot, or will not, stand. And we stand with those who would be flattened by our inherent prejudices. For we all breathe the same air.

There are those who would offer the false choice of liberty or preventing hurt feelings. They demand the right to insult and offend under a convincing veneer of free speech.

But this must be rejected. Not only because vilification harms free speech by silencing its victims, but because such behavior goes against everything we stand for as Americans.

Let us assure tomorrow's rising stars that they can grow up in a world where they don't have to fear their fellow Americans.

No matter what we look like, where we come from, or who we are we are equally entitled to our human rights and dignity. This is why we crave an America sensitive to all and where emotional distress has no abode.

Where the young Muslim in Dearborn wearing a hijab doesn't invite harassment. Where a young black man in Ferguson isn't profiled by police. Where the unemployed man collecting public assistance in Tupelo isn't shamed. And where the single mother in Duquesne can walk to the local supermarket without disapproving stares.

For too long, irrational fear of certain groups of America has trumped our ideals. We can no longer pursue policies and foster attitudes that damage and oppress these groups. No longer must such views remain endemic in our institutions.

We must be as quick to condemn discrimination on the grounds of race, color and religion at home as we are to condemn the persecution of other minorities in faraway lands.

We are a nation that believes in opportunity and equality for all. It is why we want access to health care, child care and education for every American.

Let us inaugurate a new era of civilized discourse. Ours is a nation that celebrates efforts to diminish offensive speech on our university campuses and in our workplaces. Our children must be adequately sensitized, and understand the need for collective harmony and the self-esteem of all.

Let us apply these protections to our society at large, for it is our duty to defend those with less power. In doing so, our speech will become a roadmap of our nation's most cherished principles, setting forth our expectations of every American.

We are a proud nation, but our pride must be tempered by the realities.

Too often, in our own country, we have mistreated our minorities, neglected our poor and discriminated against non-whites.

Too often, in our own country, women have been victimized by men, blacks victimized by whites and gays victimized by straights.

Too often, in our own country, we have suspected our own because of how they look or the way they pray.

But we know that America can do better. We know that America is capable of being an example of tolerance and inclusiveness for the entire world. It must be shared.

Let us resolve to eliminate material inequality to achieve our end of socioeconomic egalitarianism. Our prosperity—in all its forms—must be collective.

We should demand from our courts not only justice, but social justice. We must acknowledge that the neutral application of the law is often inadequate to ensure social progress. Our laws must reflect our values and give full voice to civility and tolerance.

In our government, we should demand the highest standards of transparency, even when they are damaging. And we must acknowledge the necessity of government in achieving a more just America. It is our duty to better the lives of others through our government.

Our nation was founded on religious freedom, and today in America, people are free to worship as they wish. But people are also free to not worship. We respect their right, and re-affirm our government to be secular. While we acknowledge the importance of a belief in God to many in our nation, we know that, too often, faith has drilled fault lines in our society, causing conflicts and endangering progress. The expectation of a shared public faith is not just anachronistic, but counter-productive. It threatens cohesion and ingrains existing discrimination. It would deny two loving partners the opportunity to marry in front of their friends, only because they share a different attraction.

The material inequality in our nation and world is attributable to big business, unforgiving capitalist competition and Western imperialism, not to mention our historic and continued support for allies who some might say impede peaceful regional solutions.

They tear at the world's social fabric. They unravel the tapestry that is our common humanity. They prompt others to engage in savage terrorism against innocents.

It is why we will pursue a different vision of international cooperation that leads to peace and harmony on our planet. This will allow for a true moral authority in world leadership. This is the context in which we steady ourselves to deal with the two greatest threats to our national security—climate change and U.S. overreach.

It is also why, as the fingerprints of America on the globe begin to fade, we should not be alarmed. The softening of American influence around the world will allow a multi-national effort that is fairer, the result of which will empower the most disenfranchised in the world, removing their motivation to injure us. In turn, we will be the recipients of their gratitude, and the inheritors of their respect.

The pessimistic believe that the world's problems will never be solved, and that deep American footprints in other lands are necessary for our security. But they show little faith in humanity. They underestimate its basic goodness. They underrate every individual's common desire for a peaceful, tolerant, open and free society. Our big dreams for the world will never be satisfied by that small-minded agenda for our country.

In the same way, our response when terrorism visits will rise above the reactionary temptation. Our response to terrorism should concern us as much as terror itself. No Muslim woman in America shall ever feel the need to remove her hijab in the days following terrorism. To engage in rhetoric that only adds fuel to the fire of anti-Muslim hate and bigotry is unpatriotic. Our nation should never accommodate a demeaning, intimidating or hostile environment toward a group.

For those who would rush to judgment and call in to question the religion of Islam, we must remind ourselves that history is replete with atrocities conducted in the name of religions. But adopting a cause does not always equate to motivation. No religion condones the killing of innocents, no matter what any self-described adherents of that faith may claim.

As Americans, we treasure fairness. To expect our Muslim brothers and sisters to condemn acts of terror supposedly in the name of Islam when we would not do the equivalent for our faith should cause serious self-reflection.

While it cannot be denied that in recent times we have witnessed barbarism in the Middle East, let us remember there are those who would deem legal capital punishment in thirty-two of our states to be barbaric.

It is important to remember that the terror threat pales in comparison with the consequences of climate change in our future.

Addressing climate change is an environmental, economic and security challenge, but it is also a moral obligation. No longer can we tolerate vested interests mudding the waters of climate science. This is the great risk we must manage. Our earth is not immutable. Our oceans are rising. Our hurricanes are more violent. Drought is more prevalent. And our weather is more unpredictable. If we look at our European neighbors, we see that we are leading from behind, when it comes to our environment.

Many among us claim we are an exceptional nation. But in doing so, we must be careful to not elevate ourselves at the expense of others. And we cannot forget our greatness is entirely subjective. Objective truth eludes us because of the eyesight of race, gender and class.

The white man in Wichita holds different truths than the black man in Baltimore. The man in Minneapolis holds different truth than the woman in Wilmington. The poor person in Phoenix holds different truths than the rich person in Rapid City.

So, our patriotism must never come at the expense of perspective.

We all aspire to a better world, and only a collective generosity and spirit on our part will achieve it.

But this lamp of generosity and spirit can only shine abroad, if it shines at home.

We welcome all who make America home. Some say, with a nod to chauvinism, that we must insist they adhere to certain traditions and customs, and would set an arbitrary level of engagement in American life.

Instead of hailing our diversity as our greatest strength, these people promote an American identity. By engaging in these efforts, they confine and constrain and show disloyalty to everything that is Americanism. They reveal their public devotions to freedom to be hollow.

For our state of the union to be strong, such jingoism has no place in America. Our borders should only seldom be used to discriminate against others. Let us never prize our American citizenship above our world citizenship.

All too much, cable news talking heads and radio controversialists divide us, rating opinion and entertainment over news, using their bully pulpit to divide us. Let us aim for a softer, gentler media, one that reports forensically rather than aggressively, and doesn't victimize and sensationalize.

In the America we envision, every child will grow up with the same opportunities. Every family will practice its faith, and every community will celebrate and welcome diversity.

We will fight inequality with the same vigor of wealth creation. We will not only view the world as a duel between good and evil, but rich and poor and strong and weak. We will understand the force of love to be greater than any family ideal before.

And our moral compass will be influenced as much by our conscience, heart and science as any religious values.

That is our promise. That is our potential. That is our America.

Thank you, and may shared prosperity bless our nation.

END

12:10 P.M. EST

There's that noise again!

But this time, the noise is different. It's the rapturous and uncontained applause and cheering of the literati. History and political science professors at universities all over the world are stampeding to the photocopy room, desperate to print off a transcript of the speech to give to their students for class. Liberal pundits laud the President for "courage" and "honesty", remarking how well-received the speech will be across the world. Al Sharpton busts out some James Brown-inspired dance moves. Sandra Fluke is so excited she even momentarily considers purchasing her own birth control. #Inauguration2017 is trending, and already being made into t-shirts. Gay activists are flinging beads around like they're at Mardi Gras.

President Obama smiles warmly throughout the speech, enthusiastically clapping. He's left the fundamental transformation of America in good hands. He's looking forward to that deep dish Chicago pizza later that afternoon, after he and Michelle step off Marine One for the final time. His work here is done.

All this as Islamists sitting opposite their super-sized America-designed flat-screen television gently and confidently stroke their beards, walk outside, raise their arms, and yell Allah Akbar, blasting off a hail of bullets into the sky just for good measure. Environmentalists drop their biodegradable, hypo-allergenic crystal ball, emerge from their caves donning grass skirts holding hands singing "We are the World," and sip fruit punch from recyclable cups. Chinese cyber warfare experts smile mischievously, slurping their noodles, preparing to launch their next attack.

Meanwhile, you're absolutely devastated, shaking your head in disgust. In fact, every one you know is shaking their head. Even politically agnostic Agnes from the local Dairy Queen who always makes your Blizzard the way you like it, appears flummoxed. Sean Hannity, Rush Limbaugh, Glenn Beck and Mark Levin are rightfully apoplectic, and you agree with them. Law enforcement cringe, bracing themselves for more of the popular culture that has seen their reputation (and lives) shot to pieces, spurred by unhelpful, if not untruthful reporting. Patriots, optimistic by nature, can barely bring themselves to look at others at the local shopping mall, in the knowledge that at least one in two must have voted for this kind of America. The despair is borne from the feeling of no longer understanding your country, or its people. It's not the America you grew up in, or the one you want to live in.

What an awful speech that would be. If you had fun reading it, just imagine how much fun I had writing it!

If this address was to be delivered, I could almost guarantee that such a speech would entrench the lethargy and division of Americans, if not exacerbate it. It would be a continuation of the previous eight years, further setting back America's fortunes, and delaying any recovery. The cultural damage it would do for the next four years, if not eight, would be almost irreparable. (I'm an optimist and believe America can come back from anything, anytime. Just look at history.) That's why we must quit equivocating, and start repudiating.

So, now you have the transcripts of two possible inauguration speeches, offering two alternative visions for America, allowing you to play "spot the difference." One is based on political correctness; the other not at all. With an objective hat, re-read each speech and decide which one you would want your President to deliver. Consider which one reflects your values and the type of nation you can be proud to live in. Which one really inspires, and which one offers real hope and change?

I firmly believe that the future of this country will depend on the next election.

Your move, America.

2

RED, WHITE AND BLUE
COMEBACK

"Survive and advance."

—JIM VALVANO,
basketball coach of North Carolina State in 1983

★

I f I was President, which can't happen for obvious reasons, I would have included the following passage somewhere in that first inauguration speech:

★

For too long now, to our great detriment, we have embraced the relative: that idea that no culture, or religion, or set of values, is superior to others. Nothing could be further from the truth. All people are equal, but all cultures are not.

Of all enemy combatants, political correctness is the most dangerous. It endangers our homeland and our culture. It emboldens our enemies and critics. It denies reality and encourages mediocrity. We give thanks for freedom of speech, press, assembly, and lobby. Our laboratory of freedom provides a daring, exuberant, risk-defying openness. This gives our system an almost miraculous capacity for self-criticism, self-correction, and self-renewal. This is what doomed slavery and defeated communism. It is the jewel of humility in our crown.

That's why my first act as President is to announce from this day forward an end to political correctness. No longer will we hesitate to name our enemies. No more will we entertain expectations of uniformity, exclusion and tolerance. Our culture of empathy must never be a culture of immunity. There are no exclusive zones in the marketplace of ideas.

I believe this can change. When it does, confidence will return. Consensus on the American identity, a must if America is to be at her best, will re-emerge.

It is a necessary inclusion, given the times and challenges facing America right now, one perhaps I see more clearly.

OUTSIDE PERSPECTIVE

It's a curious fact that on occasion in American history, a fresh set of eyes visiting from distant lands has helped Americans see themselves more accurately. As the adage goes, sometimes a spectator sees more of the game.

Alexis de Tocqueville, the prescient French nobleman, visited the United States in the 1830s when he was just 26. His book *Democracy in America* praised America's lack of a centralized government, deemed religion salutary for democracy, and described how political freedom and uninhibited commerce went hand in hand.

Likewise with Winston Churchill, the wartime British prime minister and greatest figure of the 20th century, who led the fight against Hitler and sounded the alarm on Communism. Churchill genuinely loved this nation that he called "the Great Republic." Churchill's maternal family lineage no doubt assisted, but it was the people and philosophy that sourced his immense faith in the USA. Challenging his own country's predilection for consensus and moderation, he displayed American-like leadership with indomitable will and bulldog tenacity.

And both men remarked on America's resilience. "The greatness of America lies not in her being more enlightened than any other nation, but in her ability to repair her faults," observed the Frenchman. The Briton jibed affectionately: "You can always count on Americans to do the right thing—after they've tried everything else."

Maybe it is an "outsider" thing, but I immediately discerned the same American comeback capability as they did, from the moment I set foot on U.S. soil. That is why I am sanguine about America's prospects. This is why I believe America can defeat political correctness.

EXCEPTIONAL AMERICA

My previous book, *The American Boomerang* (2014*)*, explored in great detail from a de Tocqueville perspective what makes the United States the world's pinnacle nation. You see, American exceptionalism is often derided as a phrase of partisan polemics, or worse still a mere hypothesis, or even a myth. But it is an incontrovertible reality, however unwelcome or unpalatable this might be to those whose ears are attuned to a different siren. In 5,000 years of recorded human history, no other nation has come close to resembling the United States. The American model has offered, and continues to offer a greater chance for dignity, hope, and happiness for more people than any other system.

As Margaret Thatcher, the British prime minister, put it, "Europe was created by history. America was created by philosophy." Lady Thatcher was right. The philosophy is one of individual liberty, free-market opportunity, and belief that it's all a gift from God. America is the best idea the world has ever had, the greatest value system ever devised. The greatest threat and challenge to American exceptionalism is political correctness.

AMERICAN VALUES

What are these values that make America exceptional? Individualism, not collectivism. Patriotism, not relativism. Optimism, not pessimism. Limited government, not the nanny state. God, not Caesar. Faith, not secularism. *E pluribus Unum*, not multiculturalism. Life, not death. Equality of opportunity, not equality of outcome. Goodness, not moral equivalence. America is about being bold, not bland. Brave, not meek. Striving for greatness, not mediocrity.

It is interesting that all of these values are aligned with what's called today a conservative outlook. On every single count, traditional America both viscerally and ideologically sides with conservatism. America thus represents the greatest impediment to leftist aims, and becomes the prime target of the progressive movement in all its manifestations. It is easy to love America simply for the enemies she makes.

American success, by design not accident, is the most significant refutation of leftist ideals. That's because America has fostered a society that allows its citizens the widest latitude for creativity and innovation. It rewards success without government approvals and bureaucratic interference. It embraces religious faith, aspiration, and risk. As a result, the people of America have been the most enterprising, market-oriented, individualistic and adverse to taxation and regulation that have ever walked the earth.

THE TRUTH ABOUT THE WORLD

America has also shown uncommon valor against the sword of tyranny. She has frosted the neighborhoods of tyranny and oppression, by freezing the sweat and chilling the bones of men harbouring such aspirations. From the beaches of Normandy to the sands of Iraq, America has spread more freedom and fought more evil than any other country, expending enormous treasure.

People still cross oceans to get to this country. They are as willing as ever to empty their life savings to get to America, legally or illegally. They are as prepared as ever to sell the shirt off their backs just to feel the American winds of freedom and opportunity. There is no other place where so many come with nothing and achieve anything they seek. Put simply, the world is a better place with America. This is not to say America is perfect. But contrary to the distorted portrait painted by the Left of slaveholders, robber barons, imperialists, and protectors of privilege, our country is one of fundamental goodness. America is the best thing humanity has.

Anti-Americans are like spoiled children. They confuse defectiveness with malice, loathe what belongs to others, and denounce as abuse any repudiation to indulge them—while sullenly demanding avoidance of costs and continued satisfaction of unearned benefits.

WHY IS AMERICA IN TROUBLE?

Political correctness' failures, by contrast, are equally clear. It has created economically unsustainable and character-destroying welfare states. It has undermined Western military strength. It has politicized universities and the arts. It authored the culture of complaint, and its close cousin, the self-esteem movement. Every area of our life in the world today is being downgraded because of political correctness, its agendas, and its stranglehold on elite opinion. We are less free, poorer, weaker, less innovative, less confident and less family-oriented. We are more divided and more faithless. We're well on our way to becoming Europe—fiscally, socially, and culturally.

America is therefore in the fight of its life. Individualism, patriotism, and liberty—the unique properties of American life and culture—are at diminished levels, beleaguered by the anti-American virus prevalent in schools and universities, entertainment media, and the arts. The elite's inverted priority of climate over jihad

speaks volumes of the problems that afflict the world's pinnacle
nation. The readiness of many opinion leaders to allege evil in the
local police, but not in Islamic terror, stuns many of those who
watch from abroad. We see America weaker today than she has
ever been, making the world a more dangerous place for everyone.

Sadly, in a democracy (which has now really become a *psephoc-
racy*— a system totally dominated by electoral victories and defeats where the moment you enter office, every act is framed in
your desire to win the next election), governments are a reflection
of ourselves. We've become greedy, entitled and demanding. We
want and demand everything for free, with scant regard to the real
cost. And forget social issues—that's just on the economics! We're
forcing governments to do what is best for our egotistical selves.
We are all "Me, Me, Me."

10 POINT PLAN TO AN AMERICAN BOOMERANG

What can America do to recover from its current position? The
answer is pretty simple: defy political correctness by returning to
common sense. In terms of policies, here's a plan I think American
leadership should embrace:

- End the waste
- Pay back the debt
- Limit the government
- Axe political correctness
- Protect the borders
- Preserve Judeo-Christian traditions
- End the culture of entitlement
- Cut taxes
- Exercise loyalty to the Constitution
- Keep the peace through unquestioned military advantage

You will observe that I have included a specific reference to political correctness in the plan. I did so because of the gravity I deem it to have. But don't be misled into believing it is a stand-alone issue. It isn't. The truth is that every one of the other nine objectives in this plan cannot be achieved, unless political correctness is abandoned. Protecting borders, eliminating government programs, limiting the number of people on welfare benefits, and standing up for a Judeo-Christian heritage all violate, violently, almost every single tenet of political correctness. Proponents of political correctness repeatedly imply that even merely raising such suggestions as these, indeed even asking difficult questions, betrays ignorance, intolerance, bigotry, and xenophobia.

So, you see that the underlying issue to every problem in America, and the obstacle to every necessary corresponding solution, is politically correct thoughts and sentiments.

5 POINT PLAN TO MAKE AMERICA ECONOMICALLY BOOMERANG

Right now, America's got more problems than you could list with an almost unlimited number of economic woes. If you'd started a business the day Jesus was born, and lost a million dollars every year, you'd still be in better financial shape than the American government. But there is good news. If politically correctness got out of the way, we could take some easy steps including instituting this plan:

- Cut taxes
- Cut red and green tape, and deregulate
- Stop spending so much money
- Tap into energy resources at home
- Repatriate the almost $3 trillion held by American corporations overseas

Those five actions would stimulate the economy; shaft China, boomerang the economy to the level of Reagan-era growth, and all of this would be done without tax dollars. But will the politically correct practitioners move out of the way? Would an electorate conditioned by a mainstream and social media to have politically correct instincts be prepared to accept such reform, however essential it is to America's prosperity? Would elected representatives, wary of the strongly-left mainstream media and increasing dependency of millions of Americans, have the stones and the stomach to implement such reforms? The plan may sound easy enough, but when you analyze each of its steps, you can easily predict the staunch opposition of the politically correct forces. Frack? That would probably be greeted with a different four letter f-word. Waiving a thirty-five percent tax rate to some of the biggest American corporations in the world? Over our dead body. You see political correctness isn't interested in what's good for the country or in serving the public interest; its only concern is protecting and perpetuating its hold on humanity. That's why it invariably leads to liberal math.

Hey, look, if you like your economy, you can keep your economy. But I sure preferred Reagan's.

NEEDING A SPINE, BUT GETTING A SHRUG

Talking of Reagan, he set an example that we should follow. There's a politician whose every word was not market tested and utterly non-inspirational; he loved telling jokes (the kind that would have today's political advisers in a cold sweat). He knew dry wit and good-natured satire were the right vehicles for plain truths. Imagine where the world would be today if he had followed the dictates of moral relativism, a core political correctness belief. Imagine how his jokes would be received today. Would President Reagan do an apology tour? Did he think American exceptionalism couldn't be differentiated from Greek or British? Would the September 11th terrorist attack on Benghazi have gone unpunished under his Presidency? Would the doctor who led the Navy Seals to America's most wanted man still be languishing in a Pakistani prison?

The answers are clear. All of those examples may relate to the Obama years, but they are not exclusive to the 44th President, and apply to any office-holder infected with the political correctness virus. While we need a spine, political correctness can only offer a shrug. The important thing to remember is that much like gout was known as the disease of the kings, political correctness is the disease of the elites. Between Manhattan and Malibu, the disease is rife in pockets, but it is not widespread. We can use this in our campaign against political correctness, as we're headed in a bad direction. The average American, outside the professional political/ journalist class, is still inherently conservative, but he or she is too afraid to express conservative values. How often in private conversation does someone express an opinion and then says, "But you can't say that anymore"? It happens very often. They loathe political correctness. Unfortunately, they still fear it.

We've been told many times that genuine conservatives are unelectable. For this reason, "conservative" governments tend to be faux-conservative. It's easy for the left to make faux-conservatives look bad. When conservatives point out the mess left behind by Democrats, they shouldn't be apologetic about it, almost as if they're afraid to be angry about it. I think a strong, conservative leader, who tells it like it is unapologetically, can indeed win and lead. We need leaders to get angry and encourage us to be angry together with them. That's the only way we can muster the passion to defeat political correctness.

WHERE TO GO FROM HERE

I'm convinced that an American renaissance is not as distant, or as impossible, as many speculate. But neither will it roll in on the wheels of inevitability. We must revitalize an informed patriotism across the land. We also must recover a common recognition that the principles of freedom and responsibility found in the Declaration of Independence and the Constitution are in every American's self-interest, regardless of identity politics. This must become, as it once was, the lens through which all Americans view cultural choices, political candidates and public policy.

Saving America requires bringing intellectual ammunition to the battle of ideas. Too many people have forgotten or never learned what makes America exceptional—and you cannot advocate what you cannot articulate. Reason and faith are the two wings by which the American eagle took flight. The arithmetic of the American trinity is simple: Virtue cannot be sustained in the absence of faith, and if virtue is absent, then liberty must be as well. Yet new generations of Americans are unable to write out the formula, let alone balance the equation. But once that formula is relearned, confidence will return. Consensus on the American identity, a prerequisite for any renaissance, will re-emerge.

The current season in America is confusion and uncertainty. Islamic storms, European winds, and secular clouds—all politically correct weather patterns—are battering, drifting, and distressing American life and values. Thomas Paine's words from 1776 resonate with Americans today:

> These are the times that try men's souls. The summer soldier and the sunshine patriot will, in this crisis, shrink from the service of their country; but he that stands by it now, deserves the love and thanks of man and woman.

What does America have to do to come back in these trying times of our own? How do we win this fight?

How do we vanquish the threats besetting us and restore American glory? We do it, I believe, as Americans always have: through liberty, good constitutionally-limited government, free enterprise, and traditional Judeo-Christian values. This must be our country's future. For this to happen, political correctness must be vanquished. Then, and only then can our current season become one of prosperity, saved by warm hearts, burning for America.

Who can put the country back on that path? Who can vindicate American exceptionalism? Patriotic citizens with traditional values can. People just like you. But to do it, it will require every vein of resistance and defiance in the patriot bloodlines of millions of Americans. Political correctness? Not for us! For the sake of God and country, let's resist it.

No, let's defy it.

3

UNDERSTANDING
THE ENEMY

*"Give me the liberty to know, to utter, and to argue freely
according to conscience, above all liberties."*

—JOHN MILTON,
Areopagitica (1664)

I remember it well.

It was the fourth day of the second week of my first year
at university. In American terms, I was a freshman. Students
rushed to one of the courtyards hurriedly at around 2 p.m. that
sunny Thursday afternoon. Word was going around that the U.S.
President was about to make a major announcement. The date
was the 20th of March (in America, still the 19th). Sure enough,
the President made his announcement from the Oval Office. Operation Iraqi Freedom was beginning.

Now, anyone who's been to college can tell you that a university campus is a hotbed of socialist political activity at the best of
times. But, let me tell you, it was the very best of times when the
U.S. Republican President from Texas, waged war on Iraq. *Way
to jazz them up, George.* Half a world away, protests were organized. U.S. flags were purchased for the sole purpose of setting
them alight. George W. Bush masks were somehow found (in a
country that then barely celebrated Halloween), and fake blood

was included for special effect. Marchers in the name of peace turned violent, with thousands of student activists clashing with police, leading to dozens of arrests.

Less than two weeks later, I happened to be browsing at a local newsagent, and spotted a copy of *Newsweek*. Being intellectually curious, and naïve to the political bias of the magazine, I was amazed to read this by Evan Thomas:

"The vice President has a world view, and it is not the one shared by members of the East Coast foreign-policy establishment, men and women of moderation who believe in reason and dialogue, who think that problems can be talked out. Cheney believes that the world is a dangerous place, that diplomacy can be a trap, that force is sometimes the only choice. Many, probably the majority of Americans, particularly those living in the "red states" between the coasts, agree with Cheney. More to the point, so does President George W Bush of Midland, Texas." *(Evan Thomas, Newsweek, March 30, 2003)*

Wow, I thought. This guy doesn't believe the world is dangerous? I'm sure glad he's writing for a magazine, and not working at the Pentagon. Force is sometimes the only option? Diplomacy can be a trap? These are supposed to be abnormal conclusions or opinions . . .? I racked my brains for an explanation. Is this dude on happy gas, or what?

Of course, I would come to learn that this is standard fare for *Newsweek* and its ilk, war or no war. Their worldview is very different to mine and yours. In fairness to Thomas, he acknowledges that, but sneers at it, anyway. To you and me, it's just logical. But not to the liberal appeasement lobby of the political correctness skyscraper. I'm not only talking about the Iraq war here. I'm speaking generally. Our views, our presence in culture are *persona non grata*. Unwelcome. We see things with clear eyes. Evil exists, and must be confronted. To not confront it, is to accept it. There is no in-between. Moral courage isn't dangerous; it's inspiring and

necessary for the preservation of our country and wider civilization. For us, we value our right to fight for principles. We believe
in accountability. It's a moral choice. We're the good guys, and
if we want to keep our country and the world safe, we need to
fight over there to stop the fight coming here. Victory is defined
as going in there and killing as many of the bad guys as possible,
until they lose their will to fight. We get, that if you do not destroy
evil, it will proliferate. We know if you are kind to the cruel, you
will end up being cruel to the kind.

That's where we are coming from.

But that's not the same headspace the political correctness
crowd is in. Its members don't believe the reality of absolute evil.
After all, one man's terrorist is another's freedom fighter. It's all
a matter of perspective. America's a bad place, too. They mock
us for being unsophisticated, considering our views crude. These
sentiments were again revealed in February 2015, when State
Department spokeswoman, Marie Harf, suggested that the USA
"cannot win this war by killing them. We cannot kill our way out
of this war." Instead, she said, the administration should "go after
the root causes that lead people to join these groups"—including
"lack of opportunity for jobs." Responding to widespread criticism, she doubled down the next day, suggesting her argument
"might be too nuanced . . . for some."

The implication is clear: they (the politically correct) are smarter,
more refined, and deeper than us. They know better. They know
best. It's condescending, it's smug and sometimes it makes you hope
they catch a fist with their face. But above all, it's wrong. Sometimes
you can be so open-minded, your brains fall out. Our approach
to solving problems is based on fairness, hard work and pragma-
tism. Theirs is located in some theoretical comfort zone. Many of
these guys just want to feel good about themselves. It's not about
the group they purport to protect or stand up for; it's about them.
Blaming someone for their own difficult circumstances is harsh and
insensitive, but if you give an individual a free pass, by blaming a
country or system, then you're understanding and kind. *Come on!*

The mainstream media and its editorial teams long ago flushed its objectivity down the drain. It owes the public far more than the thin breakfast, lunch, and dinner gruel it is serving. When trying to understand political correctness, the *Newsweek* piece is instructive. It refers to the rationale behind it, and exposes the political opinions that shape it. You will have noticed that right-wing political correctness or conservative censorship barely exists. This is because conservatives generally ask: "Is the statement true?" rather than: "Does this statement or position hurt anyone's feelings?"

Political correctness is an ideology invented by the Left, because although Leftism considers itself intellectual, it really is about emotion. It's about feelings. Three engines propel political correctness forward: the ideological insecurity of the Left, their natural instinct and desire to control, and their unquestioned faith in the perfectibility of mankind. Expressed another way, political correctness is a psychological hypochondria.

It is important to drill down into the tribal practices of the Left, so let me explain the last point in detail. You see, the Left believe that all problems in human life stem from an unjust society and corrections and fine-tunings of that social mechanism will eventually bring utopia. In terms of taking on national security challenges, the thinking goes that the problems in other parts of the world stem from previous US government overreach, and if this can be rectified, no problems will exist. Hence the references in *Newsweek* to "reason," "dialogue," "diplomacy," "moderation," and "talking it out." Political correctness demands that excuses be made for evil, that it be ignored and coddled. As my friend, nationally-syndicated radio host, Dennis Prager, is fond of saying: The Left doesn't fight evil, *"And when you don't confront real evil, you hate those who do."* It's true. The last time they went after evil was World War II. They deny evil, avoid its confrontation, justifying it through moral equivalence, and end up flirting with the ugly twins, pacifism and appeasement. But, hey, don't stand in the way of a liberal and a plastic shopping bag. That rumble could get hairy. Inequality and carbon emissions—now, that's where it's at. They're really worthy of hate, energy and courage. *Evil's got nothin' on them!*

This isn't my theory, or some half-baked social-psychological theory. It's reality. Look at the record of the current American leadership on the Islamic State terrorist group. If you listen closely to the Administration, and read the *National Security Strategy* outlined by Susan Rice, the President's National Security Advisor, at the Brookings Institution in February 2015, you will be stunned. Climate change and U.S. overreach, according to the Obama administration, are the two biggest threats to national security. It is delusional. How can climate change be a strategic talking point in national security? The only way climate change can be a national security threat is if the sweating polar bears end up surviving and turn out to be jihadist.

POLITICAL CORRECTNESS DEFINED

Until now, I have not really offered a specific, referenced definition to political correctness. Most of you will know political correctness immediately if you see, hear, or experience it. It is as visceral as it is intellectual. We feel it every night in our living rooms when we watch the news, as we find ourselves living in a world that leaves us shaking our heads. Not a day goes by when we don't hear about an incident of political correctness madness. Whether it's the President refusing to reference Islam in discussing terrorism, some governing authority seeking to rename Columbus Day, a school district encouraging teachers to dispense with traditional terminology in a bid to embrace gender inclusiveness, or a five-year old sent home for pointing a crayon at another while saying "pyoo, pyoo," it doesn't stop. In fact, its incredulity seems to be getting worse with each passing day. Some of it is trivial; some of it deadly serious but what is certain is that our culture has changed and continues to change in disturbing ways.

But it's always helpful to have a definition. Here's a good one by Philip Atkinson in *A Study of Our Decline*:

"Political Correctness (PC) is the communal tyranny that erupted in the 1980s. It was a spontaneous declaration that particular ideas, expressions and behavior, which were then legal, should be forbidden by law, and people who transgressed should be punished. It started with a few voices but grew in popularity until it became unwritten and written law within the community."

Remember, of all the things about this ideology, it's the punishment aspect that is front and center. It is the engine. It can't be removed, or else the whole thing falls over. It would be like trying to remove the color from a jug of paint, or eating chicken fried steak without gravy. See, this is how political correctness works: it intimidates, silences, and excludes. Burdened by lack of facts, it has authored its own "attack" lexicon, with an epithet available for every occasion. Its pages are lined with weasel words, both vacuous and dangerous. They stand ready at a moment's notice to be hurled, uncritically and automatically, at the offender.

I speak from personal experience. For a skeptical view on climate change, I have been called everything from anti-science to anti-reason to anti-intellectual. A traditional view on marriage earned me the labels of homophobic, sexist and bigoted. For a critical view on multiculturalism, I netted the titles of racist, xenophobic and intolerant. An honest and objective view on Islam saw me branded Islamophobic, fascistic, small-minded, and . . . take-your-pick-from-above-again. *Quite the pedigree, I'm sure you'd agree!* And one, you no doubt, share at least some of! But the ludicrousness aside, this is really no laughing matter. Just the accusation—untrue it might be—if it is shouted loud enough or whispered to the right people—can make you lose your job, soil your reputation and invalidate a lifetime of good work.

See, when used in full force, political correctness acts as a heavy blacksnake, whipping us into submission. Pushing us into line. Cutting us down. It squelches debate and polices speech. The anti-bullying crusaders have no problem harassing us. In this way, it is no different than a group of gatekeepers determining how far you can get in your career. I don't know about you, but the only gatekeeper I'm prepared to accept is God. I won't let others use political correctness as their tool to limit my success, because at the end of the day, that's what it is: a tool for the weak and insecure to keep us on their level. Instead of the American ideal of everyone striving to be the best they can be, the pussycats want to turn the lions into pussycats. They seek a society that no longer "does" greatness. Forget the First Amendment (just for a New York minute), and note how completely and remarkably incompatible this is with the traditional aspirational American idea.

Of course, the sophisticated Left reading this book will counter that I am cleverly switching roles here, doing exactly what I accuse them of doing. There is no political correctness, they will assert, with a straight face and great indignation. It's a concoction of the Right. A fake, a *"fogazzi." Fuhgeddaboudit.* Adams, like other white privileged men, is using the term as a tool to marginalize the legitimate arguments of the less-privileged. He's the one using words to shut down debate. Nice try, guys. Your record and the state of our culture speak for themselves. Political correctness doesn't exist? Try telling that to the 58-year old who has lived the difference, experiencing the change over decades. As for privilege, well, without wanting to be too uncharitable, have you ever considered that what you call privilege is just me being better than you? Just because you might belong to a culture, or have a mindset, that barely values personal responsibility and self-reliance, doesn't make me privileged.

The Left's word games don't stop there. You can't help but note its tendency to insert modifiers before words that change the traditional meaning of those words entirely, and allow the Left to control discussion. Huh? What do I mean? Well, consider this easy example, which fits our theme nicely. When you place "politically" in front of "correct," all of a sudden, nothing becomes correct, does it? In fact, it's the total opposite. Now, try "social" before "justice." It is the same thing. Social justice is the opposite of justice. Or try putting "oppressed" before minority—suddenly not all minorities are equal. With "oppressed" prefacing "minority," the Left is able to declare women fit that category, while ruling out Jews.

THE RULES OF POLITICAL CORRECTNESS

Abraham Lincoln wasn't joking when he said that you cannot *"strengthen the weak by weakening the strong"*. Yet, this is precisely what the ill-liberal politically-correct Left aim to achieve. Individual liberty is a necessary ingredient for a fair and prosperous society. But political correctness rips liberty, fairness and prosperity away, and redistributes it. In this way, it operates as a tax, only without a promised collective social benefit. You see the grievances of the political correctness posse center on a perceived lack of sufficient inclusivity or sensitivity when it comes to groups that have historically been oppressed.

So, it employs a divide and conquer mentality, yet another a strategy entirely alien to America's *E Pluribus Unum* tradition. The two primary modes it uses to divide and rectify its perceived societal imbalance are language and identity. Through these, it tries to re-teach us to think differently. For example, right now the Left is trying to re-teach Americans to think of race as essential, not incidental, to our characters, and that being a woman is an achievement, not merely a chance of birth. It wants society to believe that if you are non-male, non-heterosexual and non-Anglo, you have to be struggling—irrespective of other measures of success. The Left is trying to effect changes in attitudes and labels.

Much like an unjust law, political correctness doesn't equally apply. The rules of political correctness forbid equal application. Why can you tell an Irish joke, but not an African-American one? Why can you criticize every religion except Islam? Why can you suggest that a man has poor cooking skills and be met by laughter, but to suggest that women's brains may not be as wired to learn math or engineering in the same way as men's brains is met by stunned silence? It's because the Left sets the rules of discourse here, and almost everywhere else. But to be mischievous, I guess it could get confusing. Remember the 2014 celebrity nude photo hacking scandal? Just imagine if among the hacked material a video of a scantily-clad female celebrity vigorously speaking out against gay marriage was found. The confusion among the outraged classes over how to react would be delicious.

NIPPING ALLEGATIONS OF HYPOCRISY IN THE BUD

Occasionally, defenders of political correctness will try to turn the tables, and charge that it is conservatives who feel they are entitled to define "a moral and spiritual absolute" and that they are the most dangerous to our freedom. That's wrong. The politically correct thought police have their own absolutes just as you and I do. The difference is that they want a monopoly for theirs. The Judeo-Christian world view, on which America was founded, as well as the secular enlightenment which also played a role, was never monopolistic. We don't seek to coerce individuals into a collective. It's the Marxists who do that. Political correctness is Marxist to the core.

DIVIDING BY LANGUAGE AND IDENTITY

The Left is doing its best to subdivide America along the lines of ethnicity, gender, sexuality and culture. You may have heard of the culture of complaint. Maybe you've seen references to the grievance lobby. They're one and the same. Their father? Political correctness. By deviously creating a language of division, the Left sired it. Victimhood continues to reach cultish proportions, its preachers and their preaching apparently pathological. Now, almost everyone has become a victim, complaining about almost everything. Genuine discrimination—the subject of previously serious accusation—has been watered down, and stretched to include as much as possible. Remember when racism used to be just hating someone for his or her race. Well, those days are long gone. Racist now is what you are if you disagree with me.

Remember when sexual harassment was pinching a woman's butt or the boss threatening a female employee with job loss if she didn't sleep with him? Today, compliment a woman, tell a gender-related joke or show romantic attention that is unwanted, and your reputation can be destroyed for life. In fact, researchers from Northeastern University in Boston claimed in March 2015 that polite, chivalrous men who smiled at women were benevolent sexists.

Ever heard of a micro-aggression? It is, according to one Columbia University professor, an "everyday slight, putdown, indignity, or invalidation unintentionally directed toward a marginalized group." So, if you deliberately seek out an Asian tourist at a tourist location to take your family group photo, you're delivering an insulting putdown, and should probably be shot on the spot. Or something like that. *Hey, they take better photos. I think it's a compliment.* And, of course, when it comes to judging whether a micro-aggression has taken place, the only person who can determine that is the person who perceives the bias. *Sounds like a fair deal.* Either way, the logic of the micro-aggression increasingly defines the Democratic Party, because identity politics needs the oxygen of perpetual grievance.

Instances of racism and sexual harassment are real, serious, and repugnant, but political correctness has cheapened them at great expense to cultural cohesion for political gain. It has disrespected their magnitude, and instead spawned hideously false agendas with giant industries running on fabricated hysteria. All of it deliberate; all of it for its (the Left's) own agenda. First, it creates the victim group and then it perpetuates it with more laws. What does this mean? Lawsuits get filed, and government needs to expand. Guess who gets to ride in as the white knight, and play the savior? Oh, I'm sorry. I shouldn't have said that. That's racist. Guess who gets to ride in as the *tanned* knight and rescue the day? That's right: the Left, and its language. The truth is these politically-correct efforts are far more likely to provoke a backlash (which, by the way, I consider imminent and well-overdue) that actually hinders the struggle against bias.

CONSEQUENCES OF POLITICAL CORRECTNESS

Think about everything wrong in the world right now. In most cases, political correctness is part of the problem. Take my own concerns. I believe there are five major threats facing every Western country, including our own:

- identity politics
- secularism
- the expanding welfare state
- the war against national identity
- Islamic jihadist terrorism

Political correctness is behind every single one of these concerns and its influence stops them from being effectively addressed and remedied. Take the example of the Islamic threat posed to the entire world. Liberal language or "political correctness" is now a shield for evil. By screaming "racist", rather than allowing debate, our academics, commentators and politicians deafened us to the warning until it was too late. But even now, only one side considers itself at war, and it's not us. Our President plays duck-and-cover word games, and can't even bring himself to use the adjective "Islamic" when discussing terrorism. The excusing of Muslim violence is unmistakable. There's simply a conspiracy of silence amongst the caring classes when it comes to discussing the Islamic faith. As a result, America is unable to defeat the evil and defend itself effectively. Without an unwavering grasp of what is right and what is wrong, how can we ever expect to stand in judgment of our terrorist enemies?

The steep decline across America in the economy, civility and education finds itself at the feet of political correctness. We see less discipline, less motivation and less generosity because the secular religion preaches "It's all about me. There is no greater good or greater power." Whether it's soft-hearted judges insisting on seeing the diamond in every loutish lump of coal that appears before their bench or the shameless gutting of our military at a time when the world is deeply unsettled, political correctness is not just securing bad results for our country, but also striking at the heart of our values. It's making us less patriotic and more divided as well as less confident and more mediocre. It's siphoning the strength of America and feeding it to those who would do us harm. We've rapidly turning away from being a traditional country to a secular one, where politically correct thought is considered mainstream.

If America continues to abandon its roots for political correctness, it will permanently lose all the attending benefits of Christian civilization such as law, absolute moral standards, a sound economy, a limited government, and any vestige of liberty it still maintains.

TOLERANCE AND EMPATHY

I'm a deeply empathetic person. I consider it to be extremely important. In fact, I would have trouble recognizing you as a human being if you're not empathetic. There are not many things more important than the ability to put yourself in someone else's shoes. Even as we travel our individual journeys, many of our experiences are common. Dealing with a sick parent, going through a relationship break-up, losing someone to cancer, experiencing a car accident, feeling unsure in a foreign country are experiences we all understand and during which we can give support to our fellow man. When it comes to that, I'm your man. I'm there. I'm down.

But my empathy has limits. It doesn't, for example, extend to people who have made it clear they want to hurt me, my family or my country. It doesn't include formed communities within my country of those who freely chose to come here, but treat this nation as nothing more than a stretch of land, somewhere to park. It won't prevent me from unleashing an acid critique on the desert-based honor culture that wants a veto on modernity. Basically, my empathy is not a trump card that beats out truth, freedom of speech, and everything else. It shouldn't be for you, either. While empathy is important, we cannot allow a culture of empathy to become a culture immune from criticism. We can't allow other people to take advantage of our tolerance. That's when it becomes not only counter-productive, but dangerous.

I'd feel much more comfortable if so many of those calling for "tolerance" did not seem to be tolerant of the unacceptable.

As a nation, and as a people, our tolerance is robust. There will always be individuals and incidents, but no other nation can match America's plurality and harmony. This is a record we should never be afraid to tout, contrary to the politically correct mantra that considers America flawed from its inception to the present time.

AMERICA IS PUBLIC ENEMY NO. 1

The hatred of America seems implacable. Their loathing of America is somewhat "democratic." The thinking behind, "If you have a successful business, you didn't build that." corresponds to "If you have a successful nation or culture, you didn't build that." Let me explain. The thinking goes that if all people are created equal, then all outcomes should be the same. If someone ends up a murderer, something must have happened to that person. If someone has differentiated him or herself through success or wealth, something must have allowed the person to stand out. By extension, a nation is no different. If a nation or culture is evil, it must be the victim of something. If a nation or culture is successful, something must have worked to its benefit. Social justice, then, demands that successful Western civilization (of which America is the stand-out) must be at the very least weakened, and the most failed non-Western ideologies must be rewarded. But Reagan said it all, when he said: "*Of the four wars in my lifetime, none came about because the United States was too strong.*"

Thomas Jefferson would roll in his grave if he knew that in America today, people were being punished for donating money to the "wrong" causes, or that speaker appearances were being canceled on college campuses if they don't uphold politically correct mandates. When self-appointed tolerance tsars anywhere kill voices, squash opinion and squelch debate, they are effectively turning thinking into a hate crime. Oppressive, discriminatory and unjust is what it is. It's also part of an anti-American virus, imported from abroad. Political correctness was founded on the intervention of government on others; America was founded on the presumption of liberty.

Political correctness is a brazen assault on the First Amendment. Nothing is more counter to freedom of expression and freedom of press. In essence, it denies that truth and the words to express it aren't the province of individuals to believe and speak as we see fit, rather truth is to be dictated by collective coercion and force. Tolerance, diversity, and inclusion are values that sound great in the abstract until they trump free speech. Uniformity, exclusion, and intolerance are the real expectations of political correctness.

Take religious liberty as an example. It's under fire. The media and the Left insist that fair play, as well as free speech, obligate you to sponsor your opponents' message. If you object, you're a victimizer and must be broken. *If you're a Christian business and your opponents are advocating sexual liberation, look out.*

Everyone knows the First Amendment protects freedom of religion, speech, press, lobby, and assembly. Along with the Second and Tenth Amendments of the Constitution, it's what truly makes America so special among nations. Preserving these unique freedoms is essential, particularly for our children and their future. This is why we must fight this ideology and repel this foreign virus with every fiber of our being. You know, some things just don't go together—Mitt Romney and elections, feminists and families, Islam and the West—and, political correctness and America.

4

MISSING COJONES

"The crimes of the vanquished find their background and their explanation, though not, of course, their pardon, in the follies of the victors."

—WINSTON CHURCHILL,
The Gathering Storm, pg. 15

The President sits in the Oval Office, leaning back on his high-backed leather chair, his hands folded. An irate and excitable Greek ambassador is on the other end of the desk, castigating the most powerful man in the world, apparently unhappy with recent U.S. intervention in Greek-Cypriot affairs. After weathering the storm for some minutes, the President finally snaps:

> "Listen to me, Mr. Ambassador! America is an elephant. Cyprus is a flea. Greece is a flea. If those two fleas continue itching the elephant, they may just get whacked by the elephant's trunk, whacked good. . . . We pay a lot of good American dollars to the Greeks, Mr. Ambassador. If your prime minister gives me talk about democracy, parliaments, and constitutions, he, his parliament, and his constitution may not last long."

That's a true story. The year was 1967. The U.S. president was Lyndon Johnson. The Greek ambassador was . . . well, that was kind of the President's point.

Fast forward to 2009. The season is spring; the city is London. The event is the G20 summit. A journalist asks President Obama if he believes in American exceptionalism. He responds: "I believe in American exceptionalism, just as I suspect that the Brits believe in British exceptionalism and the Greeks believe in Greek exceptionalism."

In forty-two years, we went from Greece being a flea and America an elephant to the President casually equating American exceptionalism with Greek exceptionalism. That's political correctness for you.

A COURAGE DEFICIENCY

This story is re-told, not to offend the Greeks or endorse President Johnson's sentiments. Generally speaking, I don't applaud what the politically correct would no doubt deem "abuse" of foreign leaders (unless it's deserved—then, I celebrate). But I must confess I much prefer the 1967 tirade to the 2009 tragedy. The tirade had life, color, substance and, most importantly, courage in it. The antiseptic, eunuch statement of 2009 was notable only for its timidity, and what it revealed about President Obama's worldview.

But it is unfair to suggest the loss of courage and replacement of political correctness of the United States and the Western world began with the current President. It didn't. Even as far back as 1978, prominent Russian critic of Soviet totalitarianism, Alexander Solzhenitsyn, said at a Harvard graduation ceremony:

"A decline in courage may be the most striking feature that an outside observer notices in the West today. The Western world has lost its civic courage. . . . Such a decline in courage is particularly noticeable among the ruling and intellectual elite, causing an impression of a loss of courage by the entire society."

Solzhenitsyn's observational words in the earlier stages went unheeded, and the march that would lead to the complete loss of Western stamina continued unabated. The primary blazers of the trail to timidity remain the ruling and intellectual elite Solzhenitsyn singled out for criticism, with the only difference now their enormously heightened influence on the culture. Today's elites enjoy an unparalleled existence, boosted by technology and far more enhanced communication mediums. As a consequence, we live in a world and polity largely the design of such elites, almost unanimously secular and leftist.

These leaders are ironically best known for their lack of leadership (essential to courage) on all matters of real importance, such as evil and what is in the best interests of the nation. They continually seek justification for their anemic mettle, relying on their vehicles of education and media to drive home ambivalent, if not anti-American sentiment. If people can't feel love for their country or are unable to identify with its values, then irresolution naturally follows. It is why the Left with political correctness invests such substantial effort and time diminishing America. If America is just another country with a soccer team, why should we have courage and lead when we have no moral authority to do so? Who are we to be courageous, anywhere, when there are so many problems at home? This is why America, and Western nations everywhere, has been increasingly conditioned to ignore their courage instincts, and instead choose to wallow in pathetic, unhelpful and *unwarranted* self-pity. It is also why political correctness is responsible for the impending suicide of civilization. Courage requires truth, and political correctness declares war on truth every day. Responding to barbaric violence with just a cartoonist's pencil is not a mark of civilization. It is a mark of emasculation.

FIGHTING BACK—AND WHY IT'S HARD

I'm a pretty direct kind of guy. So, I'll just come out and say it. We spend too much time protecting the culture of those who join our country and far too little defending the culture they have chosen to join. Just because people decide to make America home (their choice, let me stress), America should not have to inherit the feuds of other nations. And while I'm at it, on another related matter—I'm sick of the "America is racist" mythology perpetuated around the world, and now accepted as reality. Are there real racists in America? Of course there are. Is there real racism in America? Of course there is. But here's the truth: The U.S. is the least racist society on earth. It is the best place in the world for *anyone* to live. That's why more black Africans have immigrated to the U.S. voluntarily than came as slaves. It's also why probably very few of them have decided to leave America for other countries. And one more thing, it galls me in the wake of a terrorist attack, when the liberal media focus on the supposed anti-Islamic backlash imminent or already present, rather than the terror attacks themselves. Talk about a straw man argument. This is all because of a cowering establishment that insists on denying the obvious. *It's not religion, stupid.* It's *the* religion, stupid.

I've just picked two examples close to my heart. Both take real courage to express, because they violate the sacrosanct laws of political correctness. They are logical, simple conclusions, supported by fact. They are neither controversial, nor extreme. In fact, truth be told, they're rather plain assertions. But both would not be tolerated by the allegedly tolerant politically-correct force. In fact, such statements would be mocked and scorned viciously and endlessly, at great harm to the source, by the cultural elites in whatever form they manifest. You could lose your job, and likely attract the attention of undesirable people, becoming subject to a media or electronic witch-hunt that examines every area of your life. The fallout can continue beyond your livelihood, and even affect your health and family. Why? You dared offend the Left's confected sense of intellect. You had the audacity to challenge the orthodoxy of the panting, outraged mob, in the thrall of green-left elitists. You provided an unwelcome intrusion of reality into the Left's carefully constructed fantasy world. You questioned the war on truth and reality.

TURNING OUR BACKS ON CIVILIZATION

Advocates of political correctness say they are committed to the ideology because they wish to live in a harmonious society. But criticism and civilization are inseparable. What makes us civilized is our ability to exchange opinion, and accept alternative views. To remove these characteristics from our society is not just to thumb our nose at freedom and civil rights, but is also an exercise in misanthropy. It de-humanizes us, removing the human instincts that make us individuals (such as expression, narrative, language, etc.). Therefore, anybody with an interest in preserving civilization, or with an affinity for people and life, should find political correctness repulsive.

Civilization requires courage, life and character. For civilization to flourish, it cannot yawn at evil, or take the side of the oppressor, rather than the oppressed. Civilization cannot afford to find evil in local police, but not Islamic terror. It must not allow for constraining speech rather than increasing diversity in expression. It can't afford to prefer a hashtag and hug, to truth and necessary confrontation. Nor can it take exception with exceptionalism. If history is any guide, the protection racket on behalf of empathy usually quickly turns to a protection racket of evil.

AMERICAN DREAM TO BECOME
EUROPEAN NIGHTMARE

America need not look far for evidence of the dangers. Political correctness tore through the European continent savagely, leaving it in terminal decline. With no Judeo-Christian ethic, and no capitalist economy, it is sinking rapidly into a socialist lethargy. Its vitality and aspiration to greatness are gone. Most of all, it is willfully deaf to the threats it faces, recognized for its absolute lack of courage (and interest) in defeating threats to its homeland. "*Leave it to America*" is the continental motto, in a place more interested in vacations and soccer scores.

But world affairs are not the only thing in which Europeans are uninterested. They also show almost no desire to begin or extend their own family, preferring to concentrate on what they consider 'the good life. Such cultural selfishness is a mirror reflection of the political self-regard that animates political correctness, and the self-centeredness of "professional offence takers." This self-interest comes from the pursuit of power. Where Western civilization has been about freedom, the liberal society worldview is infinitely more concerned about power, and the creation of an absolute orthodoxy. In Europe, more so than anywhere else in the world, people have embraced an ideology that rejects free speech and alternate viewpoints. A long time ago, Europe decided that rather than fight this totalitarian threat, it would shirk a bloody street fight and learn to love it.

MANNING UP

In a world where making fried chicken for Harmony Day morning tea at work would probably trigger a call from Human Resources and a reference to a "micro-aggression" and allegations of permanent trauma, my suggestion of 'manning up' probably has feminists scowling right now as they read this. But this is exactly what America needs to do, particularly the jelly-backed media. They *certainly* need to man up. Cojones or courage is essential to fighting political correctness, which is precisely why the ideology seeks to remove it. But the courage can't be counterfeit; it must be genuine. Some talk a big game, but cower nonetheless. This is no different to phone cojones (where they are forceful on the phone, but weak in person).

Political correctness is everywhere. We see it in the reaction of locals when a fast food chain plays on the turf of hipster cafes offering positional goods and acidophilus milk. It's when Starbucks offer you a popular hashtag cause, and some baristas correct you when you ask for a black coffee *(it's un-creamed coffee, Sir)*. It's the time you realize your son's school has turned into Social Justice Warrior boot camp, where English is "Gender Studies" and History and Geography are "Global inequality and the failures of capitalism." But often it's not just what you say, but who you are. You can express the same idea as someone else, but depending on your race and sex, you might receive two completely different reactions. While we see the false virtue and rank idiocy, not to mention discrimination, in this, the Left digs its heels in, inventing yet more terminology to marginalize and alienate much of America: "mansplaining," "whitesplaining" and "straightsplaining."

No matter how hard it tries to sear the illusion that the Left's thinking and reactions are the same as those of Main Street, we must remember it is nonsense. The pet peeves of the bubble that politically correct types inhabit are not those of America; in fact, much of the crocodile tears of "victimhood" that populate this tribe, alienate most of heartland America. This is why a rebellion against political correctness by traditional forces will ultimately be successful. Much like the early defeats by Britain in the War of Independence, we will lose many of the initial battles to a hostile media and establishment, but we will win the war with people power, providing our courage punches the clock.

For as long as our courage is missing, it means that the United States cannot re-capture the common sense of purpose that has always propelled it forward. The left-wing subculture has taken over America.

We must send it back, like Elvis instructed in *"Return to Sender,"* by carrier-eagle.

5

EMBOLDENING
THE ENEMY

"Me? A Cold War warrior? Well, yes—if that is how they wish to interpret my defense of values of freedoms fundamental to our way of life."

MARGARET THATCHER,
PRIME MINISTER OF ENGLAND

The sun is rising in New York City, and people are bustling to work down 7th Avenue, with only a few making a quick stop at the corner of 40th street to quickly grab a *Berliner* (similar to a jelly doughnut) from *Bakery Reich*. Doughnut in mouth, they cross the street, artfully dodging honking Volkswagen Beetle taxis. *"Hey, pass auf,"* yells one taxi driver. *"Blöde Amerikaner—können immernoch keine Regeln folgen; verstehen nur was von Freiheit,"* he mutters under his breath, shaking his head. *Hey, be careful; watch where you're going! Stupid Americans—they still just can't follow rules after all this time; they only understand freedom.*

Another couple of blocks uptown, in the Times Square bowtie, a giant black and white swastika on a brilliant red billboard covers the entire front of Times Tower. A specially made and imported German sound system blares out *"Sieg heil!"* once at 9 a.m. and again at 6 p.m. and obligingly all stop to salute the totalitarian overlords. Resistance is out of the question; the punishment too inhumane to contemplate. That's just the East Coast. It's a similar story in California, Oregon, and Washington State, but the overlords and customs are different. They're Japanese.

Much of the world now speaks German. But the Japanese empire remains substantial, with the people of Australia, India and Indonesia eating sushi, and speaking Japanese. Judaism is outlawed everywhere, and may as well be extinct. Those who threaten the Aryan Master Race within the German empire, such as the mentally and physically handicapped, or have any Jewish connection, continue to be routinely murdered.

This is the evil world that might exist if the Nazis had won World War II. It could have easily gone this way. Thank God— and America—it didn't.

WE COULDN'T DO IT TODAY

I bring this alternate historical fantasy up for one very simple reason. It would be impossible to prosecute World War II in today's culture, with its values. Utterly impossible. Politically-correct positions, increasingly ingrained in the general population, simply will not allow it. The positions, instincts, and attitudes that were present in enough people on the world then have been perpetually and actively attacked by the Left ever since. Let us cast a glance at the list of things that were, and would be required to conduct such a war:

- our own unifying nationalism, and sense of pride
- a willingness to judge another culture
- the desire to confront, fight and defeat evil, at any cost
- patience to be in it for as long as it takes
- preparedness to "go it alone," regardless of criticism from others.

See what I mean? I'm sure you do. In the last ten years, in particular, I have not seen a modicum (or in President Obama's language, a "smidgen") of evidence to suggest that any of those five things are sufficiently present within the free world to prosecute World War II again, or for that matter, World War III in the future.

Instead, I see a general culture, led by the (now, admittedly, much more powerful) latte belt, deeply antagonistic to those positions. Ironically, this antagonism is more intense than any they might harbor for the actual evil we're considering in this hypothetical. Those five virtues, courtesy of political correctness, have become:

- Multiculturalism, and a heavily diluted national identity, divided, with little knowledge of American principles (*nationalism is chauvinist bigotry and must be curbed*)
- A refusal to judge any culture, at any cost, despite any evidence (*this is not allowed, as it is racist and bigoted, and thus, 'verboten'*)
- Lack of passion, confidence and certainty, and a clear preference of pacifism. *Is it really my place? Who am I to cast stones? Does it affect me? I'm not sure I believe in aggression. Can I get away with not doing anything about it? I've got a lot on. I would really prefer to . . .*
- Impatience and selfishness. *How long will it take? I'm used to a world of instant gratification. No limits, no restraints. Things happen quickly now, I don't like waiting. What's the easiest way? This better not drag on . . .*
- Comply with the multilateralism lobby. *Only do things with an international coalition, and UN approval. We should only act, if others join us.*

This is why our country, America, and the free world we are meant to lead are in deep trouble. The attack on our national identity, secularism, moral equivalence and the age of instant gratification with technology and the practice of empty political symbolism is a lethal combination. We are better placed than anyone else in the free world right now, but every day we inch closer to disaster, thanks to political correctness. It is urgent that we return to whom we were, and what we really are.

TO INTERN, OR NOT TO INTERN—
THE CHANGE IN US

When you consider the burgeoning global jihad threat, potentially bigger than WWII, it is hard to be optimistic. Evil as they are, they are united, passionate, patient and believe in something, other than themselves. They're prepared to fight for as long as it takes and are unrestrained by convention. They can only be defeated, if we are prepared to match their intensity, patience, and faith, in our cause.

To give an indication of just how much the culture has changed, consider this. In the 1940s, America interned Japanese-Americans. Similarly, in Australia, the Japanese, as well as Italians and Germans were interned. Regardless of what you may think about those internments and the violation of civil liberties incurred (and it is true that it appears there was little evidence of disloyalty among those interned), what interests me is both countries' preparedness to take that action. By taking that action, I believe we can infer that the people and leaders of both nations were culturally confident, passionate, imbued with a desire to win, unprepared to put anything to chance and their own sense of good and evil.

Now contemplate this. Every Western country is battling radical Islam within its own national population (exacerbated by multiculturalism and poor immigration choices), while Islamic State is proving its appeal. There is significant evidence of disloyalty (unlike the WWII internments), both on the individual and mosque level. Yet never once, anywhere, to my knowledge, has the internment of Muslims as a policy idea been floated.

Let me be clear: I am not advocating for the current internment of Muslims in America, Australia or anywhere else. But I also do not believe it should never be considered, nor do I believe anyone should fear raising this concept. I simply bring it up to highlight how different we now are as a people, as a culture, and as a society. I will leave you to ponder the consequences of those changes in light of facing and defeating evil.

PATTON'S MILITARY AND YOUR MILITARY ARE NOT THE SAME

Of everything that political correctness leaves in its path of destruction, the most dangerous to civilization is the damage done to the United States military.

I love the men and women of the United States military. They are our heroes. They protect not just America, but the entire world. They are civilization's troops and freedom's defenders. They deserve our recognition and respect every second of the day.

General George Patton represented the best of the American military tradition. He is a hero of mine. His motto '*Audacity, audacity, always audacity*' is one I live by, and one I encourage others to adopt. Patton's leadership was unparalleled, and showcased the finest of America. The following quote reveals everything you need to know about the General. A will to win defined the man. He understood that for freedom to beat tyranny, it had to not only match tyranny's intensity, passion and hunger, but surpass it.

We'll win this war but we'll win only by fighting and showing the Germans that we've got more guts than they have, or ever will have. We're not just going to shoot the sons of bitches, we're going to rip out their living G-damn guts and use them to grease the treads of our tanks.

The United States needs a General Patton right now, perhaps more than ever. Yet a retired Army Colonel recently told me that when he was in Command at General Staff College, there was a consensus view that Patton would not have risen beyond the level of captain in today's Army. Political correctness has changed the military enormously, and continues to, from the way it is run, to the way wars are conducted, to the revision of rules and standards.

The warrior culture is being strangled. Lowering fitness standards for female marines, the Obama administration's repeal of "Don't Ask, Don't Tell," policy, consideration of a change to its "transgender" service policy, running 'sexism and racism' seminars and plans to shrink it to pre-WWII levels are all examples of the rampant political correctness making America and the world less safe.

In 2012, a new army manual ordered soldiers to avoid "taboo conversation topics," including "making derogatory comments about the Taliban," "advocating women's rights," "any criticism of pedophilia," "directing any criticism towards Afghans," "mentioning homosexuality and homosexual conduct" or "anything related to Islam." In 2015, a Pentagon-approved seminar taught that modern sexism is rooted in the Bible, U.S. Constitution and the Declaration of Independence.

I've just picked a few examples. There are enough to fill several pages. But you get the point. It is all outrageous, offensive and deeply disturbing.

Armed conflict is the last step of diplomacy. I believe that for the last twenty years, politics have kept the army from fulfilling its core mission of "close with and destroy the enemy." I also feel that for the past thirteen years of war, the military has been restrained from destroying the enemy. Perhaps the best example is the current farce—the ISIS campaign waged by the United States and several allies. Our military's hands are tied with the rope of political correctness. Our brave men and women want to get the job done, but they're not allowed.

We must be free to win and defeat tyranny. We can't fight in a civilized manner when we're fighting animals. In any street fight, it's the person who wants to win the most, the one who's prepared to die, who always win. Our enemies are prepared to die. Unless we can match the intensity, passion and hunger they have for their tyrannical cause, with ours for freedom and civilization, we will not win.

With a change in the White House and potentially in the Pentagon, I pray that in the coming years, the military's hands will not be tied and we will be allowed to destroy the enemy. The best defense is an awesome offense. We must bring the fight to our enemies.

It's what Patton would do.

THE WORLD RIGHT NOW

The next American President must be blunt and confident, backed up with quick action, on the world scene. It's not about shooting first, and aiming later, as President Obama is fond of suggesting. It's about shooting the bad guy before he shoots us. There are a lot of bad guys, and like the sharks they are, they have sensed our blood in the water from miles away.

As the West bleeds, continuing to lather itself in its own hate soap in the shower, and acts like it has shampoo in its eyes when it comes to evil, the world's villains splash around in the bathtub, unsupervised, unleashed and unworried. While adult pre-schools are established in New York and Eva Mendez is forced to apologize for offending women who wear sweatpants, Islamists are chopping heads off, the Chinese are cheating like crazy, the Iranians almost have a nuke, the North Koreans are mad as ever and the Russians are turning back the clock three decades. Believe me, it certainly is a great test of my Christian charity not to use profanity at this point. It is a terrible state of affairs. Heck, it's almost enough to make you consider converting to Islam!

The world is more dangerous than it has been in a long time, and the incorrigible truth is that our America and Western civilization is at a tipping point. The thought-control called political correctness isn't just annoying. It's a form of soft Marxism that is anti-truth and anti-reality, a noose around our neck, making us incapable of dealing with opponents to the civilized world. Through political correctness, we are telegraphing our weaknesses. This limp-wristedness means the enemies of America and bullies of the world provoke, test and assert in ways that once were impossible. When America is strong, the world complains. When America is weak, the world suffers. That's what we are seeing right now. It does not surprise me that at the same time America is retreating and downsizing its military, China and Russia are expanding. What has happened to our moral courage?

WHY MORAL COURAGE BARELY BREATHES

I have to tell you that I don't consider the concept of an eye for an eye, and a tooth for a tooth (a response to match, not exceed the original offence) as one of vengeance, but rather justice. Sadly, that puts me at odds with an American elite that has lost its nerve, its head, its soul, or all three. I believe moral courage is the greatest trait any person can have. In terms of leadership, I don't believe you can be great, if you don't have it. The liberal appeasement lobby worldview has always seen such courage as dangerous. If only we could ask Reagan. His opponents saw his challenging of the Soviet Union as dangerous. But imagine the world today if he had followed the dictates of moral relativism. *Don't worry: I won't go there this time!*

Moral courage cannot co-exist with political correctness. It's not even an awkward relationship or deeply unhappy marriage. There's absolutely nothing there. The two are deeply incompatible with irreconcilable differences. Moral courage contravenes not only political correctness, but its inspiration and its agenda. This is why it is not permissible for anyone wishing to stay in the good graces of the politically-correct elites to display it. It's also why the media which carry the water for the politically correct agenda mercilessly mock and deride any leader that even hints at it. And let's be honest, with political correctness in control of the political establishment, the media, and most opinion-leaders, leaders have more skin in the game in terms of staying within political correctness confines. This is why American leadership and its respect in the world are at historically low levels. To put is rather crassly, it's why we've lost our testicular fortitude.

Interestingly, it was moral courage that began the experiment of freedom in the laboratory of America, and has always animated it. It is little wonder that whenever it dissipates (think Carter and Obama), there is a national malaise. That's why it is time to ask ourselves the right questions. No one put it better than the Gipper: *"There are no easy answers, but there are simple answers. We must have the courage to do what we know is morally right."*

WHAT AMERICA NEEDS IN A PRESIDENT

I want an important President.

Allow me to explain. History should judge the next President of the United States as a defining figure who came to represent not just a set of political beliefs but a cast of mind, a cultural attitude and an image of America itself. To do that, he or she will have to be:

- at least as politically incorrect as President Reagan, if not more so
- at least as tough as Margaret Thatcher, if not more so
- at least as tenacious as Winston Churchill, if not more so and,
- at least as morally courageous as President George W. Bush, if not more so

Tough ask, I know, particularly with how much the world has changed, even in the last five years. But nevertheless, it is what is needed. The key is the absence of political correctness, an absence from which toughness, tenacity and moral courage will be allowed to emerge.

But let's back up a bit. No other leader in the world is more scrutinized or pressured than the President of the United States. The office is the greatest honor and highest responsibility anywhere on this earth. The President can set the tone for the world, and be the role model of the successful civilization he represents.

He, or she, should never seek to be popular, because the job itself makes this an impossible aim. A truly great President will be praised and vilified, admired and detested beyond leaving office. To echo the words of Churchill: *"You have enemies? Good. That means you've stood up for something, sometime in your life."* A defining President will inspire blind hatred, swooning worship, anger and adoration, but never indifference, until the day he or she dies. Such disparity of intense opinion will tell you all you need to know about the effectiveness of the Administration. That, my friends, can only be the legacy of a politically-incorrect President. Am I saying that a politically-correct President can't be a great President? Yes. You bet I am.

Personally, my ideal President is one who every morning, looks at himself in the mirror, straightens his tie, and says, *"Today, as a constitutional conservative, I am not giving an inch on my principles or on my grave concern for where this country, a nation in blithe denial, is headed."* I want someone charismatic and appealing, but viscerally and instinctively tribal. A President who believes that you will be either with him, and right, or against him, and therefore wrong. A President for whom there will be seldom a third way. Strong in principle, bold in action. A force of nature, able to carry American culture, and lead to an important Presidency.

Given my views about what we need in a President, I want to say this about the upcoming 2016 election. No candidate is perfect. The eventual nominee may cause a certain group to lose interest, but if it does, is that political maturity? Civic maturity? Do people really see the Republican as no different from the Democrat? Our goal should be to correct that fallacy. If we let the perfect be the enemy of the good, the bad will prevail.

HOW LEADERSHIP MAKES A DIFFERENCE—
CHINESE PEP TALK

The London 2012 Olympics hosted fevered speculation and attention on an American-Chinese rivalry, drummed up by the world's media, largely acting as cheerleaders for China. The talk was enhanced by the "battle" playing out for top position on the medal tally (which America won comfortably, I might add, despite being at a one billion person handicap). Adding further fuel to the fire, amidst accusations of Chinese doping, the Chinese hit out at the Americans during the swimming, saying "*The Americans are very bad; they do a lot of evil.*"

A match-up for a gold medal between the two national sides for a major sporting event at the Olympics never eventuated. But at the time, its possibility intrigued me, having grown up watching re-runs of the final moments of the Miracle Game in Lake Placid (not the gold medal game, but golden in different ways), and later Kurt Russell's brilliant performance in the 2004 Disney movie, *Miracle*. It is often said sport is life, but often sport throughout history has also been tied to politics. So, if there was a major game between China and America at the Olympics, what kind of locker room speech should a coach give the team before such an event?

Our time has arrived. The moment each of you has dreamed of is here.

Tonight we play for the gold medal. You're on the edge of glory.

I'm proud of each of you, and so is your country. Some of you hail from big cities; others of you from towns so small you can't even find them on the map.

Your journey has been long, hard, and full of setbacks and triumphs. You've wept in disappointment and screamed in elation. And your families and churches and neighborhoods have shared every moment with you. They've sacrificed and in some cases, gave you money they didn't have. Because they believed. Believed in you. Believed in your dream. Believed in their country.

Today, you are the role models of your communities. Right now, thousands of miles away, people you know in places you know are huddled around televisions ready to watch you take this game.

This is where you need to remember who you are and where you come from. Each of you has worn your shirt knowing that what's on the front is much more important than what is on the back. You don't just play for yourself; you play for the United States of America.

Tonight we play China.

Now, I don't put much stock in politics. It's not my deal. I don't like it and never have. I do sports. That's my thing. But I can tell you that sometimes sport can be more than physical; sometimes it's emotional and political. Sometimes the circumstances in the world around a game make it that way. Sometimes a whole nation can lift on the back of an improbable victory on a field or a rink. And when it does, you stir patriotism so profound, men and women that don't even know the basics of our sport are forced to wipe their streaming tears away.

It's happened before. And it needs to happen here again tonight.

It's difficult not to sense a U.S. downslide. But we're only falling behind our potential. The world tells us that we live in the Asian century. That it is only a matter of time before China overtakes America and the Communist Party of China and its ruling Politburo, and military, will be the most powerful force in the world.

I have nothing against the Chinese people. They are men and women created by God, just like us. Many of their individual objectives are the same as ours. Every individual is equal. But every culture is not.

Communism and America will never see eye to eye. We were founded on the idea of freedom through limited government, and filled with the belief that our rights come from God and are therefore inalienable. We are an optimistic, libertarian, philanthropic, individualistic, and religious nation. China is none of these. China's power comes from its sheer size of population, not its innovation. It may have opened its markets to be free, but its heart remains closed.

We may be locked in close battle with China for superiority on the medal tally but our culture and way of life, and the culture of the West, is superior. Whatever our gripes with our government, and there are rightfully many, we are free and committed to the idea that we can rise above however we were born to achieve whatever it is we want to. Our heart is open. And it's why we have no time for the government of our opponents, and the way they treat their people. They're scheming, scary, and mysterious, and if they step too far, you can be sure we will unleash a can of industrial strength-sized American whoop ass on them. It's what we do.

Our 300 million people may be dwarfed by the 1.3 billion that their government controls but our free minds, voices and hearts will always drown them out.

Tonight, use your minds, voices, and hearts to not only win the gold medal but notch a victory for freedom, and humanity.

A victory that says freedom will always triumph. A victory that celebrates our red, white and blue goodness. A victory that reminds our enemies and detractors that we are the land of the free and the home of the brave. A victory that will have opponents trembling with fear.

Tonight, you are warriors. Let's get our nation cheering again.

This is your time. Take it. No defeat; no surrender.

———————

It is highly unlikely this pep-talk would have been given at the 2012 Olympic Games—I'll get to why in a minute. But I can imagine a similar speech being given in 1980 and 1984 in a similar context about the Soviets. Genuine, effective leadership has a big hand in determining cultural consensus, by penetrating social consciousness, and making people feel comfortable in expressing their views.

The Left would be completely disgusted with this locker room speech, momentarily speechless, before finding its tongue, to brand it 'racist' and 'bigoted,' 'representing the worst traditions of America.' But they should tell someone who cares. This is exactly the kind of speech that should be given. It is powerful, patriotic, principled and confident—exactly what America and its leadership should be.

RUDY WAS RIGHT

"I do not believe, and I know this is a horrible thing to say, but I do not believe that the president loves America," Giuliani said during the dinner at the 21 Club, a former Prohibition-era speakeasy in midtown Manhattan in February 2015. *"He doesn't love you. And he doesn't love me. He wasn't brought up the way you were brought up and I was brought up through love of this country."*

The remarks prompted strong reaction from predictable quarters, with the mainstream media, Twitter and their progressive heroes seemingly taking turns to audition for apoplexy. Cowed by political correctness, even many conservative talking heads tap-danced, querying the use of Giuliani's language and suggesting it was not helpful to the Republican cause. Following the liberal playbook, few asked themselves if the statement was true, preferring to consider hurt feelings.

But Rudy was right. Our country has had the occasional president who did not believe in the truths of the Declaration or the restraints of the Constitution. But we never had one who did not believe in the essential goodness of America itself. When President Obama turned up to bat, all bases were finally loaded. And this is why the U.S.—China locker-room speech would never have been given in 2012. When the President doesn't speak of the essential goodness of America itself, you can almost guarantee sport coaches and mentors won't be prepared to do it. That is to the detriment of America, and ultimately, the world.

SECTION TWO

6

THE DEFILING OF CITIZENSHIP AND HUMANITY

"When you can't make them see the light, make them feel the heat."

—RONALD REAGAN

The 26th President of the United States was a New Yorker by the name of Theodore Roosevelt, and from all accounts, he was an *E Pluribus Unum* kind of guy. Although the poison of multiculturalism and cultural relativism weren't yet around, we can pretty much work out where good old (or young, I should say!) Teddy stood, when he let loose with this priceless gem:

> The man who loves other countries as much as his own stands on a level with the man who loves other women as much as he loves his own wife.

Oops, don't tell that one to Michelle. In today's *Twittersphere* that would probably trend as *#owned*. But in the good old days, Teddy was probably just slapped on the back by friends and toasted with raucous approval, as they sat drinking mint juleps and chomping cigars on fold out chairs, eyeing the renovations happening at the White House. How civilization has declined . . . Anyway, I digress. Seriously, though, we can probably notch that Roosevelt zinger as the earliest recorded rebuke of the so-called cultural harmonist.

In defending citizenship, the President's visceral disdain for what he equated with a deficiency of patriotism was intellectually sound and honest. It is no surprise that the reverse is true. Political correctness, through its intellectual laziness and downright dishonesty, is attacking the borders of citizenship and humanity. It's why our society isn't seeing learning honored, churches energized, families strengthened, multiculturalism outgrown and charities expanded. Without that foundation, America remains firmly at sea, and this one isn't shining, blemishing America's beauty.

CONTAGIOUS CITIZENSHIP

Cus D'Amato, the legendary boxing trainer, was talking to his thirteen year-old prodigy Mike Tyson about the effect of fear on a person:

> Fear is like fire. You can make it work for you: it can warm you in the winter, cook your food when you're hungry, give you light when you are in the dark, and produce energy. Let it go out of control and it can hurt you, even kill you. . . . Fear is a friend of exceptional people.

Citizenship—either robust or conspicuously absent—has a similar effect on a country. If it's healthy, it will have people burning for their country from the soles of their feet. If it's absent, it will burn a country up, destroying everything in its path. It is for these reasons that the pushback against citizenship by the Left is deeply disturbing and unpatriotic. It is uninterested in authentic or traditional citizenship. Instead, it seeks to have Americans identify as citizens of the world, considering any conception of American exceptionalism conceited and chauvinistic. It matters little that the Left is unable to point to another nation with a greater record in identifying or confronting evil; in fact, those in its good graces tend to be the custodians of far poorer records on such matters.

The implication of the Left's positions is crystal clear: it is wrong to consider your nation the best. It is wrong to have any expectations of those choosing to make your country their home. In fact, it is reasonable for you and your country to change, or make exceptions, to accommodate these new people. As a result, Western countries are increasingly full of people who accept the benefits of their chosen nation, while alleging racism and harboring nothing but animosity to their hosts. Perhaps the greatest irony of this tragedy is that where a dilution of citizenship was sought to remove beautiful passion from the hearts of the harmless, all it delivered was ugly passion in the heartless harmful.

THE IDEAL IMMIGRANT

The *ideal* immigrant to America from Mexico, upon receiving news that he has been granted a Green Card, might want to write this open letter to his new country:

MY OPEN LETTER TO AMERICA

My fellow American,

I did it! I just got my Green Card!

It was one of the most difficult things I have ever done, taking years and costing me my life's savings. This step was critical, but not the end.

In five years' time, and not a day later (the law requires me to have lived in America for exactly five years), I will knock on the door of my local USCIS office, dressed in my best suit and one bought specifically for the occasion, and cry throughout my naturalization ceremony. With enormous pride, I will recite the Oath of Allegiance, an oath I have memorized by heart already, and been practicing since I was a child.

I want to be clear.

It is important for me to acknowledge that I have come to America to be American. If I wanted to be Mexican, I would have stayed in Mexico. I acknowledge I am coming to America because she is a better country than the one I was born in. She offers more opportunity and the American Dream. I don't come to America to change it; I come to enhance it. My new countrymen: I come to make, not take.

I will speak English, because this is the language of your country. I have no interest in breaking the law in America, as to do so would mean I will not be allowed to become an American citizen, which is the dream God put in my heart.

I want you to know I was never tempted to break the law and enter the country illegally (although you should probably make it easier for people like me to come to your country, and less easy for others). My first interaction with the country that I love would never be to break her law.

The United States of America is the greatest country in the world, and I am prepared to do everything I have to do to keep it that way. Your challenge is mine, and I will work as hard, if not harder, than anyone in overcoming America's threats and defeating its enemies.

I will work hard to own my own house, taking on as many jobs as I need to. The American flag will fly outside every day, and I will make sure the children I plan to have learn flag protocol, this nation's history and are raised as Americans.

God bless you, and God bless the greatest nation on this earth—our United States of America.

Sincerely,
Jorge Gomez

Now, Jorge is exactly the type of legal immigrant we want in America. Yet the Left and political correctness suggest that almost any expectation we have for immigrants coming to our nation is unreasonable, and a product of our privilege. But when did it become prejudiced and unreasonable to ask that those coming to your home abide by your customs and rules? Here's another example. Islamic immigration is proving to be problematic for Western societies. Why is it not logical to ask, "If we can meet our needs for migrants with people from cultures where this is not something we need to worry about, why don't we?"

But whatever you do, be sure you don't refer to Jorge, or any other immigrant, as an "alien." At least in California, that is. Governor Brown has signed a bill banning the word in the state's labor laws.

Banning language in America? What an alien concept.

LAY OFF THE DECAF

"Dear Sir:
   Regarding your article 'What's Wrong with the World?'
   I am.
      Yours truly,
      G. K. Chesterton."

When some magazine asked famous people 100 years ago for wise comments about the mess we're in, Chesterton's answer was the shortest, truest, and most honest of all. The truth is that in order to renew itself, America needs a higher order of statesmanship from politicians in both parties than what we're now getting— and a higher order of citizenship from "we the people" than what you and I see in the mirror.

But the greatest obstacle to a higher level of citizenship is political correctness—it wages war on the very idea of citizenship. It doesn't believe in borders, national values, personal religious commitments or patriotic responsibilities of any kind. This is reinforced by the nothing-to-see-here, religion-of-peace, all-the-colors-bleed-into one line taken after every incident of violence by the leftist media. It is an ideology that has emptied and plundered citizenship and humanity, including passion. It has removed the caffeine from life. Yet my advice to Americans is: one of the greatest things about America is bottomless coffee (compared to being charged for each cup, like in the rest of the world)—but make sure you lay off the decaf.

There are many questions that are never asked of the pedestrian ideology that is political correctness. Why does it, for example, embrace the value of new ideas, while simultaneously denigrating common historic accomplishments of humanity?

Why does it embrace agendas of special interest groups, while simultaneously seeking to marginalize, if not expunge, mainstream values? Much like multiculturalism, it claims to be founded on the protection of diversity, but is profoundly mono-cultural in its promotion of its values. Why does political correctness insist that free speech cannot advance social justice, when it so clearly can?

Why are the conditions that led to America changing the world—an entrepreneurial spirit, self-empowerment and true Americanism—so loathed and denigrated? Unless you want to deliberately diminish America, why would you want to remove the circumstances that saw Edison, all alone, failing his 2,000th time to create the lightbulb?

As Western civilization is discovering, the Left is the San Andreas Fault of the nation. Anything built on its loyalty is subject to extreme earthquake risk.

7

PLASTIC PEOPLE

"People are either charming or tedious."

—OSCAR WILDE

The alarm on my Blackberry went off at 4:45 a.m. I sat up in the bed of my New York hotel room, trying to open my eyes. I felt terrible. This was the cold to end all colds. I'd had it for days, and despite buying up the entire cold remedy shelf at the drug store, this damn thing wasn't going away. I looked over at my impressive collection of lozenges, tablets, sprays, and syrups, and sighed. Being sick away from home is one thing; having to go on national television for an interview *while you're sick* is quite another. But I had no choice. I made it to the shower, after further depleting my medical stores. Allowing myself to be inspired by some Italian opera on my iPod, I managed to get dressed, and make my way to the lobby where a car was waiting for me. To add insult to (literal) injury, this early January morning was certainly no advertisement for global warming.

The show was *Fox and Friends,* on Fox News. Elisabeth Hasselbeck and Clayton Morris were on the couch. We were to discuss a recent *Daily Caller* interview in which I had explained that masculinity had declined, and that it was a dangerous time to be a man. I remember waiting in the Green Room, furiously sipping coffee, desperately hoping for some kind of kick to disguise my complete lack of energy. I was afraid it was completely transparent. As I was ushered in studio, and mic'd up, I gave myself a pep talk, said a quick prayer, and mercifully, the interview went extremely well.

In fact, as it turns out, it went a little too well. Before long, the Huffington Post had run a story on the interview, and from there . . . well, things just exploded. The interview went viral. The Left was apoplectic, inconsolable, and livid with both Hasselbeck and me. It took particular umbrage at Hasselbeck asking me a serious question about the effect a decline in masculinity could have on American national security. From what I understand, my observations that "*all feminism has delivered is angry women and feminine men*" and "*wimps and wusses deliver mediocrity, and men win*" also didn't earn me a spot on their *Happy Holidays* card list. For three days, the political correctness brigade teamed up with the rainbow mafia and handbag hit squad, to mercilessly pound away. As my friend, retired Lt Col. Allen West, told me at the time, "Spot on, Nick, always remember you don't take flak, unless you are over the target!"

Welcome to political correctness.

TOP HOST, LOSER LEFT

Jeremy Clarkson can definitely relate. The former host of *Top-Gear*, was sacked by the BBC in March 2014, following an alleged physical altercation with a producer. But his real offence? Being perpetually politically incorrect, yet remaining popular and successful among sections of society the chattering classes would rather didn't exist. *You know, those car-loving, free-speaking, eco-unfriendly and un-PC folk are just dreadful . . .*

As Richard Littlejohn astutely put it in the *Daily Mail*, speaking of BBC chief Danny Cohen's desire to get rid of Clarkson, two weeks before the decision was made:

If he succeeds he'll be the toast of fashionable Shoreditch salons, a folk hero to the Guardianistas and all those who despise Top Gear for being too white, too male and, frankly, too damned British. The Lilliputian Lefties who infest the BBC see Clarkson as an embarrassment— a racist, sexist, homophobic, xenophobic caveman, who shouldn't be given house room by a 'liberal' publicly funded broadcaster.

When news of Clarkson's dismissal came, I was in Australia, having breakfast, watching the national broadcaster's breakfast program. The show has two hosts, one of whom is a woman whose first instincts while covering the breaking news of the Boston bombing was to suggest *"we are overly focusing on what happens to rich white people in the West"*—were clearly chuffed with BBC's decision. The male presenter, who'd have to stand up twice to cast a shadow, gleefully remarked of the decision, "And it's a good thing, too!"

Not being able to help it, I blurted out between cereal bites in the direction of the television: "You just don't like him because he's a man, and you're a pussy!" What I said wasn't politically correct and rather uncharitable, but as a fan of Clarkson, it was how I felt. Besides, why would you want to be politically correct, when you can be right?

CAN'T MUZZLE A MAVERICK

During my time in Australian politics, I was referred to as a "maverick," a "cowboy," and a "rebel." Some people probably threw in "loose cannon" just for good measure, or to get their tautology fix. Anyway, you get the picture. You see, in Australia, a political party is full of gatekeepers (well, little totalitarians, actually), making endless rules and arbitrarily enforcing them. They're also obsessed with centralization and micromanagement, and employ an illogical one-size-fits-all campaign model, justified in part by the compulsory voting system that exists (the one President Obama lavishly praised, by the way!).

Anyone deemed unconventional in approach, unorthodox in style, and nonconformist in action is immediately labeled with such "pejoratives," as is anyone who isn't plastic, and has a bit of character. By the way, the quotation marks are deliberate. I see great virtue in being an individualist, a free thinker, and taking an independent stand. It's part of why I love America so much. And why I will fight to the death to make sure that thinking never permeates substantially in the land of opportunity. I want America to remain the country of characters, individuals, and yes, mavericks, not robots. That's how it stays exceptional; that's what provides its magic.

BEING A "CHARACTER"

I've always been a character. I have a nickname for just about everyone. If I disagree with current practice or accepted wisdom, I'm not afraid to speak up. I call things as I see them. I'm not afraid to call it how I see it. I'm almost always polite (I can think of a couple of notable exceptions!), but sometimes disrespectful of the establishment when warranted, and occasionally lacking in deference. It's probably this trait that has led me to clash with the politically correct establishment just about everywhere I've encountered its members.

I don't have much time for what I, admittedly rather unkindly, refer to as 'boring, nothing' people. I just can't help it; I've never been a robot. Actually, I'm about as far from being one as possible. Growing up, I loved tennis, but always related much more to Andre Agassi than Pete Sampras. I preferred Lleyton Hewitt over Pat Rafter. In recent times, I've always admired the tennis talent of Roger Federer, but never find myself fired up about him. Of course, no one can compare to John McEnroe in the personality stakes, but unfortunately I only caught his twilight years, mostly on YouTube . . . Anyway, you get my point. I much prefer people with personality and panache even if the former aren't as successful as their contemporaries.

The tragic reality is that there has long been a war on 'characters.' So far, this war has been more successful in other countries than in America, but political correctness has become rampant in this country as well. One of the incredible advantages of the United States to visitors is its many "characters"—"larger than life" individuals who stay with you, long after they or you leave. *Uncle Ray* of Texas, a retired, partially deaf (thanks to Vietnam) veteran springs to mind. He has a heart of gold, and is loved among his friends, but he isn't everyone's cup of tea. He's loud, brash and with a propensity to offend. I suspect that's just the way he likes it. In that part of the world, most people have someone like that in their life. If you don't, you should try to find someone like *Uncle Ray*, because you're poorer for not knowing someone like him.

Even the British liberal comedian Stephen Fry observes this uniqueness about America:

'In Maine we don't always follow the rules. We sometimes make our own. In Maine we think different.' Those words, surely somewhat overblown in the context of a television advertisement for a local phone network, confirmed my suspicions about American statal (sic) pride. 'We think different in Tennessee', 'South Dakotans march to a different drum', 'We don't follow the pack in New Mexico', 'I guess you can call us Missourians mavericks' . . . and so on.

We all like to think ourselves different, 'I'm unconventional like everybody else,' as Wilde once almost said, but it seems particularly important to Americans to remind themselves of their separateness, their uniqueness, their rebel spirit and they do it, not so much as a nation, but state by state.

THE COST OF BEING DIFFERENT

At this point, it probably doesn't warrant a Fox News alert that I loved the legendary conservative, blue-collar character Archie Bunker of "All in the Family." So did my dad. Sadly, I doubt that show would even be aired today. But ABC's "Last Man Standing" with Tim Allen's character, Mike Baxter, has somehow slipped through. It comes pretty close!

Sadly, away from the screen, in the real world, where political correctness is not lampooned but either embraced or cowed to, individuals who differentiate themselves from the collective are treated worse than second-class citizens by the elite.

I first noticed this phenomenon while in high school. I wasn't an angel, by any means, but my sins were never serious. I wasn't a bully. I didn't steal. I didn't cheat. I didn't vandalize property. I didn't skip school. But I did challenge teachers, disobey what I considered unfair or unreasonable commands and enjoyed either playing the class clown, or facilitating someone else to fulfill that role. Meanwhile, there were other students, who did bully, steal, cheat, vandalize, and skip school. Yet I found the kids guilty of these serious transgressions were better received by the teachers and broader school community than I was. Also, given the magnitude of their misdemeanors, they appeared to get away with 'stuff' far more easily than I did when I committed far lesser offences. Why? Despite their "crimes," they were fairly characterless and not seen as much as a threat to school cohesion. The sad reality? Due to the influence of political correctness on culture and society, bad people who are plastic draw less ire and are more popular than good people who aren't plastic.

PUTTING THE LEFT ELBOW ON
THE DINNER TABLE

Charlton Heston, the great actor and political activist, once quipped that "political correctness is tyranny with manners." As much as I am loathe to be quibbling with the legendary Heston, I think he may have been being a little too charitable.

Like many of you, growing up, I was taught to address ladies as "Ma'am" and men as "Sir. " Admittedly, I have often done so with gritted teeth, particularly when I felt the person didn't warrant such respect. But I have never considered my use of those terms to be that remarkable. I certainly never considered them to reflect my politics, my worldview or my intelligence. Yet in formal interviews, I have often been asked to stop using that form of address, with some people suggesting it makes them uncomfortable or they find it intimidating. Amazing, I know. People get funny when you call them 'Sir' and 'Ma'am,' viewing these phrases as esoteric, old-fashioned or anachronistic.

The irony, of course, is that political correctness, according to its staunchest defenders, is simply politeness—an agenda apparently seeking to promote a discourse that is more polite, and congenial.

As for my use of "Sir" and "Ma'am," I say what Charlton would say: "Out of my cold, dead hands."

BOYCOTTS FOR BULLIES LEAD TO BLANDNESS

It's not just politicians who have to be bland. Everyone has to be. It's the great tragedy of modern society.

It's simply not worth the risk to be anything other than extremely bland. Conformity is the new black. If you're not conformist, you're basically buying a home in Tornado Alley. Make a comment, offer an opinion or hold a view that is seen as progressive, and what I call the "outrage" machine kicks into full throttle. It acts like a tornado, roaring through people's lives, displacing them, ripping through their home, community and place of employment. In no time at all, lives and businesses are thrown into turmoil. Careers, revenue streams, sponsors, anonymity, and freedom—theirs and often, their families'—are lost.

If the outrage machine is a tornado, social media (which I'll discuss in detail in the next chapter) is a match that spreads confected outrage explosively, immediately and uncontrollably, into a ubiquitous fire.

Once you have a reputation and online record, your ability to find a job is affected. Old friends distance themselves. If it's possible to find alternatives, your customers, clients, and professional associations most likely will. The funny looks you receive are no longer just confined to those walking their manicured, prize-winning poodles past your house when they observe your flag; but also from ordinary punters who simply assume: "*Where there is smoke, there must be fire.*"

The examples are endless. Just weeks apart in April and May 2014, Rutgers and Brandeis universities' faculty and students, by online petitions and protests, respectively shunned former Secretary of State Condoleezza Rice and Ayaan Hirsi Ali, a women's rights activist, from delivering commencement addresses due to political incompatibility. It's worth noting that not one feminist said as much as "Man!" in response. All the way on the other side of the country, in Silicon Valley (fittingly, for all its plastic people), around the same time, Mozilla Firefox CEO, Brendan Eich, was effectively forced to resign after it was revealed he had made a $1000 donation six years before to an anti-gay marriage campaign in California.

In early April 2015, there was a deluge of publicity surrounding Indiana's religious freedom law that claimed it would allow discrimination against gays and lesbians. Following this, New York Governor Andrew Cuomo banned non-essential state-funded travel to Indiana, and several businesses, including Apple, and performers canceled events and announced boycotts of Indiana. Even businesses based in Indiana felt the heat. Memories Pizza, a small pizza shop run by a husband and wife in the northern part of the state, were forced to go into hiding, after one of the co-owners said she would refuse to cater a wedding for a gay or lesbian couple because of her religious beliefs. (Thankfully, in an example of American exceptionalism that could only happen here, an Internet crowdfunding page for the pizza shop raised more than $800,000 and it ended well. God bless America).

But this is an exception. Ordinarily, it ends very badly for those guilty of earning the wrath of the politically correct elite. Boycotts and social media shaming are the elite's chief bullying tactics. It's plain and simple. Those tactics are devastatingly successful because our uninformed and illiterate culture communicates and reacts to current events like junior high girls. Sadly, social media has given a voice to the undeserving uninformed and illiterate, granting them a greater platform than those more deserving.

HOW THE TABLES HAVE TURNED

"Are you now, or have you ever been, a member of the Communist party?" The question was asked by congressional panel, after congressional panel, to thousands of Americans. Senator Joseph McCarthy, in a speech at the 1952 Republican National Convention, spelled it out for all to hear: *"Our job as Americans and as Republicans is to dislodge the traitors from every place where they've been sent to do their traitorous work."*

It's funny, you know. The way things change.

Years ago, if you were a communist, or anyone associated to you was a communist, you couldn't get a job, or you'd lose your business. Now, we've come full circle. It's the other way around. If you're a conservative, or associate with known conservatives, you can't get a job. Or you lose your business, or are denied opportunities, or suspected first for wrongdoing. Conservatives in America in 2016 are the 'communists' of 1950s America. *Hey, at least, McCarthy was upfront about it. It's more than you can say for today's gutless Left.*

WE'RE THE TOLERANT ONES

The reason the tables have turned is that the culture war has been effectively won by the totalitarian Left, which perpetuate the merciless and uncompromising approach that saw it achieve the power it now wields. The difference between the Left and the rest of us is that on the rare occasion, we do have one of them on the floor, our foot on his throat, we offer a hand to pull the person back up. But when positions are swapped, the Left not only proceeds to step into our throat, it does so in such a way that we'll never get up again.

"Co-exist" is often the catch cry of the modern Left. Personally, I find it a ponytail word, and you won't find me using it anytime soon. But the truth is, we politically-incorrect conservatives are far more prepared to co-exist than those waving the "co-exist" banners, or driving a car with that very bumper sticker, wedged among others "Hillary 2016," "Michelle 2024," "Sasha 2040" and "Malia 2048." We're the tolerant ones. If we don't like something, we look away. We grumble to ourselves, and on a rare occasion, might share it with a friend. The same goes for a person with views we don't share. But if a leftist doesn't like something or somebody, he wants to eliminate it. The Left will take away your job, your reputation, and everything you have ever worked toward. It will stop at nothing.

That's why we've got to stop the Leftists. It's time for us to be intolerant of their intolerance. The symptoms of tyranny such as these brazen attacks on free speech have threatened Republics through our time. Fortunately, America, and only America, has the vaccine: the American ideal.

8

CONTROL, ALTER, DELETE

"You're going to be up against people who have an opinion, a modem and a bathrobe. All of my life, developing credentials to cover my field of work, and now I'm up against a guy named Vinny in an efficiency apartment in the Bronx who hasn't left the efficiency apartment in two years."

—BRIAN WILLIAMS,
Former NBC News star

Imagine September 11, 2001, with social media, in today's culture.

Twitter hashtags going viral insisting that people should not be afraid of Muslims, but should be afraid of being labeled a bigot. Facebook memes shared tens of thousands of times expressing solidarity with Islam, implying America had it coming. Facebook pages created to express solidarity with Islam, possibly titled *'Americans Against Islamophobia'* and *'I love Allah, and I'm proud of it.'* Celebrities beginning a *'Take a selfie with a Muslim'* campaign, tweeting about the number of people killed in the Middle East on the same day, and complaining about the lack of coverage.

None of this is fanciful, nor can I be accused of taking creative license. My assertions were not scribbled on the back of a cocktail napkin, after a few drinks. These things are a reality today. In fact, I have taken them from the world's real life experience. In the immediate aftermath of attacks in Boston, Paris, Ottawa, Sydney and the murder of Lee Rigby on the streets of south London, we have seen *exactly* this type of social media activity. (*#JeSuisCharlie* may be the Twitter hashtag everyone remembers following Paris, but pro-Muslim *#voyageavecmoi*, translated to "travel with me," trended, too).

One can only assume that after the worst terrorist attack in world history, such activity would only have been more heightened and ubiquitous. The need of the Left to invent victims, instead of allowing us to mourn for the real ones, would have been greater than ever. Its preference to return to platitudes of tolerance, rather than learning from evil would have been more on display than ever. As Brendan O'Neil put it in the *National Review*:

> It's the same after every terrorist attack: from 9/11 to 7/7 in London to last year's Sydney siege to Paris today: Liberals' instant, almost Pavlovian response to Islamist terror attacks in the West is to worry about a violent uprising of the ill-educated against Muslims. The uprising never comes, but that doesn't halt their fantasy fears.

In this way, they're like the drunk at the bar who keeps going back to the jukebox to play the same old song: '*Backlash*'.

The point is it is almost universally accepted that the best of the American way—unity, strength, resolve and patriotism—emerged in the days, weeks and months following the evil of September 11. It might be a stretch to say but I believe if those attacks happened today, in today's politically correct culture fueled by social media, I don't believe the perception of such unity and strength would be possible. This is not to say I don't believe middle-America would have galvanized in the way it clearly was, but that the voices without a platform then, would be deafening and organized now, would have muddled the consensus substantially.

Let's face it. Social media, with all its trolls, has changed the world, strengthened political correctness, and is increasingly becoming a clear and present danger to Western civilization.

PERSONAL BIAS

Now, let me get this out of the way first. It is confession time.

I'm probably biased. You'll never hear me say, I long for the day when my phone becomes obsolete. I still insist on checking in with a real person at an airport, usually in the hope that if I flash a smile and be nice, I might just get bumped up to business class, or the employee may turn a blind eye to my overweight luggage. After all, there's no chance of getting a break if you're dealing with a machine, or using your phone as a boarding pass. The last time I played a video game was on a Super Nintendo in 1994, at the age of ten, I prefer spending my money on inspirational sports memorabilia from *Hobby Lobby*, than paying for a premium version of some dating site. Professionally, I've been more interested in pursuing an old-fashioned career (a path withering away, I might add), writing books, and appearing on television, rather than building an online presence and seeking to harvest new media. This may make me sound rather square, but I think by now you've probably worked out, I'm anything but. I just have traditional tastes, instincts and values—ones I'm not only proud of, but I consider superior to the new ones on offer. Oh, and I find *Twitter* an airheaded and repetitive medium.

I might sound like a grumpy, old man, but I'm not. I'm just a culturally conservative millennial (there's not many of us!) who is clear-eyed. I like technology, but I like people more. Certainly, some of the benefits of technology like information at your fingertips and increased convenience are utterly peerless, but some of its unintended consequences have been downright awful. I like personal interaction, and worldliness, both of which I fear are going by the wayside, in large part due to technology.

MIRROR, MIRROR ON THE WALL—WHO IS
THE DUMBEST OF US ALL?

I obviously belong to the most over-documented generation in history. Just think about it. Neil Armstrong landed on the moon, with hardly any pictures; now a young girl takes five "selfies" just walking out the door of her family home on her way to *Chili's* to meet friends. It's fair to say that increasing numbers of people today are ignorant, self-absorbed, and distracted, as a result of mobile technology.

I think it started with the iPod, when I was at college (although I'm sure the *Walkman* was anti-social as well). I recall certain students, even the daughter of a prominent Australian politician, walking through campus, with their white earphones *permanently* plugged in. I remember thinking: so much for the university experience. For me, it was all about socializing, and I couldn't imagine shutting myself off to the world like that. Fast forward thirteen years, and those students are no longer the exception, and the iPod is now the least guilty culprit in the distraction, or lack of engagement, stakes. Think of the hypnotizing effect of the iPhone.

When I was growing up in Australia, American children and teenagers were renowned for their civic and citizenship knowledge. In fact, I remember a 15-year old American exchange student at my school who could name every President in order, and recite the capital city of every state. How things change. Now, one television program after the other (although none as comprehensively as the Watters World segment on "The O'Reilly Factor"), showcases the ignorance of America's young on the street, on college campuses, and on the beach. Kids think Boko Harem is a restaurant. Benghazi is a person. They don't know who Joe Biden is. You know what I'm talking about. You've seen it.

And I've seen it, too.

I visit high schools and universities in America all the time speaking to students about the history of the country and why the U.S. is an exceptional nation. Students are more interested in taking "selfies," than learning about American inventions. Rather than copy down their homework, they take a photo of the whiteboard with their phone. The overwhelming majority of them are amazed when I explain I can speak English only because of American involvement in World War II. Their general knowledge is confined to remembering only catchy politically-correct positions they first heard in a classroom, and were reinforced by some meme they caught floating around their Facebook feed. At Argyle High School in Denton County, Texas, in early March 2011, one student reveled in an opportunity she saw to trip me up. "How," she boomed across the auditorium, "can you say 'America has everything to be proud about, and nothing to be ashamed about when we interned the Japanese?" Sitting back, she smiled smugly, clearly pleased with herself, congratulated by her girlfriends sitting either side of her. It turned out the student had no idea that the Japanese had without provocation bombed Pearl Harbor, had incredibly brutal prisoner of war camps during World War II, or any appreciation of the climate of fear that gripped the world at that time.

Unfortunately, this is the culture of today's America.

SMARTPHONE, DUMB PEOPLE

Technology has changed our world.

Some of it has been advantageous, but only a blind supporter (sorry—*visually impaired*) would deny its shortcomings are significant. Off the top of my head, I can rattle off three:

- Social media has given a voice to those who don't deserve one.
- Technology has made it easier for the media and the public to punish anyone who is interesting.
- The bland have been encouraged; the vanilla validated.

It's impossible to be a giant anymore. As we've already discussed, an online mafia has only made a bad situation worse. The best way to describe it is indignation overreach. It has given a greater voice and bigger platform to people who do not deserve it. Tolerance totalitarians are now able to conduct witch hunts and act as lynch mobs. Corporations, sponsors, universities and politicians have shown little stomach for the bad publicity these irrational and unsavory campaigns cause, emboldening its practitioners.

But, in spite of their serious nature, these are essentially boutique complaints. The real problem with the Internet and technology is that it is weakening and endangering America by creating a generation living inside a bubble. These people are in their own world, separated from reality. Intellectual curiosity has been replaced by instant gratification. Most importantly, the drug-like addiction to technology is changing the way citizens are participating in the democratic process.

For those of us who love our nation, and spend nights continuously flipping our pillows over to the cold side as we worry about the state of the union, this is an enormous problem. Whenever I am asked how America could be transformed, I maintain that we need to see a nation where:

- Citizenship will be revived
- Government will be re-limited
- Freedom of conscience will be upheld
- Exceptionalism will be re-embraced
- Defenses will be re-built, and,
- Sovereignty will be re-asserted

But these are aims that specifically require robust engagement in the democratic process. Without it, they are impossible to achieve. Sadly and frighteningly, the trend is firmly against this great need. For the first time in American history, despite their civic-minded tradition, many Americans are unaware of what their government is doing, or what is happening in their community. It sounds crazy, but the smartphone is actually threatening American exceptionalism.

The traditional American has virtues such as: selflessness, individual responsibility, work ethic, neighborly involvement, etc. But I would say technology is radically transforming people and creating unproductive, lazy, and less intelligent citizens. The combined consequence of this is a national decline. To use a football analogy, America is down on the scoreboard at half-time, showing no signs of improvement, and injuries to most of the team hamper its prospects of a comeback. To further the analogy, right now, the way America is playing, it doesn't have enough momentum to even make the playoffs.

The hypnotic effect of the latest technology is helping turn America soft. It's breeding bad citizens. It's a recipe America's enemies might soon have framed in their offices.

IN THE PAST . . .

I am firmly of the belief that with the advent of the social media medium and political correctness in general, Churchill, Reagan and Thatcher would not have survived, politically. In the case of Reagan, he may not have even won a primary. On a different note, just imagine the latter years of the Bill Clinton Presidency with social media and today's Internet (and a 24-7 news cycle). The pressure would have been far more intense, and one can only speculate whether it would have led to his impeachment, or his resignation . . .

IN THE FUTURE

I could be wrong, but my bet is that President Obama will be the last two-term President, unless there are extraordinary electoral circumstances. The incessant, unforgiving scrutiny offered by the 24-hour news cycle and social media, means that the conversion of human years to dog years applies to holding office.

When people hear and read about someone non-stop, with every minor slip replayed endlessly, it is impossible to overcome the 'it's time for a change' sentiment that sweeps across the electorate. The media and information overload that exists today is a minefield for politicians, a party for the politically correct, a bonanza for the culture of complaint, and a source of frustration for the everyday person. In today's online world that we carry with us in our pockets, which Bill O'Reilly correctly describes as a "sewer," where hate, envy and negativity collide, it is easy to build momentum for any cause, particularly over unpopular decisions of a political leader. The scope for error is enormous, but doesn't only include politicians. It includes an electorate that is open to change, purely for change sake.

NOSINESS

I have to tell you: one thing I can't stand is nosiness. It's the libertarian in me. I'm *big* on minding my own business. Generally speaking, I don't care what others do, and therefore expect that others don't care what I do. Firstly, I don't have the time, and secondly, I'm so focused on my own ambition, being noisy is simply distracting and pointless. In fact, I think if people spent less time worrying about what is happening in other people's lives and focused on themselves, they'd accomplish far more. Dreaming and achieving is far more useful to yourself and the world, than sitting around, turning a deep shade of green about someone else's perceived success. But human nature is what it is, and unfortunately, nosiness has always been with us.

Only now, nosiness is on steroids. Forget waiting to make sure the neighbors drive away with everyone in the car, and sneaking a peek over the fence by standing on your tippy toes to look into your neighbor's yard; now everyone stands naked, in full sight of anyone who wants to look. Technology has encouraged nosiness and it has given people the tools to be nosy. Today, no one minds their own business, and your business is everybody's business. The world has grown smaller. This nosiness and accessibility to the information of others enriches the *"I'm-A-Victim-And-Must-Complain-And-Bring-Someone-Down-In-The-Process"* program. All of a sudden, people have ammunition on others, and the reality is, the bigger the target, the more information there is likely to be. This reality means that it pays to be mediocre. This is a terrible message. It is another reason why 'greatness' in this era belongs only to Kanye West and his Instagram pictures of the 'overly-distressed jeans' he wears.

HEAR THAT ECHO . . . ECHO . . . ECHO

Following the defeat of Mitt Romney at the hands of President Obama in November 2012, I determined that as a constitutional conservative, I was not giving an inch on my principles or on my grave concern for where this country, a nation in blithe denial, was headed. *Nothing has changed.* But it gave me cause to pause. It was an electoral outcome that cautioned me against living in an echo chamber.

Why? Mea culpa: I never saw the Romney defeat coming. I was convinced President Obama was gone. But I was wrong, not just by a little but by a great deal! Part of the reason was that, unconsciously, my social media bubble had made me see only what I wanted to see.

It is troublesome that it is now increasingly difficult for anyone to properly gauge national sentiment, or live in the "real world." We're all guilty of this. After the victory of the Conservative Party in England in May 2015, earning David Cameron the ability to govern in his own right, scores of violent Leftist protesters took to the streets, even desecrating a WW II memorial. Clearly, they were in disbelief. In Britain's *The Telegraph*, it was best explained by Bryony Gordon:

> Writing off 11.3 million people as nothing more than Tory scum is both insulting and arrogant. But then perhaps it is merely a

symptom of the blinkers that social media has put on us. When you live your life on Twitter and Facebook, and are only friends with like—minded people on Twitter and Facebook, you are not living in the real world. You are living in a narcissistic echo chamber. No wonder it has come as such a surprise to so many that not everyone shares the same world view.

Enough said.

PETITION THIS

Now, let me be clear: I'm not talking about the *right to petition government*, a fundamental freedom and guaranteed by the First Amendment. This is about something different. I don't know about you, but I don't like petitions. I think the last one I signed was about ten years ago as a university student, and truth be told, it had more to do with the young woman who was asking for my signature, than the benign cause it sought to promote.

Once upon a time, petitions were useful, genuine tools to effect change, or draw attention to a matter. But with social change, and technological advance, I can't help but see them as the embodiment of the complaint society of which we now live. Online petition websites have now sprung up everywhere, billing themselves as agents of social change. If you look at them, the petitions featured are almost always framed around the insistence that somebody has to apologize for something, or that something has to be banned.

These sites, visited by tens of millions, work snugly with Twitter and Facebook to propel the outrage in order to shut down debate, manipulate voters and make us less free. To use a baseball analogy, they provide the baseball bat free of-charge, and then permit un-limited free swings, but instead of hitting the ball, they're slugging the player with whom they disagree. All, without any oversight or objectivity, I might add.

Then, of course, the lapdog media comes in to treat the news of such a petition's existence as an *actual* news story. "*An online petition calling for The Tallahassee Gazette's Jack Simpson to be fired for his anti-immigrant column has garnered more than 150,000 signatures,"* the media will scream. Or if half a dozen Twitter generals have swung the aforementioned bat at a prominent figure, you're likely to hear or read: *"An ugly war of words has erupted after Jimmy Fallon told an off-color joke on Monday night."*

When reality can be distorted by a handful of grubs carrying on like a frog in a sock on social media, defaming a good person in the process, you know you've got a problem.

BLOGGER SAYS IT BEST

Blogger Andrew Sullivan captures it perfectly within this piece in January 2015:

> Twitter and Facebook encourage mutually reassuring group-think, in which individuals are required to "like" anything that isn't white, male, cisgendered, etc., in which an ideology is enforced by un-friending those with other views instead of engaging them, and in which large numbers of Twitter-users can descend on a racist/sexist/homophobic etc. miscreant and destroy his or her career and social life in pursuit of racial/gender/orientation "social justice."

My dad is fond of saying: *Once you're in the dance, you've got to dance*, meaning once you've started a process, you have to accept the consequences and roll with it. Or to paraphrase Hyman Roth in *The Godfather II*, *"This is the business I've chosen."* I expect to be labeled, libeled and lampooned. But not everyone is, a point Sullivan makes as well:

> I'm an established blogger with an independent site and have witnessed several such campaigns now—and they cannot but exact a toll. I'm fine with being called a self-hating gay or homophobe or misogynist or racist or anti-Semite, but what of those with

much less independence? People with media jobs in which any deviation from the p.c. norm renders them anathema to their peers, those in the academy who are terrified of committing a 'micro-aggression,' those in minorities who may actually have a different non-leftist view of reality: what pressure are they being put under right now?

CLICKING THE 'LIKE' BUTTON— THE VIRTUAL CHARITY WRISTBAND

From petitions to wristbands, the world is changing. Just as I don't like petitions, it would take a cold July day in Texas for me to wear a "charity" wristband. To me, they represent a disturbing trend and do a disservice to genuine charitable activity.

Disturbingly, the advent of social media is threatening genuine charitable activity, such as volunteering time to the Red Cross, doing missionary work in Africa, feeding the homeless, or visiting sick kids in hospital. This real action is being supplanted by people clicking "like" on a Facebook page or post, or retweeting on Twitter, and feeling absolved of any further obligation. The legitimate sacrifice of time or money of the old days for real charity is gone, replaced by a "wristband society" prepared to give every social justice (*read*: left wing) cause its day in the sun. The extension of this is the wristband's virtual equivalent of social media-driven faux cause campaigns. The sad thing is that those engaged in these meaningless acts today seem to derive the same satisfaction as those who legitimately participate in helping actual charities.

The same can even be said of social activism. In the past, social activism involved physical movement, such as amassing a group in a square or protesting. Today liking a Facebook page or clicking "accept" to an event invitation for something that isn't even an event is considered sufficient.

This is further evidence of how social media is softening and weakening an American value: the culture of giving. Statistics have regularly revealed that Americans are the most generous people on earth. A philanthropic spirit is as American as baseball and hot dogs. Yet political correctness is diluting it.

THE UNDER-EDUCATED ELITE

The dilution doesn't only extend to community service, but to intelligent, considered discussion and attention. People today are more vocal than ever before, yet also at their most uninformed. Let me explain.

Previously, people debating grand themes and topics of our society publicly had deep knowledge of subject matter but now they have an extremely superficial understanding. This is attributable predominantly to social media, where people passionately take up causes they know nothing about, other than one or two talking points they've heard repeatedly bleated. They only see these matters discussed in snippets, and have never taken the time to look at their context or history.

"America is to blame for the ills of the world" and "Islamic fundamentalism is created by American democracy" shout the politically correct crowd. The crowd members do this, in the context of Islamic jihadism (if you take offence to that term, I'm not sorry). How many of these people dumping on America from around the world on social media and blogs know that for nearly 1400 years, Islam has sought to conquer alternative civilization? How many of them have even heard of the *Battle of Vienna* or the *Battle of Tripoli*? Yet, get them in a room, and they'll vehemently and genuinely insist until they are red-in-the-face that it is the United States who is responsible for Islamic terrorism. They're blind, and willfully so (it's a lie that excuses those who are the real criminals and blames us for the attacks made upon us). In this way, the role social media serves is to facilitate and indoctrinate politically correct positions to the point where they become second-nature.

OH, THE WRETCHED IRONY

The world has changed, and it's almost all due to the United States. Think of virtually any technology you use every day. It's safe to assume it's American by birth—and not usually an anchor baby, although sometimes it takes others to come to America to be able to get the chance to develop their ideas. So, it is a horrible irony that these innovations have come back to bite America in the butt. The innovators could never have foreseen it. They never could have imagined that the technology they wanted to change the world with would be an unfortunate equalizer for many of America's fiercest enemies and harshest detractors. Or that at home, it would threaten citizenship and challenge exceptionalism. They never would have thought that terror groups rooted in Islam would use social media to plan, plot and inspire attacks on American soil like they did in Garland, Texas. They never could have predicted that the culture of complaint, currently bringing America to its knees, would have been so empowered by their innovations.

I'm often asked what it will take for America to boomerang. Essentially, it needs to forge a new generation that guarantees the American Dream for another 200 years.

America needs a reboot. It's the only way we're going to take it back.

Or, as they call it, #Win.

9

PANSY POLITICIANS

"When decency defeats dynamism, and inoffensiveness trumps inspiration every time, the politician who prospers best will be the one who makes the least mistakes, who provides the least grist for the media mill, and who can best put on the air of quiet substance that will—if not necessarily do the greatest good—at least do the least damage."

—PETER FITZSIMONS,
Sydney Morning Herald

NUKING THE MOON

America was once prepared to blow up the moon with a nuke, simply as a display of muscle.

Not that long ago, either. No, I'm not joking and I didn't see it in a movie, either. I read about it in a declassified 1959 report called "A Study of Lunar Research Flights" written by physicist and former NASA deputy director, Leonard Reiffel. But it was best known as "Project A-119."

A top secret U.S. Air Force plan at the height of the space race would see a "missile carrying a small nuclear device launched from an undisclosed location and travel 238,000 miles to the moon, where it would be detonated upon impact." It was 1958, when America was lagging in the space race. Yuri Gagarin, Sputnik, and Soviet success had American scientists hoping that a giant flash on the moon would intimidate their Soviet rivals, and assure the

American people that the U.S. could maintain a mutually-assured deterrence.

The report explained, "The motivation for such a detonation is clearly threefold: scientific, military and political." Of the three, perhaps the most interesting were the military considerations and visionary thinking of America's leadership. Information from the impact, according to Reiffel's report, would yield information "concerning the capability of nuclear weapons for space warfare." In military circles at the time, there was, according to Reiffel, "discussion of the moon as military high ground. That included talk of having nuclear launch sites on the moon." Reiffel told CNN in 2012, "The thinking was that if the Soviets hit the United States with nuclear weapons first and wiped out U.S. ability to strike back, the U.S. could launch warheads from the moon."

In the end, the project was abandoned.

VISION, HUNGER, CLARITY AND MANLY THINKING

Now, I'm probably showing my age, and I don't know about you, but I find all of this remarkable and fantastic. In fact, it makes me love America even more. Let me explain. There are five ingredients to this story, which I believe exemplify American exceptionalism. They are:

- clarity
- hunger/determination to win
- vision
- audacity/boldness, and;
- out of-the-box thinking

These are the traits of the consummate leader; these are the characteristics of the most successful people. From reading this anecdote, and getting a feel for the mindset of the leaders at the time, it is abundantly clear why America was able to defeat communism, and win the Cold War. It's no surprise that it became the world's pinnacle nation.

Interestingly, along with faith, these were the same values and principles on which America was founded and helped it move to the top, quicker than any other nation before it. In 1959, the founders' spirit still existed.

But here's the question. What happened? In less than sixty years, how did we go from being prepared to blow up the moon, or considering having nuclear warheads on the moon in case of necessity, to a pussycat, apologist nation with a leading-from-behind foreign policy?

How far we have fallen.

POLITICAL CORRECTNESS BLIND TO VISION

The answer, of course, is the now leading star in the otherwise glittering galaxy of America: political correctness. Big ideas and bold actions have been replaced by the safe and mediocre. In our world of instant gratification, people live only for the "now," unprepared to consider the "future." "Vision" is considered grandiose, at best, dangerous and zany, at worst. Yet without men of vision, America would never be where it is today. I believe that every elected leader should have a little futurist in them.

Political correctness celebrates the conventional, narrowing the thoughts and expectations of people, and the media is quick to reinforce these perceptions. In America, we the people, with our distrust and inherent dislike of politicians and government, have added to this in both our reactions to such ideas and the reluctance of leaders to take a risk. Vision and optimism are married, and so it is not surprising that the political correctness campaign is defined, like all political campaigns these days, mostly by its negativity.

When Speaker Gingrich promised a manned moon base by 2020, if he was elected President in 2012, he was mocked, derided and scorned. The idea, itself, was dismissed out of hand. This was a bad look for America. Regardless of your views on the idea (and I can appreciate the concern of straining the federal budget, at a time of fiscal belt-tightening), any bold proposal encouraging a nationalistic adventure in the hope of building a bigger and better future should never be scoffed at. Re-building America is not going to happen if its business as usual. It's going to take a refusal to color in between the lines.

The overall point is that vision, hunger, clarity, audacity and creativity are at record lows among those in American political leadership. Consequently, the world is infinitely more dangerous, and America worryingly weak.

CHURCHILLIAN LEADERSHIP

The five leadership values bring me to one of the greatest figures of the twentieth century, and a man that I love. Sir Winston Churchill.

Sorry, President Obama, but it is Churchill's speeches that are on my iPod, not yours. While both are heralded for their oratory, Sir Winston never required a teleprompter, wrote his own speeches, and was as much a man in his actions as he was in his rhetoric. And, I have to say that the British Prime Minister made the world a much safer place, while the current U.S. President has done the exact opposite.

But politics and history aside, what I love most about Churchill is that he wasn't one of these plastic people with no character. He had flair and charisma and was fearless. He was more than prepared to put people in their place when they deserved it. Even when things went wrong, he stalked the prize like a wounded lion, pulling off historic victories. He loved port, smoking cigars and women. He ate too much; he drank too much. In fact, he loved life so much, he'd often be struck down with gout! Not to mention, he had a brain the size of a small planet, a larrikin streak and a rapier wit. He also had an unparalleled mastery of words, theater and occasion. He was a bit of a rebel who wasn't afraid to believe in something even if it wasn't a popular position.

Not surprisingly, even in that era, this panache made him a controversial figure, often landing him in trouble, and out of the good graces of the establishment. One of the lesser known anecdotes relating to Churchill was this exchange he had with the press, and it is one that American leaders, current and aspiring, would do well to copy. Before the election of 1945, *The Times* newspaper in London decided it did not want to support Churchill's Conservative government. The newspaper's management penned an editorial suggesting that Churchill campaign as a non-partisan world leader and then retire gracefully quickly afterward. The editor informed Churchill of the editorial, and its content, in the hope it might sway him. *"Mr. Editor,"* Churchill replied, *"I fight for my corner and I leave when the pub closes."* Boom.

GOING NUCLEAR ON THE LIBERAL MEDIA

Imagine this fictional interview between a conservative Washington state politician (Jim Levendi) and a local television host (Veronica Mole). To set the scene, Levendi is doing the interview from a remote street location, with Mole in-studio. Both are white. They are discussing current Seattle race riots that have occurred followed the death of a young African-American male at the hands of police. Mole is well-known for carrying the water for the Left, and her network has similar politics to CNN and MSNBC. The interview has been testy, with Mole seldom letting Levendi answer her questions, preferring to interrupt him with her own opinion. We join the interview about midway through. Here's the transcript:

> **REP. LEVENDI:** The behavior of the rioters is deplorable, and I believe the police should round up and lock up anyone breaking the law. I think—

MOLE: Don't the rioters have a point? And aren't we in this situation because of the police in the first place?

■

REP. LEVENDI: Absolutely not. What a crock. That's the greatest baloney I've ever heard. Our police are the finest and put themselves in harm's—

■

MOLE: *(voice raised)* So, the police have no responsibility here, is that what you're saying, Rep. Levendi? Isn't the truth that there is long pattern of police abuse, harassment and violence toward our city's African-American community in the context of systemic class inequality, custodial citizenship and mass incarceration?

■

REP LEVENDI: I'm sorry, but I entirely reject that. You're reading the Left's talking points. America is the greatest country in the world for a black person to live. As it is for everyone, no matter, what race, color or sexual orientation. It's why more Africans have come to our country voluntarily than came as sla-

■

MOLE: *(voice raised further)* That's irrelevant. You're in denial. You clearly have no historical perspective and a very short-term memory, Sir. Michael Brown, Eric Garner, Freddie Gray, Rodney King. Do I need to go on?

■

REP: LEVENDI: Please let me finish. The police allow us to sleep at night. We call them when there is a problem. I will not allow smears on our policemen and women go unanswered. The real issues here are within the black community, where there are absent black fathers, broken homes and an urban culture of poverty and violence. Now, I do have sympathy for bla-

■

MOLE: *(yelling)* It's all their fault? They're not even human to you, are they, Representative?

REP. LEVENDI: Ma'am, do you want to yell and have a soliloquy, or do you want to have an interview? You have a choice.

■

MOLE: Do you have a problem with me because I'm a woman, Rep. Levendi? Maybe that's what it is, maybe that's the difference.

■

REP. LEVENDI: Ma'am, this is the last interview you will do with me. I have not interrupted you once, yet you have interrupted me almost every answer. You have been discourteous, biased and unreasonable. Please extend to me the same courtesy I have offered you while I give this answer.

No, I don't have a problem with you because you're a woman. I have a problem with you because you aren't a patriot. In this interview, you are exemplifying the culture of complaint and victimhood—and you do it to the detriment of your own county. I get it. I'm a white, educated, middle-class male. I'm not supposed to have a voice in your world. But guess what? I do. And it's louder, more articulate and more coherent than yours. Now, let me explain something to you. When I look at our nation's flag, I see greatness, sacrifice and opportunity. When you look at the flag, you see white guilt and slavery. I'll tell you the difference between us, ma'am. I seek a strong America; you seek a weak America. I seek a united America. You seek a divided America. I lionize patriots, not thugs. You're prepared to allow people to use their race as a sword and a shield as it suits them, while I believe it should be neither. I'm tired of the untruths peddled by media outlets like yours, and media personalities like you. Now you can sit there and throw any label you want at me—sexist, racist—be my guest. But all it does is expose the poverty of your intellect, and the malnourishment of your *morality*.

We're done here. Thank you.

■

(Levendi, clearly fired up but calm, removes microphone, and walks off camera.)

STANDING UP TO MEDIA BULLIES

That's the way it's done. At this point, it's probably redundant for me to tell you Representative Levendi is my type of guy! If he was running for President this time around, I'd vote for him. But more importantly, he's the type of leader America needs. He's politically incorrect, confident, and confrontational when he needs to be and, like Churchill, he doesn't take his cues from the liberal media. He calls them out for their bias and their lack of civility, refusing to do the interview on their terms, ending it on his. And despite the provocation and his passion, he manages to do it politely. That's a leader. That's strength.

BAN 'EM

Sadly, politicians today are too fearful of having their actions interpreted as arrogant or authoritarian. We, the people, probably share much of the blame for this, and have unwittingly played into the hands of liberal media bullies, who have been able to intimidate with relative impunity (notable exceptions being Governor Chris Christie of New Jersey, and the epic frontal attack of Speaker Gingrich on CNN during a 2012 Presidential debate).

I, for one, would love to see a governor holding a press conference, but regularly refusing to begin until certain journalists from particular media outlets who had proven themselves deliberately antagonistic, deceptive or repeatedly biased, had removed themselves. They're free to report, but they aren't welcome at official press conferences; they have to get their news from the other outlets. Sure, it's controversial, and would generate heat. But it's also the type of strong-arm leadership America could use right now. It would galvanize mainstream Americans by sending a message that they, too, no longer need to put up with it. It would also signal to the Left and the elites that they've got a fight on their hands. With all the mainstream media, with the exception of Fox News, having chosen their side a long time ago and only wanting to play unopposed, sometimes it is worth changing the rules of the game.

It takes big cojones, but it must be done.

STRAIGHT TALK

Like it has us, political correctness has robbed our politicians of their identity, their freedom and their character. It's also the reason why almost every country in the world has two liberal parties as major contenders in national politics.

As a result of these realities, America is suffering.

I understand that it's hard. In politics, enemies on your own side, and even in your own political party, are waiting to jump on any gaffe, or a bad analogy. Indignation overreach on social media is permanently in a crouch position, leading with its left, prepared to pounce. The media is constantly squawking and waiting for you to slip, like chickens that need to be fed. These days everyone has a video camera or tape recorder so you must be very careful.

For national conservative leaders in America, it is even more difficult. Political correctness has made them appear as professional controversialists. Not only does the Left dominate the news media in America; outside of America, left-wing media are often the only major news media. In addition to protecting themselves, they're also concerned with the reputation of America.

But leadership requires, above all else, a firm gaze and straight talk. You need to have a steely determination to do the right thing, even when it is unpopular and tough. When you say something, you have to mean it. It's the only way people will follow and support you, and the only way you will earn the respect of your detractors and enemies. Mincing words as a leader only weakens your country, and strengthens less desirable trends, causes or people. Clear and unambiguous language is indispensable to leadership. It can create the unity and commitment necessary to enable necessary prosecution of all enemies, foreign and domestic.

In 2014, when Putin invaded the Crimea, it is rumored President Obama considered defriending him on Facebook. No, really. Well, not quite—but the fact you momentarily entertained it tells you all you need to know. It was straight out of the PPP (Pussycat Politician Playbook).

Moral confusion, cowardice and appeasement of evil in the context of political correctness are normal. A loathing for moral absolutes, judgments, language, and those that offer them, also exists. That's all the more reason for U.S. politicians to speak freely and candidly, lest they be mistaken for members of the European Parliament in Strasbourg.

ALL TALK AND NO ACTION

In our politically correct world today, politicians love holding conventions, conferences, summits, councils, delegations, inquiries, reviews, symposiums, and assemblies. They gather as many in a given field as they possibly can. The wider the composition of the collaboration the better. They spend tons to promote the event to all the media. They love it because this political puffery gives them the appearance of action, when in reality, convening these talkfests benefit the conference and hospitality industries, but nobody else.

GOVERNMENT BY POLL

Another newfound development of the wonderful world of political correctness is the way political polls now govern the government. With highly publicized new polls coming out virtually every day, leaders have become more interested in making popular decisions, rather than the right ones. They announce a policy, and then walk it back when they're hit with a slide in approval ratings. This, in effect, is government by polling, a terrible outcome for everyone, and an embodiment of the undependable nature of political leaders we have come to know.

SEVERING SHACKLES ON SPEECH

Yes, politicians are the living, breathing proof that America is less free, less feisty and less fun due to political correctness. The chains that now exist on speech must be dropped.

I believe I speak for the world when I say we don't want the next President of the United States to refer to Islamic terrorism as "violent extremism," or "workplace violence," or "zealots randomly shooting folks at a deli." Nor do we want the moral and cultural equivalence that compares Christianity to Islam, and American exceptionalism with British and Greek exceptionalism, as if America was just a number on a roulette table.

We don't want a President who has more sympathy for Muslims than Jews, and takes potshots at Christianity every chance he gets while they are being slaughtered in the Middle East. Christians use "less than loving expressions," and lest anyone get on a "high horse," religious violence is not limited to one group, according to the current "theologian" occupying the White House. There are, of course other religions currently engaged in mass murder, systematic rape, slavery, beheading innocents, bombing public events, shooting up school children, and wiping out whole religious communities. *It's just, well, we've never heard about them.*

This stuff is not only absurd, it makes America look like a headless chicken. The next President needs to call a spade a spade, if not a shovel, from time to time. It's the only way to lead.

C'MON, SAY IT

Earlier in the book, I offered two competing speeches. To add to that, here are eight simple things I believe genuine American leaders must say, for the good of the American people. When you cast a vote in a primary or Presidential election this year, ask yourself who has said, or would be prepared to say the following:

- "Education is not the answer to 'every problem we confront.' The answer to every problem we confront depends on an individual's values, character development, moral education, wisdom and common sense. It is not education per se, unless its purposes are instruction, passing on the wisdom of the ages, and developing common sense. Since the Left took over education, these have not been taught."

- "'Money politics' has clearly failed. It is the behavior of individual human beings, not big government that leads to success. Liberal policies that have created dependence and entitlement, promoting victimization, and anger, have failed to help Americans who desperately need help."

- "Anyone who ignores the threat of radicalized Islam simply plays into their strategy. Radical Islam is counting on political correctness in Western civilization. No one is talking in absolutes, but there is a disturbing percentage of Muslims who support varying degrees of terror and subjugation. Robust and serious public opinion polling shows that. No one should be making excuses for Islamist fanatics in the Middle East or their imitators anywhere. Radical Islam needs to be confronted culturally and militarily. It isn't going away; this fight has been with us since the beginning of time."

- "The Left and the media would have us believe that Islamic violence is simply a function of racial discrimination, lack of opportunities and poverty. They downplay the role of Islam, even if the perpetrators explicitly say so. This is ridiculous, but also dangerous. Let me tell you why they do it: if they put the moral responsibility on the Islamists who were violent, they would violate the media doctrines of moral neutrality between good and evil when the evil is anti-Western. There are many peaceful and law-abiding Muslims, but this does not make Islam a religion of peace. Our enemy is Islamic jihadism."

- "The best and the only answer to making a better world is the American value system. Nothing approaches the American value system as humanity's best hope. The fact that America has not always lived up to its promise or any of its noblest values proves only that Americans are flawed, not that American values are not better than other value systems."

- "America has been the center of energy and creativity in almost every area of life because it has remained far more religious than any other industrialized Western democracy and because enough of its citizens, until recently at least, have rejected the welfare state model and its mentality."

- "America was always a religious country, and it remains the most religious of industrialized Western democracies. America derived its strength from religion, not secularism. It is a rewriting of history to deny the religious origins and purposes of America, or to claim that America was founded to be a secular state. The oft-cited charge that belief in God and religion has led to more wars and evil than anything else is as untrue as it is widely believed. Secular movements in the twentieth century alone killed and enslaved more people than any other movement in any century in history."

- "People who come to this country are free to live as they choose, provided they don't steal that same freedom from others. Those who come here must be as open and accepting of their adopted country, as we are of them. Those who live here must be as tolerant of others as we are of them. No one should live in our country while denying our values and rejecting the very idea of a free and open society."

CAUTIONARY NOTE

Political correctness prevents real leadership and that's a key reason why elected leaders around the world tend to be weak, pathetic and unpopular. Within America, there is a deep-seated disdain of political leaders of both major parties. This is certainly understandable. The quality of leadership in America, especially of late, has been lacking. For real change, we are going to need precisely the form of leadership I have outlined here.

But to do that, we may have to cut our political hopefuls or representatives a little slack. If we don't want to cower and default to de facto obedience under the guise of political correctness, then we shouldn't expect them to, either. We may not realize it, but when it comes to non-ideological matters, many of our expectations of our politicians are quite politically correct. If we want solid, strong, conservative leaders, we need to permit them to be themselves, and have the courage to not adhere to politically correct standards. If allowing our politicians a certain amount of the grandiose will lead to them feeling confident and compelled to do great things for our country and as a result, we have better outcomes, then that is a small price to pay. We must entertain their big ideas and bold actions, even if they appear to contradict some of our ideological commitments, without immediately writing them off. We can't allow the perfect to be the enemy of the good. Only then we will get the results that will benefit everyone.

HITTING BACK

The U.S. needs to stop wimping around and worrying about talk and start walking the walk. Political correctness be damned. We are at war. To echo Churchill's leadership words in these times for America: *"I never worry about action, but only about inaction."*

I believe it is time for us to stand up and be counted. We can no longer be passive. It is time to set aside political correctness and replace it with bold values and principles. America can remain the greatest nation on earth, if we chose confidence over fearfulness and innovation over complacency. We must stop apologizing and start leading because the world is in desperate need of fair, ethical and inspirational leadership.

10

THE AMERICAN DREAM
v PC NIGHTMARE

"Success is the American Dream. And that success is not something to be ashamed of, or to demonize."

—GOV. SUSANA MARTINEZ

I f you asked me write a personal creed, this is what you'd read:

Life is short. Fill it with adventure. Explore this world. Dream big. Take risks. Reach high. Embrace challenges. Never quit until life quits you.

But if I were to write the personal creed of political correctness, it would sound something like this:

Embrace mediocrity. Push causes. Extinguish life's little pleasures. Don't stand out. Find actions to condemn and ban. Take offence. Control everything (except abortion and sex).

Now, let me ask you: which sounds more American?

CHOOSE ONE OR THE OTHER; CAN'T CO-EXIST

Like tens of millions of others, I came to America for the American dream. I came to secure the destiny I believe God put me on this earth to fulfill. I came to America to be the best because I knew that to join and beat the best; you had to first learn from the best. As the lyrics of the Alicia Keys song "*New York*" state, "If I can make it here, I can make it anywhere, that's what they say."

This is America's rightful reputation. After freedom, America's next greatest export is the American Dream. But all of this is in jeopardy. All of this teeters on the brink of extinction unless America squashes an ideology that is anathema to its own creed. Today, if you wish to chart, like Columbus, new horizons in your chosen field, political correctness will sink you. I can't say it any more simply. Political correctness is preventing Americans from achieving their dreams, and stopping Americans from being free to pursue their happiness by:

- limiting the opportunity for their success
- encouraging mediocrity
- punishing mistakes,
- demonizing those with the audacity to pursue their dreams.

Political correctness sees people as liabilities to manage, not assets to develop. That's never been what America is about.

MEANWHILE, ACROSS THE ATLANTIC . . .

Once upon a time, there was a dynamic civilization living in a majestic continent. Like a very old lady, once beautiful in her youth, whose eyes still reveal a glimpse of her beauty, the continent still bears breathtaking and inspirational architecture of earlier eras. There was a time where talent, greatness, vibrancy and intellectual excitement reigned in her lands, and where enterprise lived.

That civilization is the European. The continent's name remains Europe, but its culture is vastly different. It is now a group of nations in disarray, and irreversible decline. Its heroes are bureaucrats; its villains, entrepreneurs; its demographics seriously problematic; its national identity and culture dead. It is best to live here, not there.

Even Pope Francis alluded to Europe's morbidity in a speech to the European Parliament in November, 2014:

> In many quarters we encounter a general impression of weariness and aging, of a Europe which is now a 'grandmother,' no longer fertile and vibrant.

But Europe didn't get here alone. Just as America's success has not been accidental, Europe's failures have not been mere misfortune. Dennis Prager puts it best in his book, *Still The Best Hope,* when he writes:

> This happened thanks to secularism, the big and powerful welfare state, and the war against national identity culture. Any one of them alone is destructive. Together they are lethal.

It doesn't need to be pointed out that the three reasons Prager offers for Europe's decline are all products of political correctness. In fact, if political correctness were a proud single mother, Secularism, Welfare State, and Unpatriotic would be her three children. Fortunately, America's founders birthed a rather large, and exceptional family: Liberty, Hope, Faith, Risk, Bravery, Entrepreneur, Dynamic, Individual, and Patriot.

But this will change, if political correctness continues its uninterrupted march toward the fundamental transformation of our country. Americans upset that the borders of their country are not properly enforced should realize the matter will become purely academic. If the trends continue, America will simply be an extension of Europe. Heck, we might even do away with those sturdy, blue passports, and get one of those burgundy-colored European passports to flash around, too.

No, not for us. No one put it better than former President of the Colorado Senate, John Andrews, when he wrote in a *Denver Post* column:

> For many of us, though, the watchword is still 'America without apologies, America as it was meant to be.' Our land shines bright even as it strives toward unrealized ideals. Not for us the elite vision of convergence with Europe: borders erased, enterprise stifled, liberty fading, birth rates falling, Islam ascendant, faith censored and secularism supreme.

GREATNESS, NOT HIPSTER-ISM

Hipsters love to do things that are in fashion. They'll sport a new hairstyle, order a different coffee, buy a scarf and fly "carbon neutral" by offsetting their flight, all if it's the "in" thing to do. They have no anchor, and little sense of historical perspective, yet consider themselves morally grounded and socially superior, or in their terms, "too cool for school."

Like all good subjects of the Socialist Republic of Political Correctness, they follow the crowd. It's what is asked and expected of them. Superficial, and simply not up to task for the real world, they are excited by newness and change.

I'm not. I don't think America should be either. I'll tell you what cranks my tractor (*or blows my dress up, added for gender equality and neutrality*). I'm excited by greatness. Show me time-tested, historically superior thoughts and ideas, and I'll defend them.

For me, there is no intrinsic value to newness or change, just for their own sake. It's the contest of the "old thing versus the new thing." It's a question of the *nature* of the change—what you're proposing to change to—that needs evaluation. Being new is not equivalent to being better, and change is only 'good' if you presume that the old thing is not 'good' (which is usually not proven by the advocates of change). 'Change' is always offered to us as a word and an idea with intrinsic value. But it has none. Its value is dependent on both the value of the old thing and the value of the thing that is proposed to replace it.

No matter what the politically correct parrot, 'change' is not intrinsically valuable, and if you believe that it is, you devalue what holds Western civilization together—the pursuit of greatness.

MESSING WITH MEDIOCRITY

In asking you to follow the crowd, curb your speech and adjust your actions, all to suit the tastes of self-appointed cultural dieticians, political correctness makes you a friend of mediocrity.

Western civilization has triumphed and thrived due to trailblazers, change agents, and restless warriors who refuse to simply go through the motions, visionaries who see "it" when no one else does. People prepared to gamble on new ideas. But the politically correct mindset propagates that such people are crazy. This view is that they should give up and settle; that they are mavericks, cowboys, and non-team players who are dangerous, and therefore must be contained.

Independent thought is the greatest threat to the politically-correct establishment because it is contagious, powerful, and endangers their control. It is what permits people to have faith and ambition, traits that when acted out, help ensure money, talent, and resources end up where they are needed. An enthusiasm for entrepreneurship and subsequent job creation is what has always propelled America forward economically. Economic woes, for example, can often be traced back to a loss of entrepreneurial nerve.

It's important to note that our country has not only been full of great risk takers; it's been replete with small risk takers, too, including "workers who quit their jobs to find better ones, companies that expand payrolls and families that move from sluggish economic regions to ones with low unemployment rates." In other words, risk and confidence are very American. I don't know about you, but if I'm going to ever follow anyone, it will be someone that exudes these two qualities and says, "Come *with me. This is going to be incredible.'*"

HATING RISK, BANNING FAILURE AND STEALING CONFIDENCE

If political correctness dislikes truth, it positively hates risk. In the politically correct sphere, risk is an offense punishable by jail, without parole. Despised, condemned and unwelcome, it fits neither the spirit, nor the agenda of Leftists. But risk-aversion is not in the spirit or the agenda of America. In fact, traditionally, nothing has been more un-American. But this is changing as this *Wall Street Journal* piece pointed out in 2013:

> "Americans have long taken pride in their willingness to bet it all on a dream. But that risk-taking spirit appears to be fading."

It went on to offer this explanation of the genesis of American economic success:

> "The U.S. has succeeded in part because of its dynamism, its high pace of job creation and destruction, and its high pace of churning of workers," said John Haltiwanger, a University of Maryland economist who has studied the decline in American entrepreneurship. "The pessimistic view is we've lost our mojo" . . . Companies that gamble on new ideas are more likely to fail, but also more likely to hit it big. Entrepreneurs face long odds, but those that achieve success create jobs for many others."

Nothing ventured, nothing gained. A lack of risk puts America at risk. Motivational speakers often say, "*You have to fail your way to success,"* and then name a long list of famous and successful people who failed at first. Failure is a likely outcome of risk, but hardly a reason to settle for less. In life, failure is unavoidable, and as it turns out, a necessary element for growth. But political correctness not only dissuades you from failing to succeed, the culture it fosters is mercilessly unforgiving to instances of failure.

The totalitarian DNA of the Left also makes it disdainful of those with self-confidence. Confidence, connected to risk and a preparedness to fall flat on your face in pursuit of something better, has no place within an ideology that prays on weakness and counts on submission. Yet, without self-confidence, an individual is inadequate, and constrained, and the nation suffers.

In fact, without acts of faith and ambition, this country would never exist.

COMMENT ON CONFIDENCE

Confidence, I have always firmly believed, lies at the heart of everything great. Think about it for a minute. It takes confidence to be an individual and not conform. To be patriotic. To have faith. To be politically incorrect. To not care what others think. To fend for yourself, and not use government as your anchor. To behave like a man, and not a pus.. pushover.

Jumping back to Europe for a minute let me tell you—I've seen it firsthand there. In the absence of confidence, conformity is a virtue. Fitting in, not standing out, not being too loud, just believing in polite nothings—this is today's Europe, to a tee.

HAPPY OPTIMISTS OR UNHAPPY PESSIMISTS?

In my introduction, I told you about my love for life. Life is not always easy, but I have always lived by the mantra—*need something to be thankful for? Check your pulse.* Gratitude and happiness are not just inseparable, but American qualities. I find the people in this country to be among the happiest and most energetic

I have ever encountered. Whenever my Australian friends visit America, they always come back and say, *"Everyone's so upbeat, so happy. No one complains. Even the guy sweeping the floors or cleaning the bathroom has got such pride and energy in his work. Everyone seems to just be high on life over there. It's pretty intense. It's actually fired me up for my own life back home. The optimism is amazing!"*

It's unmistakable, and it's catching. America wouldn't be America without optimism. A positive outlook requires a level of happiness and a love of life. It celebrates every minor pleasure in life, and finds a silver lining in every situation.

That's the American people.

But the politically-correct are a miserable bunch. They blow up every mistake in life, and find offense in every situation. They don't like humor. They don't like meat. They don't like cars. Or children playing games at school. Or smoking (either do I, but I would never dream of stopping people, if that's their thing). They don't like wood-burning fireplaces. Or certain lightbulbs. The list goes on. There is no joy in political correctness. Just as it robs us of our character, it takes away the joy in our life, too. *(Just a side note. The funny thing is the Left's problem with these things often doesn't extend the personal lives of those in the Left. There's one rule for them and another for everyone else.)*

Again, I say: we need, and want none of it—not the misery, not the hypocrisy.

DREAMING OF NO MORE PC NIGHTMARES

If Americans are going to build a better life for their children, and begin to dream again, it's pretty clear what needs to happen. The American dream will only be rediscovered in the absence of political correctness. I want Americans to understand that its brick and mortar will be completely sledgehammered, if something doesn't change. It's happened in Europe, and in England and in Australia. It will happen here, too. Every element of American greatness is challenged, divided, countered, undermined and constricted by political correctness. Views, actions and predilections must be in accordance with the arbitrary tastes of self-appointed cultural shepherds. Risk, confidence, optimism, happiness, entrepreneurial spirit and love of country are not possible. That's why the American dream is turning into the politically-correct nightmare.

It's time to wake up.

11

ENID BLYTON

"There are, in the body politic, economic and social, many and grave evils, and there is urgent necessity for the sternest war upon them."

—THEODORE ROOSEVELT

A s a little boy, I loved reading. In fact, almost no force in the world could bring me to put a book down. At night, I would wait until everyone was asleep, and then use a hidden flashlight to continue reading, so as to not be discovered. It eventually caught up with me at high school, when it turned out my eyesight had taken a hit, and I was the first person in the family to need glasses. I read just about everything I could get my hands on from *The Hardy Boys* to *Biggles* to *Calvin & Hobbes*. I read all the classics, but as the recent opening of boxes closed a long time ago revealed, also lots of nineties American teenage stuff such as *The Babysitter's Club*, *Goosebumps* and *Sweet Valley High*. Hey, I had moments of weakness; John Grisham, Scott Turow and Harold Robbins were also in the mix.

More than anything else, though, I was hooked on Enid Blyton. She was the author who most enthralled me as a child. Her books were (and remain) terrific page-turners, uncomplicated, and fun. She was one of, if not the, most prolific children's writers ever, translated into dozens of languages and selling more than 600 million books. British, she was the author of *The Famous Five, The Secret Seven, The Faraway Tree, The Five Find-Outers,* and many other titles. She wrote of adventures and life of children and teenagers at British boarding schools, on islands and even characters in nurseries. Most Americans are not familiar with her work, but if you were a kid in any Commonwealth country anytime in the last seventy years, Enid Blyton was a name you knew. I read, and re-read every one of her books and immersed myself in the intrepid adventures of her characters, always adventuring in the absence of adult supervision. They were cracking stories capturing your imagination.

TRAGEDY STRIKES

Of course, this story doesn't have a nice ending. How could it, when political correctness makes it its duty to actively seek to spoil everything, even the simple pleasure of a child's bedtime reading? It always manages to find a way to side with the lesser over the better, wrong over right and ugly over beautiful, no matter what the question.

The Enid Blyton story is powerful. Not only is it an embodiment of politically correct ideology, it pulls back the curtain on the coalition of liberal blowhards and busybodies that make up the outrage industry. This is why it's worth its own chapter. To warm you up for what is to come, here's a 2012 quote written by some third-rate mediocrity in *The Guardian*:

> You cannot get much more anachronistic in children's literature in 2012 than Enid Blyton, a rosy throwback to simpler times when the working class could still be scoffed at and rudeness to people of colour was commonplace . . .

And here's a gem from *The New Stateman*, Britain's leading weekly magazine, where Blyton is accused of being responsible for alleged institutionalized racism in the UK police force:

Enid Blyton was a priceless bigot. It is unarguably the case that without the persistence of her slothfully vile characterisations, the Macpherson report would never have been necessary.

Now, I'm sure you see where this is going as well as the awful people involved. But let's take a step back—a long way back—to when the censoring began.

ESTABLISHMENT BULLIES

In the 1930s, it was the British Broadcasting Corporation (BBC), the country's public-service broadcast network that started the strong-arm strategy for silencing Blyton. The producers and executives of that time made a collective decision to refuse to interview the author, or broadcast any of her plays or works, keeping her off the airwaves completely for thirty years. Why? Blyton was deemed a "second-rater," her work supposedly lacked "literary value," and as was stated in one memo written by a BBC employee at the time, *"It really is odd to think that this woman is a best-seller. It is all such very small beer."*

You can't make this stuff up. Here was a woman, astronomically successful with unprecedented popularity, and these media elites were writing memos to each other from their Chesterfield lounges in some bizarre hate orgy.

Yes, these guys were the politically correct before there was political correctness! Or, looking at it differently, maybe the establishment has always been this way, and our fight is not new. It simply has become mainstream. As Sharmini Brookes explains,

> During the 1950s, the BBC was not alone in its Blyton ban; several libraries refused to stock the author's work because it lacked literary merit. The literary world and the chattering classes recoiled from Blyton's prewar moral certainty and turned their noses up at a middle-class teacher who was raised

above a shop in London's East Dulwich and churned out popular children's books like whipping cream from a spray can.

Talk about a war on a woman!

CONTROL, ALTER, DELETE

But the remarkable persecution and vilification of Blyton was only beginning. The elite pack mentality started spreading. Brookes continues:

> By the 1960s and 1970s, Blyton's work remained the object of censorship, but the literary dismissal of Blyton's books had been replaced by concerns that it was 'sexist' and 'classist'.
>
> As the British Library put it, 'publishers began demanding that Blyton change her characters to fit the multicultural society that Britain boasted. Libraries removed her work from their shelves for her "political incorrectness" and alleged racism, classism and sexism. Some critics believed that her work was harmful to young readers.' By the 1980s, her work had returned to library shelves, but it had not done so unaltered. For example, the Golliwogs' names in her Golliwogs series were changed to Wiggie, Waggie and Wollie.

So, there you have it. Pre-school teacher, mother, and grandmother, Enid Blyton is not suitable for children. Her work had to be controlled, altered, and deleted to the extent possible. According to her critics, she was a homophobe, a racist, a sexist, and just plain offensive. Her *Noddy* series was homophobic, the character playing a Pixie called Chinky in *The Wishing Chair* was racist and the "golliwog" toys were xenophobic. With stunning chronological bigotry, the Left determined it time to bring Blyton and her books into line with modern thought and sensitivities.

REVISED, YET STILL REVILED

Well, you know what they say about a leftist inch, it becomes a mile.

At first, they came for Blyton's turns of phrase which they categorized as "outdated language," or "difficult and challenging words." Changes were made so "queer" became "odd" and "gay" was translated as "happy." Then the names of her characters were altered. "Dame Slap" transformed into "Dame Snap," "Bessie" (a name associated with slavery) was replaced with "Beth." Then her settings and characters were attacked: "Dame Snap" now scolds naughty children in preference to smacking them, and the household chores have been newly reassigned so that the boys share the housework with the girls. Andy of *The Adventurous Four*, who worked for his dad full-time as a fisherman is now suddenly at school, and only helps Dad on weekends, so he's not a truant or violating child labor laws.

It's all unbelievable.

Blyton's official biographer, Barbara Stoney, sums it up best:

> How utterly ridiculous it all is. Blyton wrote the bulk of her fiction in the Forties and Fifties. The settings and the characters' names and attitudes reflect the time in which they were written . . . Where will it all end? The whole Blyton oeuvre will have to be rewritten to appease the muddled thinking of a politically-correct minority who believe children cannot make an imaginative leap into the past . . . She wrote about the childhood she knew, which was dependably middle-class, and she peopled her fiction with characters that belonged to the era in which she lived.

Yet, despite reason, Blyton remains untenable for the politically correct, intent on behaving like the mafia. While passing away almost half a century ago, to this day Blyton critics still seek to intimidate and silence her legacy, by trying to shut down any celebration of her life, whether in the form of a festival or an exhibit, or sending hate mail to a store opened in her honor.

ALL THE WHILE . . .

There have never been, to Stoney's knowledge, *"any complaints from her many readers in Asian and African countries"* and *"not one of those voices raised in clamorous complaint against her belongs to a child"*. Indeed, *"had she written about a teddy bears' insurrection, she would doubtless have incurred the wrath of the wildlife lobby"*, Stoney frustratingly opines, going on to explain: *"It is all palpable madness. The fact is that no child has been rendered racist or sexist by reading Enid Blyton."*

I can vouch for that. I loved Enid Blyton as a child, and I turned out to be a lovely, non-racist, non-bigoted person. And, as a child, I was nowhere near as nuanced or critical to pick up even one of these so-called "offences." Nor was any other child I know who read them. Can't we give children some credit and a chance for discussion, for heaven's sake!

IT'S PERSONAL

For me, it's personal. I wouldn't be the person I am today if it wasn't for Enid Blyton. She brought untold numbers of children incredible joy. She was responsible for turning the most reluctant readers into avid ones. There's even evidence that the safe world with nuclear families living happily ever after she depicts gives comfort to "damaged children." Why would you want to take away that happiness, all in the name of some ideological straitjacket that dislikes nuclear families and the way things once were?

I'll tell you this.

I'll always have happy memories of Enid Blyton, and take the happy, uncomplicated, adventurous Blyton view of the world, over the grey, complicated reality of today anytime. I have preserved all my editions of Blyton's books for my own children to read.

This censoring reveals the depths only the politically correct can plumb, turning the happily united imagination of children into the bitterly divided opinion of adults. It is all deeply unnecessary and frighteningly totalitarian.

QUICK WORD ON BIGGLES

Earlier in the chapter, I referenced William Earle Johns' *Biggles*, another book series that I read as a child. If you think that only Blyton was afflicted by the political correctness disease, that's not the case. The *Biggles* books which present a pre-war world-view of honor and decency became deeply offensive to the liberal intelligentsia of the 1960s, and guess what? They, too, disappeared from libraries, and have become collector's items. Graham Reid explains:

> In the past two decades Biggles has fallen from favour . . . Johns' 150-odd books about him disappeared from library shelves amid accusations of racism and sexism . . . their appeal is nostalgic because they speak of a world of old values and a sense of decency, and the fact they were ripping good stories.

Where will this stop? When will this stop? It will stop where and when we stop it.

FINAL WORD

I'll give the final word to an American friend, who upon learning of Enid Blyton and her journey from me, offered these fine words, "She sounds lovely! What a tragedy, though, that her books have been 'revised.' What pish."

I really couldn't say it better myself.

SECTION THREE

12

PERSONAL STORIES

"It's somewhat disturbing how controversial it's become to have commencement speakers, particularly if they're identified with one political side or the other. If any controversy means that person isn't going to be invited . . . or it's going to cause a problem, we'll end up with some commencement speeches that are pretty boring . . . and full of platitudes instead of substantive commentaries."

—ROBERT SHIBLEY,
senior vice president of the Foundation for
Individual Rights in Education in Philadelphia

"They did not feel you would be a good fit for a public school setting. Sorry."

This was the message I received one cold Saturday afternoon in early May of 2015, while I was sitting at home in the Australian countryside.

HOT, THEN FROZEN OUT

A month earlier, on April 7, after arriving in Los Angeles, I turned on my Blackberry and found this email which had been forwarded from my website:

From: Adriana Moon <MoonA@whitehouseisd.org>
Date: Wed, Apr 8, 2015 at 2:01 AM
Subject: Speaker for District-wide In-service
To: speaking@nickadamsinamerica.com

Good morning,

I wanted to get some information in regards
to cost and availability of Nick Adams. In
Whitehouse Independent School District, a public
school district in East Texas, we hold an annual
District-wide In-service for all of our em-
ployees to kick-off the new school year. This
year our In-service is scheduled for Friday,
August 21. We would need Nick Adams to give a 45
minute speech. What would the cost be for this
and would Mr. Adams be available?

Adriana Moon
PR/Communications Specialist
Whitehouse ISD

Turns out a good friend who lived within the ISD and was friends with the Superintendent had recommended me as a speaker. In turn, the school had reached out to invite me. These types of requests are not unusual, but what followed was. Despite my response, and several emails over a month, there was suddenly silence. I decided to ask the friend who had recommended me to find out what had happened. He finally reached them.

That's when I got that message. I was the latest victim in a long line of conservatives who had been canceled as a speaker because of their politics. To borrow Goose's line in one of my favorite movies of all time, *Top Gun*: '*the list is long, but distinguished.*'

EVEN IN TEXAS . . .

I love Texas. In fact, I plan on living there one day. For me, it's the greatest civilization has to offer. I think it's heaven on earth, and I will defend it to my last breath.

But it's obvious that sometimes with things I love, I'm guilty of wearing rose-colored glasses. Because *that* school? It's in Texas. It's not in New York, or Chicago or San Francisco. And it's not in Dallas or Austin or Houston or San Antonio, either. It's in *real* Texas. You expect this stuff in other places, but not there, even if it is a public school.

If there isn't any freedom of speech left even in Texas, what in God's name has happened to America?

PAINFUL REMINDERS

My first reaction? Oh no, it's happening again. And then: it happens here, too.

Outside of the United States, these things happen every day. Reports of this type of treatment don't even raise an eyebrow.

Just ask me. I became accustomed to it. It happened over and over again to me. It's why I came to America to escape it, or at least try. It's also why I set up the Foundation for Liberty and American Greatness (FLAG), an organization dedicated to speaking events at as many high schools and universities across America as possible.

HIGH SCHOOL, ACT I

One year after finishing high school at the age of nineteen, I was publicly elected to local government, having been the equivalent of a Republican nominee. My high school was part of the local government area. After being re-elected, I ending up serving eight-and-a-half years, one of them as Deputy Mayor. In that time, there were many occasions when decisions relating to my school came up, and every time without fail, and at great political expense to me, I supported them. In spite of my support, four-teen years of schooling, making history as the youngest Deputy Mayor in the country's history, and even having my name on an academic honor board in the school hall, I was never once invited back.

In fact, during that time, the school decided to create a business directory for the school community, giving alumni the opportu-nity to promote their business and search for others. I submitted my entry as a local Councilor, stating my willingness to assist any families of the school community (many of which lived in the electorate) on any council issue. When the business directory was printed, my name was omitted.

Why? I never got a direct response but I know I was excluded because of my conservative politics, my outspoken attitude in a national political culture that prized timidity and moderation, and probably that a few teachers still had their noses out of joint from a few run-ins with me.

UNIVERSITY, ACT II

My time completing two degrees at the University of Sydney was easily the happiest I can ever remember. It is where my politics took shape, and where my journey began. The University also happens to be home to Fisher Library, the largest library in the Southern hemisphere.

In the spirit of giving back to an institution that I felt had given much to me, I offered to donate a couple of copies of my first book to the library. In fact, I even visited in person, and left a copy with library staff, along with my contact details. A few weeks later, I received back this email:

From: Rena McGrogan
Sent: Monday, 12 September 2011 4:44 PM
To: speaking@nickadamsinamerica.com
Subject: Donation of your book «America: the Greatest Good»

Dear Mr Adams

Thank you for offering to donate a copy of your book "America: the Greatest Good" to the University of Sydney Library. I have been in contact with academics from the Faculty of Arts and Social Sciences. They advise that it does not match their current research or teaching needs, so I will not be processing it for the collection.

Would you like the book posted back to you, or would you like to come and pick it up?

Regards
Rena

RENA McGROGAN | Faculty Liaison Librarian, SOPHI
Arts Library Services Team | University Library
THE UNIVERSITY OF SYDNEY
Fisher Library | The University of Sydney | NSW
| 2006 | AUSTRALIA |
T +61 2 9351 5859 | F +61 2 9351 4328 |M +61 414 606 890
E rena.mcgrogan@sydney.edu.au | W http: //sydney.edu.au/library

Incredible. Hitler's *Mein Kampf* is there. *Quotations from Chairman Mao* is there. Marx and Engels' *The Communist Manifesto* also line the shelves. Just about any other book ever published is available in Fisher Library, including books essentially bound at a local office supply shop.

But my little book (now *The American Boomerang*) on American exceptionalism? A book on America's role in the world by an alumnus? One that would end up being endorsed by *The National Review*, *The Washington Examiner*, *The Dartmouth Review*, Ben Carson, and The Heritage Foundation, to name a few? By an author, Ed Feulner, the founder of The Heritage Foundation and one of the fathers of the conservative movement in America would call "*the de Tocqueville traveler of our times*"? Who, in his 2012 book, *The American Spirit*, quotes an extract of my book.

Sorry. No can do. We don't want it.

In case you're wondering, I never responded. The librarian probably just threw it away.

But not all is lost . . .

I was hurt, I must confess.

But I've never been one to sit around, licking my wounds, for long. I said that I needed to forget this small-fry stuff and shoot for the top. So, I reached out to the largest library in the world, and in a story that should give you hope for America, the Library of Congress said it would be "honored" to hold my book. Here's what I got after sending off my book:

LIBRARY OF CONGRESS

101 Independence Avenue, S.E
Washington, DC 20540-4271

SECTION HEAD, CANADA & OCEANIA SECTION
U.S./ DIVISION
202 707-3239 (Voice)
202 252-3418 (Fax)
phah@loc.gov (E-mail)

March 2, 2012
Our reference: A-AUS

Dear Mr. Adams:

Pursuant to the authority delegated to me by the Librarian of Congress, I accept and

acknowledge the receipt of the kind gift of your publication: America: the Greatest Good (2010).

We greatly appreciate your thoughtfulness in making this publication available to this
Library.

Once again, thank you for considering the Library of Congress.

Sincerely,

Paul Hahn
Section Head, Canada and Oceania

The Texas tale is tough. But never give up on America, or its
leading light, Texas. We'll take 'em back to the extent they're gone.

13

GETTING SCHOOLED

"It speaks volumes about our schools and colleges that far-left radical Howard Zinn's pretentiously titled book, 'A People's History of the United States,' is widely used across the country. It is one indictment, complaint, and distortion after another . . . The one virtue of Zinn's book is that it helps you identify unmistakably which teachers are using their classrooms as propaganda centers."

—THOMAS SOWELL

The year is 1980, and George is in the ninth grade.

The bell to mark the end of recess has sounded. George is misbehaving outside the lockers. Poor behavior at school is not uncharacteristic for George. The teacher, Mr. Weremy, who was on duty, also happened to be George's math teacher. Weremy was known as a no-nonsense, old-style teacher, with a voice box that enabled him to compete with the best in shouting. He apparently had no use for first names, referring to all students, and even himself, simply by last name. Frustrated at George's lack of decorum now spilling over from class to the locker area, the teacher begins to loudly scold him, making his displeasure at the lack of discipline clear. Rather than staying silent, George chooses to defend himself. In a show of authority, and to make his point, Weremy walks up close to George, and begins poking him in the chest, almost always in the same spot.

When George arrives home from school at the end of the day, he amplifies the story as much as possible in a bid for sympathy.

To seal the deal and prove his persecution, he takes off his shirt to reveal the small area of his chest Weremy had poked, now starting to show signs of bruising. His mother is alarmed, but says little. Later, almost as soon as his dad arrives home, George's mother fills him in, with George happily standing by, ready to pull off his shirt and attest to the evil of his teacher.

Right on cue, his dad asks him to take off his shirt, so he can have a look. After taking a long, hard look, George's dad asks, "What did you do for this teacher, Mr. Weremy, to do this?" Shocked by this question, George stumbles over his answer. The question gets asked again, this time more sharply, with both parents closing in on him. George folds, and confesses reluctantly, explaining that he was misbehaving and talking back to the teacher. His dad begins poking him in the same spot, his punishment for George misbehaving at school!

HOW THE TIMES CHANGE . . .

I laugh every time my family friend, Uncle George, tells me this story. He's one of the funniest guys I know, and this anecdote is hilarious, but it also has a serious point, which is the context in which he recounts it. *"Times have changed, Nick,"* he tells me. *"Back in the day, parents backed up the teachers. Whatever punishment you got in school, when your parents found out about it, you got double. Discipline was a serious matter. Now, parents back up their kids, no matter what, and see the teachers as enemies."*

CHANGE HAS COME

He's right. From parents belting their children after seeing what provoked their teachers to the point of becoming somewhat physical, there are now lawsuits, rights and responsibilities, and detailed codes of conduct that would likely see the teacher lose his job.

But that's just the start of it. High schools and universities across the world have changed. From the daily traditions of schools, to collectivist school mottos ("together we are stronger"), to what's taught in the classroom, to the expectations of parents, to affirmative action, to the causes that are promoted at school assemblies, learning institutions in America have undergone dramatic surgery to the point of being barely recognizable.

They are now, as Dennis Prager likes to point out, "left-wing seminaries." Today, schools and universities battle with the media to see who wins the prize for being the most politically correct. Multiculturalism, gay pride, feminism and the blame America movement battle for top spot in the school gymnasium, hallways and classrooms.

WHAT'S REALLY HAPPENING IN OUR SCHOOLS

In May 2014, Kareem Abdul-Jabbar, a six-time NBA champion and Islamic convert wrote in *Time* magazine:

> The best way to combat racism in the face of selective attention and situational racism is to seek it out every minute of every day and expose every instance we find; and not just racism, but also sexism, homophobia and every other kind of injustice.

In doing so, Abdul-Jabbar prescribed precisely what principals and teaching staff at high schools across the world strongly encourage their students to do, almost word for word. At universities, student conduct codes defining 'acceptable' conduct are also designed to accommodate this activism.

And that's precisely what it is: activism. These schools and universities are not seeking to protect students; they are turning students into witch-hunting activists, eagerly prepared to arbitrarily define and expose every instance of perceived "injustice." From virtually the first day at school, students are taught the language of political correctness intimidation, and how to wield it in the culture of complaint. School administrators at all-girl schools organize frequent visits from anti-domestic violence campaigners.

While these visits may serve as a vital defense against violence by providing knowledge on the reporting process, at the same time it encourages a feeling of victimhood and equips these young ladies with the ability to abuse the process, and unjustifiably cause real harm to men. During these same visits, girls are encouraged to leave a relationship at any time, even if no abuse has occurred.

COMING TO AN ADULT WORLD NEAR YOU

Not only have I been a teacher, but I have close ties to the profession. The stories I can tell are alarming. The fruits of the political correctness transformation of school curriculum and traditions are becoming clear. The instincts and attitudes of high school students today are both startling and distressing. As young as the age of twelve, students call out their teachers on "micro-aggressions," understand the power of complaint in damaging professional reputation, how to "hold" something over their teacher, and they insist on promoting social issues in their classwork.

Students today already instinctively want to write on the back of a page they've already written on, instead of starting a new one. At the end of a lesson, without request, students hand back to the teacher the worksheet distributed earlier in the lesson. Why? *"Because, Sir, we can't waste paper."* So powerfully and repetitively has environmental consciousness as a virtue been drilled into them at school, they have changed their habits. Some of you may consider this a positive step. I don't and I think it's sick. If students determine of their own volition, after extensive reading and studying that the environment is in peril, and they wish to do their part, that's reasonable. But they shouldn't do something because it's become fashionable and thirteen-year-olds have been given a guilt trip practically from birth.

It's frightening when the politically-correct environment of schools leads to innocuous commentary within the classroom being branded "racist." Take this real life example that I heard from a friend who teaches at an all-boys school. This teacher set up eighth grade students with group work. Each group had to design a poster; students were left to get in their groups and choose their own work area in the classroom. As students often do, they didn't listen very carefully, and several groups were seated close together all trying to work on their large posters, leading to a dispute between them about sharing the pens. Meanwhile, there was plenty of open space in the classroom. "*Come on, guys, there's no need for you to be sitting so close together,*" the teacher said. "*We're not in China, or anything. There's lots of space. Ben, your group—pick up your stuff and move here.*" The reply from the students was swift in the form of shouts from across the class: "That's racist, Sir!" they yelled. "Oh, racism, Sir!" one exclaimed. Another: "That's discrimination!" Just a note: there was not *a* single foreign student in the class. You can guarantee these fourteen-year-olds didn't even know the meaning of the words they were using. But the utterance of a semi-racial comparison had these once fearless boys caterwauling like spinsters who saw a mouse.

From racism to sexism. Here's another story related to me by a math teacher who had more than three decades experience. A few years ago, at the start of one school year, he noticed a new trend. Students had swapped the full-length ruler they traditionally carried around in their pencil case for a small ruler (probably a result of the Left's pressure movement to downsize everything, but that's another story). During a seventh-grade geometry lesson in the first week, he observed that students were finding it more difficult to draw pyramids because of the small rulers. So, he announced to the class, "You shouldn't be using these small rulers. They just make your life difficult. From now on, please bring to class a man-sized ruler." Within seconds, one of the twelve-year old students in her very first week of high school raised her hand. "Why are you being sexist?" she asked. Yes, these are the kids coming to our adult world very soon. Cranking the outrage machine from the age of twelve.

But I've even got that beat! A third-grader from New York City went on a family vacation to Disneyland in Anaheim, and was disturbed by the racial bias in some of the attractions at the theme park. When he returned to class at the end of vacation, he discovered his classmate had had a similar experience in Orlando at Disney. The two nine-year olds decided to write to Disney outlining their complaints, and urging the theme park to make it more 'inclusive and magical for all'. Within their letter, they wrote:

We are third graders from New York City at The Cathedral School. We learn about stereotypes, and the impact they have on people's identities. For instance, in the jungle cruise, all the robotic people have dark skin and are throwing spears at you. We think this reinforces some negative associations . . . We noticed that on our trips to Disneyland and Disneyworld that all the cast members call people Prince, Princess, or Knight, judging by what the child "looks like" and assuming gender . . . With the Princess Makeovers, we think you are excluding other people who might want a makeover to be something else, including boys and transgender people."

Truly unbelievable. You couldn't make this stuff up!

JUST ASK SEINFELD

During an interview with ESPN host Colin Cowherd, Jerry Seinfeld revealed that he believes political correctness hurts comedy and suggested comedians avoid college campus performances. In the same interview, he also shared this personal anecdote:

I don't play colleges but I hear a lot of people tell me, 'Don't go near colleges, they're so pc.' Hey, I'll give you an example. My daughter's 14. My wife says to her, 'Well, you know, in the next couple of years, I think maybe you're going to want to hang around the city more on the weekends so you can see boys.' You know, my daughter says, 'That's sexist.' They just want to use these words. 'That's racist. That's sexist. That's prejudice.' They don't even know what they're talking about.

The *Seinfeld* TV show co-creator is right. Young people today use these words as arrows, but don't know what they mean. They are weasel words, designed to make excuses and pretend intelligence.

NUMBER LINE

But the capper? My favorite story: Sticking with math, it is the story of the "Number Line." A mathematics teacher is introducing his students to integers, and explaining what a number line is. For those that may have forgotten, writing numbers down on a Number Line makes it easy to tell which numbers are bigger or smaller.

To provide his students with a visual representation of this, he selects several students and asks them to stand at the front of the classroom. He then organizes them by height, shortest to the tallest, from left to right.

Days later, he is hauled in front of the school's leadership. The parents of the shortest child have made an official complaint to the school, charging that the teacher deliberately made fun of their child's height, even having the child brought to the front of the class to highlight his height. Nowhere in the complaint was the context of the Number Line mentioned.

Yes, you can't even be a good teacher any more, without political correctness biting you.

DATED DISCIPLINE

At my high school, if another teacher appeared at the door of the classroom while class was in progress, the entire class had to stand up until they were told they could sit down. When you entered the classroom as a student, you walked and stood behind your chair, and waited for the teacher to tell you that you could sit down. And when the lesson ended, you stood behind your chair, and you waited until you were dismissed.

Every teacher had to be called 'Sir,', 'Ma'am,' or be addressed by their title and name. School uniform was worn, with strict adherence even to the point of how far your sleeves could be rolled up if you wished to wear them that way, and there were specific restrictions for haircuts and hairstyles. Talking back to a teacher was a non-negotiable; you simply were not allowed to do it (something I certainly struggled with!).

Admittedly, I went to a school founded on Christian principles that demanded high standards of behavior and dress. The school insisted on these standards as they considered them the only way to preserve a secure and disciplined environment conducive to effective education. That's the point.

Discipline requires a strong hand, and in today's schools, only a limp wrist is permitted. Sadly, the resulting self-respect and self-discipline of young women and men that was omnipresent a generation or two ago, is disappearing, and diminished. Generally speaking, the approach of our young to their schoolwork and their presentation has declined dramatically and leaves much to be desired.

BREEDING PINHEADS, INSTEAD OF PATRIOTS

As if this weren't enough, perhaps the most egregious of politically correct movements in schools and universities hasn't even been covered here yet. It is "America-bashing"—the self-loathing poison imported from abroad. It best described as a concerted campaign, using false but fashionable smears, to deny to its own people that their country is a force for good in the world and a noble chapter in human history.

It has already done inestimable cultural, national and international damage in the United States. There is an entire generation that has been sold liberal lies about their country, its history and its impact on the world. These people have been told America is a racist, genocidal, land-raping nation built on stolen land. Australian students hear the same thing about their country. As for British students, knowing England, they're probably provided with a lighter, the flag, and a box of matches, just to be sure.

The self-loathing disease is not unique to America; in fact, it has come to America because the politically correct have been buoyed by the success of their infection in countries similar to America. It has yet to have the same impact on the national culture that it has had in these places, but it is only a matter of time. In Western countries, national identity hangs on by a thread, suffering from the multicultural delusion and leftist apologia.

The greatest embodiment of this effort to disavow America's fundamental goodness is the book *A People's History of the United States*, taught in colleges and high schools across America, written by leftist Howard Zinn. It has sold over a million copies, and even received prominence in popular culture, with cameos in *The Sopranos* and *Good Will Hunting*. This incredibly influential book carries the message that America has always been, and remains, an evil and exploitative nation.

As Zinn himself put it, his book tells American history from the perspective of winners and losers:

> the discovery of America from the viewpoint of the Arawak's, of the Constitution from the standpoint of the slaves, of Andrew Jackson as seen by the Cherokees, of the Civil War as seen by the New York Irish . . . the Gilded Age as seen by southern farmers, the First World War as seen by socialists, the Second World War as seen by pacifists, the New Deal as seen by blacks in Harlem, the postwar American empire as seen by peons in Latin America.

The book and its message of self-loathing is an insult to American values. Of course, Zinn and all his cheerleaders never stopped to see the danger of teaching the next generation to hate America. Why would they? It's what they wanted.

No clearer example exists than the University of New Hampshire "Bias Free Language Guide," listed on their website. It finds the use of the term 'American' to be problematic, as it "assumes the U.S. is the only country inside the continents of North and South America," and encouraged the alternatives "U.S. citizen" or "Resident of the U.S."

FROM THE IDIOTIC TO THE ISLAMIC; UNEXPECTED CONSEQUENCES

Throughout Western countries, radical Islamic recruitment is snapping up young men, born and raised beyond the Middle East, at record pace. These new recruits have North American, British, Australian, German, French and Dutch accents. They were educated in these countries. They worked in these countries. Yet they rush overseas to countries they have never visited, to pick up AK-47s, behead Westerners, and oversee blindfolded gay men thrown off the top of buildings.

It all sounds rather strange, doesn't it? What could possibly attract these young men, products of the West, to take up arms, effectively against their own countries? Maybe we should ask the Left in those countries. After all, abattoir workers have less blood on their hands after a 12-hour shift slaughtering hemophiliac cattle.

It is the Left, and their *Qur'an of political correctness* that has taught, drilled, conditioned, and inseminated young men that there is little reason to be proud of their country, or feel an allegiance. Worse than that, they have actively fostered and encouraged a distorted, critical view of the homelands of these young men and the culture in these places. In doing so, they have ignored human nature and (especially) the male need for identity. Young men, since the beginning of time, seek an identity and passionate cause. Individuals refused both go out and seek them. Right now in the world, the radical Islamic identity is almost exclusive in its offer. This must change if civilization is not to collapse.

14

EXAMPLES EVERYWHERE

"... political correctness ... is back at hurricane force ...
"Furthermore, it's being amplified to unprecedented levels by
social media. From there, mainstream news and the blogo-
sphere fall into lockstep, putting forth a kind of reflexive,
'anger at the white man' righteousness ... So what have we
got? Insatiable aggrievedness? Compulsive didacticism? Sanc-
timonious kneejerkery?"

—MEGHAN DAUM

Paul Weston climbs the steps of a local town hall, megaphone in hand, hoping to get the attention of passers-by.

He's running for the European Parliament.

On a cool April day, sporting a black windbreaker with one hand stuffed in his pocket, he raises the megaphone to his mouth. He's in his native England, sixty miles out of London. Reciting from heart, he clears his throat, and quotes a passage concerning Islam from Winston Churchill's 1899 book, *The River War*:

How dreadful are the curses which Mohammedanism lays on its votaries! Besides the fanatical frenzy, which is as dangerous in a man as hydrophobia in a dog, there is this fearful fatalistic apathy.

The effects are apparent in many countries. Improvident habits, slovenly systems of agriculture, sluggish methods of commerce, and insecurity of property exist wherever the followers of the Prophet rule or live. A degraded sensualism deprives this life of its grace and refinement; the next of its dignity and sanctity.

The fact that in Mohammedan law every woman must belong to some man as his absolute property—either as a child, a wife, or a concubine—must delay the final extinction of slavery until the faith of Islam has ceased to be a great power among men.

Individual Moslems may show splendid qualities, but the influence of the religion paralyses the social development of those who follow it. No stronger retrograde force exists in the world.

Far from being moribund, Mohammedanism is a militant and proselytizing faith. It has already spread throughout Central Africa, raising fearless warriors at every step; and were it not that Christianity is sheltered in the strong arms of science, the science against which it had vainly struggled, the civilization of modern Europe might fall, as fell the civilization of ancient Rome.

Not one other word is uttered into the megaphone. A member of the public, happening to walk by, takes offence at the quote, and calls the police. Soon, they arrive on the scene.

Weston is arrested, and charged on suspicion of religious or racial harassment.

FLACCID ENGLAND

As incredible as it is to believe, this isn't fiction. This *actually* happened in April, 2014 at Winchester Guildhall, south-west of London. Yes, that's right, a man was arrested in England for quoting one of his former Prime Ministers in an open space. Talk about a black eye for freedom.

In the United Kingdom, as I understand it, if any member of the public overhears something he or she takes offence to and lodges a complaint with the police, the person who makes the comment will be arrested. Let me explain. Imagine two good friends messing with each other on the bus on the way to get a meal:

(Two twenty-three year olds are talking about a girl they've just seen walking down the street from the bus window. Rohan is British, with Indian heritage. James is Scottish.)

Rohan: She was hot, man. I coulda' married her.

James: Oh, be quiet, you silly black bastard. You fall in love at the drop of a hat! As your best man, anyway, I get the final approval . . . and I say . . . she's mine!

Rohan: *(laughing)* Sure, Jim-Haven't-Had-A-Girlfriend-In-Three-Years-All-The-Good-Girls-Are-Gone. You can have the final say . . . she's all yours and who knows I might end up with that sister of yours!

Now, it's clear that Rohan has not taken any offence to what James said. Both have nicknames for each other. The two are friends. They give each other as good as they get. This type of conversation is probably standard fare. But let's say someone else on the bus was offended by James referring to his best friend as "a silly black bastard" and considered the comment racist. If that member of the public reports the comment to police, even though Rohan will tell police he took no offence and it's just part of their banter, James will still be arrested.

Such are the racial and religious harassment laws that exist in England. Thankfully, America is nowhere near that point yet. But, it's not far behind.

GOING DOWN THE SAME SISSY PATH

Pulitzer-prize winning journalist Bret Stephens nailed it when he wrote:

> We live in an era where people like the idea of rights, so long as there is no price to their practice. We want to speak truth to power—so long as "truth" is some shopworn cliché and "power"

comes in the form of an institution that will never harm you. Perhaps it was always so. But from time to time we need people to remind us that free speech is not some shibboleth to be piously invoked, but a right that needs to be exercised if it is to survive as a right.

He's right. And that's why America is heading down the wrong path. Remember Pamela Geller? She was the woman who organized the "Draw Mohammed" contest in Garland, Texas. It was the infamous event where two would-be Jihadis rocked up, all the way from Phoenix, AK-47s in hand, prepared to shoot the place up, but then were promptly dispatched by an unidentified traffic cop wielding just a .45 caliber Glock Pistol.

The point of the event was to illustrate the Islamic assault on free speech, a premise validated by the ensuing events. Such events may seem insensitive to those who value political correctness, and who see these things as offensive but that's the exact point Geller and her supporters were making. Whether you like it or not, radicalized elements of Islam will kill you simply for expressing an opinion, or to quote Bill Maher, it's *"the only religion that acts like the mafia, that will f**king kill you if you say the wrong thing"*. But Geller was pilloried from pillar to post, left to right, uniting large sections of both the Left and Right establishment. She asked for it, they said. It wasn't wise, they scolded. It was poor judgment, they claimed. She endangered lives, they exclaimed. She was derided as a self-promoter and a provocateur.

WHAT THE ELITES SHOULD HAVE SAID

Respectable opinion, conservative and liberal alike, should have been united in rallying around Geller. Here's what the consensus should have been—and what the talking points for any organization should have looked like:

—Insert Organization Logo Here—

TALKING POINTS

KEY MESSAGES

- We stand unequivocally for free speech. Fighting back against a deliberate and highly visible attempt to silence that freedom—an attempt to which too many in this country are too cravenly willing to submit—is courageous and noble. The events in Garland are symbolic of the way America deals with those that threaten our Constitution and our culture—we defeat them, and we defend our liberty.

- To say Pamela Geller is at fault is no different from saying that the woman dressed provocatively and caused her own rape. To suggest Geller has made us less safe is also non-sense. Radical Muslims perpetrate violence because they believe that if they kill enough Muhammad cartoonists, soon people will stop drawing cartoons of Muhammad. But this will not happen in America. We will remain a country where people are free to draw whatever they want.

MORAL CONFUSION

- In two thousand years of Christianity, never have more Christians been killed in a shorter time than in this time right now. Thousands upon thousands of Christians are being slaughtered—purposefully, publicly, as a lesson to other Christians around the world, to submit to Islam or die. The men who dedicate themselves to that cause deserve everything they get.

- Some say Geller's event—to mock Islam—wasn't the Christian thing to do. This is deep moral confusion. Some days, more than one hundred Christians are killed at the hands of these evil terrible people. And, yet, we should be concerned about offending them with words? The Christian thing to do is to oppose them with whatever tools are at hand, to do whatever we can do to diminish their influence, to turn the tide against them, and therefore stop their depredations on humanity and on Christian humanity in particular.

TRUTH

- Telling the truth is the best way to diminish their influence, for those who are unable to apply a more direct and effective method, as the officer did in Garland that night. Truth resonates, truth has power and truth must always be spoken and encouraged.

- We cannot hope to combat radicalized Islam if we don't squeeze truth and release the political correctness surrounding this issue. The reality is that if radicalized Islam wasn't a problem, none of these people would have been at this event, and there wouldn't even be an event.

Of course, I'm sure you heard the news. Pamela Geller said she will never again draw Mohammed, and Islamic terrorism immediately ceased. Another feather in political correctness' cap!

NOTHING NEW FOR AMERICA

The fight against Islamic tyranny is not new, even for America. Just ask Thomas Jefferson and John Adams.

In 1788, when the United States was barely a country, its ships were being stopped. Its crews carried off into slavery. Who by? The Barbary states of the Ottoman Empire and North Africa. Jefferson and Adams, upset and confused, went to London to visit Tripoli's envoy. *"Mr. Ambassador,"* they asked, *"Why do you do this to us? The United States has never had a quarrel with the Muslim world of any kind. We weren't in the Crusades. We weren't in the war in Spain. Why do you do this to our people and our ships? Why do you plunder and enslave our people?"*

The Ambassador, Mr. Abdrahaman, his voice dripping in disdain, responded with a smile on his face: *"Because the Koran gives us permission to do so. Because you are infidels. That's our answer."*

To which Jefferson basically responded: *"Very well, Mr. Ambassador, in that case, I will send a navy which will crush your state."* And he did.

Never heard that story before? I didn't make it up. Take it from Jefferson's report delivered to the Congress and Secretary of State John Jay:

> The ambassador answered us that [the right] was founded on the Laws of the Prophet, that it was written in their Koran, that all nations who should not have answered their authority were sinners, that it was their right and duty to make war upon them wherever they could be found, and to make slaves of all they could take as prisoners, and that every Mussulman who should be slain in battle was sure to go to Paradise.

This is a story every American should know. Unfortunately, a change in time has brought about a change in the style of leadership. Back then, there was honorable, clear, and courageous leadership by statesmen, not dithering politicians strangled by political correctness.

HOW TO CRUSH ISIS

The war against the Islamic State can be won quickly. However, the 60-nation coalition is proving itself impotent. This is because the United States will not allow its military to do what is needed to get the job done. If political correctness wasn't bombing the U.S. military daily, there would be four simple methods to finish the war in that region as it currently presents itself. They are:

- Capturing and interrogating IS leaders
- Running repeated targeted special operations
- Sending in ground combat forces
- Using American air power effectively

BALTIMORE RIOTS

Baltimore, following Ferguson and New York, endured riots in late April, following the death of African-American 25-year old, Freddie Gray, while he was in police custody. In fact, the riots spiraled so out of control that Baltimore declared a state of emergency.

A racially prejudiced Baltimore police department that continues to torment the city's poor minority neighborhoods was blamed. From President Obama to the Baltimore Mayor to the Maryland attorney-general to U.S. Attorney-General Lynch, all expressed a level of sympathy with this view.

So, let me get this straight.

In a forty-three percent black police department, under a black female Mayor, with a black female state attorney, in a city ruled by Democrats for more than fifty years, with the first black female U.S. attorney-general appointed by the first black President, the blame is . . . racism.

DAMN STRAIGHT, BLACK LIVES MATTER . . .

Of course, black lives matter. All lives matter. And, I am very interested in protecting them. That is why I wish we would discard the red herring of racist white police, and focus our energy on the real issue: all the black murderers taking black lives. Don't just take it from me. A 2010 Bureau of Justice Statistics report concluded that ninety-three percent of black homicide victims from 1980 through 2008 were killed by black offenders. A 2013 FBI Uniform Report found that ninety percent of black victims were killed by black offenders. Yet this appalling reality is almost never raised. The national media refuses to acknowledge it. Political correctness dictates it must be avoided at all cost. But if a white American kills a black American or any other minority, the story is covered endlessly, stoking racial resentment and division.

In the month following the protest arising from Freddie Gray's death, it was revealed that it had become Baltimore's most deadly month in fifteen years. The local headlines screamed *"Baltimore Gets Bloodier As Arrests Drop Post-Freddie Gray,"* *"Murders Rise As Arrests Plunge In Baltimore,"* and *"Baltimore police union: Cops more afraid of going to jail than getting shot"*. No clearer example exists of how political correctness handcuffs the wrong people.

On the matter of policing, but just to switch continents and move across the Atlantic for a moment, let's re-visit the evil tragedy of the Charlie Hebdo assassinations. In France, political correctness arrested the police a long time ago, confiscating their ability to carry guns. As a result, they arrived at the scene of the terror with nothing but a croissant in their mouths and a baguette as a baton, and yet the terrorists had polished AK-47s. Contrast this to the would-be terrorists in Garland three months later, who instead had some lead introduced into their halal diet.

Since black lives matter, the best thing to do is to actively police political correctness, put it in jail, and throw away that key made in Europe.

HOW CRAZY IT HAS BECOME

"Black lives matter. White lives matter. All lives matter."

In my view, this is a moral, reasonable, true and entirely non-controversial statement to make. I could not imagine it being offensive to anyone. But in proof of the extremes political correctness has reached through the "Black Lives Matter" movement, a Presidential candidate apologized for making that exact statement in July 2015.

Former Maryland Governor Martin O'Malley, in a pathetic display of weakness, begged for forgiveness: "I meant no disrespect.

That was a mistake on my part and I meant no disrespect. I did not mean to be insensitive in any way or communicate that I did not understand the tremendous passion, commitment and feeling and depth of feeling that all of us should be attaching to this issue."

FIRST LADY CHIMES IN

Blacks, the narrative goes, are constantly the victim of micro-aggressions, such as a woman clutching her purse when a black man walks by. Blacks, the narrative goes, are victims of racial profiling, and a racist criminal justice system. Blacks, the narrative goes, do it tougher.

This is the politically correct narrative that supposedly must not be challenged. It is sustained by whites and blacks, primarily interested in defaming America and depicting white police as racists.

As Baltimore was still smoldering, First Lady Michelle Obama deliver a characteristically self-pitying commencement speech, feeding and reinforcing the narrative, by fanning the flames of racial tension:

Instead they will make assumptions about who they think you are based on their limited notion of the world. And my husband and I know how frustrating that experience can be. We've both felt the sting of those daily slights throughout our entire lives —the folks who crossed the street in fear of their safety; the clerks who kept a close eye on us in all those department stores; the people at formal events who assumed we were the "help" —and those who have questioned our intelligence, our honesty, even our love of this country.

And I know that these little indignities are obviously nothing compared to what folks across the country are dealing with every single day —those nagging worries that you're going to get stopped or pulled over for absolutely no reason; the fear that your job application will be overlooked because of the way your name sounds; the agony of sending your kids to schools that may no longer be separate, but are far from equal; the realization that no matter how far you rise in life, how hard you work to be a good person, a good parent, a good citizen —for some folks, it will never be enough.

WHAT THE FIRST LADY SHOULD HAVE SAID

The First Lady has earned the right to say whatever she wants to say. But I believe this particular section of her Commencement Speech should have sought to unite, rather than divide. Instead of striking an aggrieved note, I feel it was an opportunity for warmth, inspiration and patriotism. In its place, she chose political correctness and identity politics.

Here's what I think she should have said—and what would have waved away the unhelpful political correctness:

Life will not always be easy. Setbacks will stop you, hurdles will halt you and obstacles will obstruct you. But nothing that lies before you or ahead of you can compete with what lies within you.

You should all be comforted by the fact that you are Americans. And this is the greatest country in the world for any person—black, white, gay, transgender or disabled—to live. This is the country where you can obtain, procure, reach and score. Not even the sky or the moon are the limits.

Life will not always be fair. You will encounter unpleasant and difficult people. Sometimes your industriousness won't be rewarded. Sometimes the luck you were working so hard to create just won't be there. Sometimes the path will seem all uphill. But trust in God's plan for you. Activate your faith, not your fear. Work harder. Fight more ferociously. Rest, if you may. But don't you quit.

And never look to blame someone for your predicament. That's not the American way. That's not who we are as a people.

Believe in the beauty of America. Anyone can rise above the circumstances of their birth and achieve whatever it is they want to achieve.

HITTING THE JACKPOT—DIFFERENT PREMISE, SAME NARRATIVE

Just days after the First Lady's Tuskegee University Commencement Address, President Obama referred to high earners as 'society's lottery winners.' The lesson: be irresponsible, because your success or failure is pure luck. Again, we see a politically-correct narrative advanced, where individual agency is undermined and imaginary social forces are overhyped. This allows for people to feel better about themselves, and appeases yet another politically correct strain: relativism. That everyone is the same; just some have had more luck. Surely, a more Presidential and American (and by virtue, less politically-correct) sentiment would have involved refraining from the cheap shot.

IN OBAMA'S FOXHOLE

While we're on the subject of cheap shots, at the same summit on poverty at Georgetown University where these remarks were made, the President once more referenced Fox News, the number one cable news network. This was not the first time the President singled out the network for criticism; in fact, it has been a recurring theme in the seven years of his Presidency.

Yet again, the President is perpetuating a politically correct narrative that is patently false. For years now, upset that Fox News does not advance the liberal agenda and at its commercial success, the Left has manufactured the lie or exaggeration that Fox is biased. This narrative has been repeated endlessly in the mainstream media, social media, and left-wing groups, with academics holding conferences and writing thoughtful-sounding opinion pieces about it. As Russian communist revolutionary, Vladimir

Lenin, said, "A lie told often enough, becomes the truth." But this is how politically-correct narratives are bred.

Meanwhile, the majority of the mainstream media incentivizes riots and Islamic massacres for ratings, and political correctness. It's a terrible show all around.

THE SEASONS OF CLIMATE CHANGE

No better example exists of this formula than the cult of climate change. The falsehood was manufactured and pumped up like a football to the point where it has largely penetrated popular culture and the individual psyche. I don't believe in it. I think climate change is a tool of the Left, designed to redistribute wealth, and calls for action on so-called anthropogenic climate change is designed to weaken America.

SPOILING THE SEASON

I love Christmas. That's why it pains me no end that for most of the last decade, there has been an unceasing assault on Christmas. Politically correct losers maintain the use of the word is offensive to non-Christians, and therefore politically incorrect. What a joke.

The Christmas tree is the "Holiday Tree" and "Season's Greetings" or "Happy Holidays" replace "Merry Christmas." Christmas decorations in shops and display windows of stores are frowned upon. Funny looks are received from those walking past your house on their way to the café for their soy chai latte and daily admiration of street art, when they notice your Christmas lights.

Those behind the war on Christmas are urban dwellers who consider themselves the sophisticated gatekeepers of the common good. They tend to be awful people without even a trace of the spirit of the season. Rather than leaving a nation whose traditions so clearly irritate them and perhaps moving to another that does not celebrate Christmas, say Iran, perhaps (where their views on feminism, gays and drugs would be most welcome), they remain and have the audacity to try and change their country. What exactly does 'Happy Holidays' mean? What on earth is a 'Holiday Tree'?

I will always wish people a 'Merry Christmas.' If they don't like it, they can either live with it, or go away.

IT ISN'T ALWAYS WHAT YOU THINK

Even political correctness's unintended consequences are disastrous. I remember one conversation I had with a Muslim taxi driver in London one December afternoon. We had been making small talk about the weather which was abysmal, typical for that time of year. Grey covered the sky, rain hit the roof and it looked bleak. I sat back, and checked my Blackberry. As I looked out of the window filled with water drops, I realized the traffic was just starting to set in. This wasn't going to be a short trip so I might as well chat with the driver. Having noticed his slight accent, I leaned forward toward the front seat, and asked, *"Where are you from?"*

"Pakistan," he responded, with a quick glance in my direction. *OK, so he's a Muslim*, I said to myself.

"How long have you lived here?" I followed up.

"I came when I was three. For thirty years," he said with a grin.

"Do you like it?" I prodded.

"Why yes," he quickly answered. *"I do. But this country is going downhill."*

Even though I agreed with him for my own reasons, I stayed quiet.

"This year they've decided not to have a Nativity Play at my son's school," he said with disgust.

Huh?

"And that offends you?" I inquired, a bit perplexed, thinking I must be the victim of jetlag.

"Of course," he said. *"Absolutely, that offends me! I went to that school myself. I played Joseph!"*

I couldn't suppress a grin. *"So, why did they cancel the play?"*

"They said they didn't want to offend the non-Christian families. In particular, they didn't want to offend the Muslim families. They meant people like me! Little do they realize that Muslims believe in the nativity of Jesus, in his virgin birth, that to us, he is a special prophet."

Oh, the irony. The politically-correct didn't want to offend Muslim families, but they ended up doing just that. Political correctness is, as they say in my home state of Texas, all hat and no cattle. Absent knowledge, but misplaced zeal abound.

THE DEATH PENALTY

When I learned that a Boston jury had sentenced Dzhokhar Tsarnaev to death for his role in the Boston Marathon bombing of 2013, I enjoyed a cold beer. Political correctness has long waged war on capital punishment, deeming it barbaric and morally wrong. But I believe it is a just sentence. I believe in executing convicted murderers, and see it not only as a matter of law, but a matter of values. For me, it fits into my world of justice. Losing one's life early is the greatest injustice, and the punishment should match this injustice I would much prefer to live in a society where murder is seen so awful that it takes away that murderer's life, than a society that allows all its murderers to live, thereby sending a message that it considers murder less awful.

REDSKINS

Let me close this chapter with perhaps the most well-known example of political correctness in recent years in America. A fight over symbols and names reflects the bigger fight America has for what it wants to symbolize and be known by.

I'm referring to the controversy over the name and logo of the Washington Redskins football team. For more than eight decades, the club existed without protest until some racial agitators, sports media elites and politicians made it an issue. For years now, this matter has dragged on, with President and U.S. Senators weighing in, and a new national chorus urging a name change. It has even escalated to the point of the Obama administration sending lawyers to court to oppose the team's trademarks, and the U.S. Patent's Office canceling the team's trademarks for being "disparaging to Native Americans." Not to be outdone, the lawmakers of the Socialist Republic of California decided to try their hand at playing the heavily-tattooed, tight-shirted enforcer, pushing a formal resolution to pressure Redskins' team owner Dan Snyder.

But here's the thing. When used in relation to the team, the R-word is never used as abuse, or with offensive intent. It may have once been a pejorative term for Indian-Americans, but it certainly isn't anymore. You would think that in order for the use of the R-word to be a racial slur, there must be intent to slur, and to be racist. Not so, for the puritans of imperious political correctness. For them, context is nil, and the 'right' for one group to not be offended trumps all other liberty.

Pressuring a NFL team to change its name shows that political correctness is on steroids. Every American should be offended at the idea of any American government lecturing owners of a private enterprise. Every American should choke on his or her morning cereal, pancakes, waffles or grits at an attempt by the government to interfere in the exercise of free will, and meddle in the management of that business. In a free market in a free country, let the consumers and the owners be the final arbiters of whether or not they should change a name.

The lesson is wherever political correctness is found, it must be crushed. If it's on the football field, punt it out of the stadium. If it's in a police force, arrest it. If it's in the workplace, sack it. If it's in a war, bomb it. If it's in a school, send it home. If it's in an environment, flood it. If it's in a newsroom, spike it. If it's on a university campus, expel it.

Since it's in America, deport it.

15

HILLARY FEMINISM

"It is about a socialist, anti-family political movement that encourages women to leave their husbands, kill their children, practice witchcraft, destroy capitalism and become lesbians."

PAT ROBERTSON,
on the subject of "feminism"

In *The American Boomerang*, I offered this critique of feminism:

Men are to be the leaders and the head of their families, not in a domineering way but in a strong gentle manner that imbues a sense of stability and security. When you force a change on the natural roles and disrupt the order of society, it brings chaos and destruction. Feminism has done nothing, but tear the family apart and emasculate men. There is no celebration of the feminine in feminism.

So, you know pretty much where I stand. Without wanting to belabor the point and be too uncharitable, I don't like left inner-city feminists. I dislike what they represent, their appearance, their manner, and their ideological ambitions. I'm also dismayed at the way men are routinely portrayed on sitcoms as weak, feckless, infantile, idle, incapable, unintelligent Neanderthals. Feminism is, of course, a politically-correct construct.

NO FOOTHOLD IN FEMINISM

Part of the problem is that feminism has no moral anchor, and therefore often serves contradictory ends. Let me give you an example. As a man, I want to see women protected. I want to make sure women are safe. So, to me, it's just plain offensive that feminism attacks those who try to protect women, accusing them of blaming the victim all because they suggest women should take responsibility for their own personal safety. We've seen it before. Take these possible scenarios. If a beauty queen encourages women to take up karate for self-defense, the feminist commentators jump from their siestas, aggressively kicking to one side their open copies of Virginia Woolf's, *A Room of One's Own*, and proceed to angrily finger bash the helpless keys of their keyboards. If a Sheriff advises women to always have someone with them when they walk after dark in a particular area, feminists all over wrinkle their studded noses, toss their short hair back, pinch their glasses, ignore the crying baby in the next room, and proceed to let the well-meaning police officer have it. This behavior leads to fewer people speaking out, and greater chance of predator success.

Feminism has a record of achieving bad outcomes as a result of its campaigns. Take its crusade against 'rape culture' on university campuses. Cathy Young writes an incredibly powerful plea in the *Washington Post*, headlined: *"Feminists want us to define these ugly sexual encounters as rape. Don't let them. We need to stop prosecuting bad behavior as rape."* As she continues to explain:

> Ultimately, ensuring that sexual consent is always free of pressure is an impossible goal. Consent advocates already fret that even an explicit "yes" may not be given freely enough. A series of educational campus posters includes the warning that "if they don't feel free to say 'No,' it's not consent"; a Canadian college campaign cautions that consent is invalid if it's "muted" or "uncertain" rather than "loud and clear."

This advocacy creates a world where virtually any regretted sexual encounter can be reconstructed as assault (unless the person who regrets it initiated it while fully sober) and retroactive perceptions of coercion must always be credited over contemporaneous perceptions of consent— even though we know that memory often "edits" the past to fit present biases . . . The quest for perfect consent is profoundly utopian. Like all such quests that ignore human realities, it points the way to dystopian nightmare.

But if you thought these kinds of ugly problems were confined to the cocoons of university grounds or a few media articles, and would never penetrate the mainstream, you haven't seen anything yet. Political feminism is about to come to America in a big way.

CLINTON CRAFTINESS

When Hillary Clinton becomes the Democratic nominee next year, she and her team will frame the election as 'historically significant.' In doing so, they will ignite a great social movement to elect the first Madame President. You can guarantee it.

Even before she announced her intention to contest the Presidential election in April 2015, Secretary Clinton's public speeches and commentary had discernibly shifted in focus and content to female empowerment, pay equity, and her 'grandmotherly glow.' Never far away with a ready and helping hand, the media have shown their intent to advance the Clinton 2016 'historical' and feminist narrative.

MEDIA TO BE NO MILLSTONE

In March, 2015, a month before her official announcement, following the conclusion of her prepared remarks at her own press conference addressing the email scandal, her first exchange with the media began like this:

"It's wonderful to see you here again. Why did you opt out of using two devices at the time?" *the Turkish reporter asked, after Clinton spoke at the United Nations in New York.*

"My second follow up question— if you were a man today, would all the fuss being made, be made?"

The question prompted Bill O'Reilly to tell *Factor* viewers that night:

"Now, I truly hope this bogus sexism business is not going to be part of Hillary Clinton's campaign. I mean, that would just be awful."

But I *know* it will, as I suspect O'Reilly probably does.

AUSTRALIAN ANALOGY

As I watched the Clinton announcement and see the signs, it feels like *déjà vu.*

I've been there. I've experienced it. So has my former country. And I'm here to tell you: it *is* awful.

In 2010, Julia Gillard knifed an elected prime minister in his first term to take on the job of Prime Minister of Australia. A few months later, she went on to form a minority government after an election. Gillard was possibly the worst Prime Minister Australia ever had: dishonest, untrustworthy, incompetent, and unworthy of the job.

But the greatest damage she wrought was on the national culture with her poisonous war on men. Her deliberate divisiveness was on full display when she gave what became known as the "Misogyny Speech" in the Australian parliament in October, 2012, the video of which went viral attracting international media attention, accusing the then Opposition Leader (now Prime Minister) Tony Abbott of sexism and misogyny which was totally baseless.

Unfortunately, it didn't end there. She persistently misrepresented criticism of her performance and the performance of her government as examples of sexism and misogyny. She set up a fund-raising group called "Women for Gillard." At its launch in 2013, she cautioned against "a government led by men in blue ties":

> On that day, 14 September, we are going to make a big decision as a nation," *she said.* "It's a decision about whether, once again, we will banish women's voices from our political life.

After listing a series of Labor policy advances she claimed would be "slashed" by an Abbott government, including childcare rebates and superannuation for low-income women, she said:

> We don't want to live in an Australia where abortion again becomes the political plaything of men who think they know better. . . . A prime minister—a man in a blue tie—who goes on holidays to be replaced by a man in a blue tie. A treasurer, who delivers a budget wearing a blue tie, to be supported by a finance minister—another man in a blue tie. Women once again banished from the center of Australia's political life.

GILLARD MATES WITH CLINTON

It will surprise few that Gillard and Clinton are friends, coming from the same political tribe: liberal feminism. Like Clinton, Gillard struggled with a public perception of dishonesty and untrustworthiness. In fact, Gillard has pledged to "barrack (*US: root*) loudly from the sidelines for Hillary", and in her 2014 memoir, *Hard Choices,* Clinton referenced Gillard:

> Nonetheless, it's an unfortunate reality that women in public life still face an unfair double standard. Even leaders like former Prime Minister Julia Gillard of Australia have faced outrageous sexism, which shouldn't be tolerated in any country.

But Gillard left perhaps her best argument for a Clinton Presidency for an interview on *Fox Business* with Maria Bartiromo in late May, 2015:

> . . . I also think there is something enormous for the world here about having the US elect the first woman, particularly at this moment in history. We, the US, Australia, so many other countries, are involved in this struggle with ISIS, the Islamic State so-called, and when you unpack it, what is it about? Well, at the core of that ideology is really the subjugation of women. So, in the face of that, for the US to say we are going to endorse the first woman as our leader, I think will be a powerful message to the world.

Gillard's talking points, or Hillary's? Gillard's personal opinion, or is she acting as a campaign surrogate? Who knows? And, of course, what difference, at this point, does it make? The "only—women-bleed" professional victimhood operation fraud is already underway.

FEMALE LEADERSHIP AND FEMINIST LEADERSHIP DIFFERENT

Detractors will be quick to accuse me of misogyny, and unwilling to accept female leadership. Not true. If Condoleezza Rice was running for President, I would vote for her. So, too, former Hewlett-Packard head, Carly Fiorina, should she be the nominee. I would have happily voted for Margaret Thatcher. After all, she repeatedly observed: *"I owe nothing to women's lib."*

Therein lays the point.

Feminist leadership is different from female leadership in that it seeks to settle scores with male counterparts by rectifying perceived injustice and imbalance. Australia learned through Julia Gillard that such leadership is cultural poison for a nation, unpleasant, dangerous, and destructive, causing long-term fear, uncertainty, and division within the electorate. Its agenda is pervasive and is impossible to counteract, rendering men impotent. The damage done in terms of the cultural expectations this agenda set unnecessarily changed the way conservative political figures conduct themselves forever.

TAKE-HOME MESSAGE

Count on every woman's magazine and the sea of very successful blogs by women, for women, and about women, to wildly champion a Hillary Clinton presidency. The so-called "mommy bloggers" will pump Hillary up until they turn blue in the face, and will scream and whine every time a media report or political candidate is supposedly guilty of a 'micro-aggression.' Secretary Clinton will know this, and just as with Gillard, she will have a formal, secret media and political strategy for women. Hollywood will reinforce it, with a ton of symbolic cement, meant to bury America into choosing symbols over skilled leadership.

So, the next time you are told by Hollywood, pop culture, and the media you will be 'voting to make history,' and you hear that your vote will be used as a 'hammer to break through the glass ceiling of the Oval Office, you would do well to recall the Australian example. Remember Julia Gillard, and her 'sister from another mister,' Hillary Clinton.

Gillard's brand of victim feminism helped to kill her leadership in Australia.

Pray that it won't help to kill U.S. leadership in the world.

Consider yourself warned.

BATTLE OF SEXES FUTILITY

As Henry Kissinger is rumored to have pithily said: "*Nobody will ever win the Battle of the Sexes. There's just too much fraternizing with the enemy.*"

Just ask Bill.

16

THE TERMS OF OUR SURRENDER

"I do not agree with what you have to say, but I'll defend to the death your right to say it."

FRANCOIS VOLTAIRE,
renowned French philosopher

In June 2015, Dylan Roof massacred nine black churchgoers in Charleston, South Carolina. On his website, Roof voiced his racist views toward African-Americans and in photos, posed with firearms and the Confederate battle flag. Roof's actions shocked people across the United States, and set off a nationwide conversation about race relations which ultimately led to the removal of the flag from the South Carolina statehouse grounds on July 10.

But it didn't stop there.

Ebay, Sears, Walmart and Amazon prohibited sales of the flag, or any "Confederate Flag merchandise." Apple removed any applications from its iTunes store that included imagery of the flag. Warner Brothers announced it will remove the Confederate Flag from atop one of the most famous cars (from "Dukes of Hazzard") in television history. The *New York Post* called for the civil war film *Gone with the Wind* to be banned. Lawmakers considered renaming schools and parks and streets named after Confederate war heroes. The *Washington Post's* Sally Jenkins opined, *"The Confederate battle flag is an American swastika, the relic of traitors and totalitarians, symbol of a brutal regime, not a republic. The Confederacy was treason in defense of a still deeper crime against humanity: slavery."*

But it still wasn't over.

Confederate graves were desecrated, headstones overturned, and statues vandalized. CNN host Don Lemon said he'd have the conversation to remove the Jefferson Memorial in the nation's capital. The Connecticut Democratic Party stripped the names of Jefferson and Jackson from its annual fundraising dinner. In Tennessee, the removal of the bust of Nathan Bedford Forrest from the Capitol building was called for, as well as trees and brush to block a Confederate Statue on private land from the interstate highway.

This was political correctness, gone mad.

DEFENDING THE SOUTH

I love the South.

What's not to love?

I can't get enough of the gospel music, mint juleps, devoured accents, and Southern belles. Not to mention the hospitality or friendliness. Don't get me started on the food, fourteen-lane highways or dually trucks!

But the most redeeming aspect of the region is its pride. America is patriotic, but the South takes it to a whole new level. I did some quick math: out of the 2,356 men and women who have died in Operation Enduring Freedom, 868 were from Southern states (I excluded states which remained with the Union). That means 36.8% of all combat deaths were from former Confederate territory, more than any other region in the country. Who wants to talk to us about loyalty and contribution to the U.S.?

I've spent time in Virginia, South Carolina, North Carolina, Georgia, Alabama, Mississippi, Tennessee, Louisiana, and Arkansas. (Let me stretch the definition of Southern, and throw in Texas, too, even though that's a whole other entity!).

Some of the nicest people I have ever met live in those states. Some of my greatest memories are from those places. Some of my best friends reside in those locations. The Confederate Flag was a representation of Southern pride and way of life according to what my Southern friends told me. It was never anything else. Of all my friends who displayed the flag in some way, I never once discerned nostalgia for the Confederacy or its cause.

I know the flag was re-appropriated in the cause of violent racism in the 1960s. But this does not mean that the overwhelming number of those who fly the flag see it as a symbol of hate. They see it as a symbol of heritage. Yet we are supposed to believe that those who fly the flag do so because they want slavery back? And, if you have a t-shirt or coffee cup with a battle flag print you hate black people? Give me a break.

It would be laughable, if it wasn't so insulting, or part of an awful, systematic cultural cleansing, in tune with the goals of political correctness.

THE ASSAULT
ON SOUTHERN IDENTITY

There is an all-out assault on Southern heritage, and while it has started with the Confederate Flag, it won't end there. The South is the last region, with 'regional pride.' This is why the collectivist Left feels it must destroy this last remnant of the old America to fully nationalize us. They feel it necessary to make Southern culture offensive, in and of itself. This is part of the overall effort to demonize the national past and poison the American people's belief in their own history.

After all, the South is America, without apologies. The food could be considered unhealthy. The people are religious. They embody a culture of honor. They venerate their ancestors. They take pride in a warrior ethos. They honor the fallen. They contribute more soldiers to the United States Armed Forces than any other region. They believe in liberty and the decentralization of power. But more than anything, the people of the South, more than anywhere else, embrace the concept of resistance to tyrants. The social revolution sweeping this country sees Southern identity as a symbol of resistance, and resistance cannot be countenanced.

The real issue, here, is not a piece of cloth, but a desire by social justice warriors to attack and dismantle Southern honor and force Americans into a permanent state of guilt. The ultimate goal is to ensure that all mention of the Confederacy be removed from the public consciousness, and that the honor retained by Southerners be sacrificed at the altar of political correctness and the New History. The South is everything the coastal elites hate.

So they call them racist. When will the Left learn it is pointless to take the moral high ground to accuse others of something as intangible as racism or sexism, when all it does is stoke resentment, without offering a solution? Are we to believe racism does not exist among non-Southerners? Why would we allow anybody to reduce all of Southern history and culture to bigotry? If the rhetoric and actions concerning the banning of the Confederate Flag are anything to go by, the flag is more a target of hate, than a symbol of hate.

Yet so many Republicans I know are silent on these cultural issues. They would rather capitulate than risk losing the potential dog catcher office they might run for in 20 years.

I don't know about you, but I will not cede any more ground to those who want to sanitize history and make it palatable to modern sensibilities. I won't retreat, and I won't run, and I won't support anyone who does.

IN FACE OF PC,
A REBELLIOUS SPIRIT REQUIRED

Karl Marx observed: "A people without heritage are easily persuaded." He's was absolutely right. The first step in persuading a people is to divorce them from their heritage. It's simple. If your goal is to dictate the future, you must destroy the past. It is why, right now, ISIS is removing historical roots.

But while ISIS is in the business of purging historical and cultural heritage, how is the behavior of the American Left different? It isn't. The Left's goals and values may be different, but the mentality is the same. In this way, it is the same beast that eradicates all memory that stands in its path of total domination.

Pat Buchanan puts it best:

> The world is turned upside down. The new dogma of the cultural Marxists: Columbus was a genocidal racist. Three of our Founding Fathers—Washington, Jefferson, Madison—were slave owners. Andrew Jackson was an ethnic cleanser of Indians. The great Confederate generals ——Lee, Jackson, Forrest—fought to preserve an evil institution. You have nothing to be proud of and much to be ashamed of if your ancestors fought for the South. And, oh yes, your battle flag is the moral equivalent of a Nazi swastika . . .
>
> If we are to preserve our republic, future generations are going to need what that battle flag truly stands for: pride in our history and defiance in the face of the arrogance of power.

ONE OTHER THOUGHT . . .

If we are in the business of removing symbols of "racism" and "bigotry," where are the calls to remove the 10 foot tall bronze statue of Democrat Robert C. Byrd that currently resides in the West Virginia Capitol Rotunda?

Byrd was a racist and former Exalted Cyclops of the Ku Klux Klan; yet for some reason his statue remains. Where are the impassioned pleas from the House floor to remove the racist Democrat from the premises? Where are the petitions and social media movements?

AND ONE MORE . . .

To our gallant veterans of Iraq: if you think that people won't take down your monuments in 131 years, think again. For the first time in American history, the precedent is now being set to remove monuments to war heroes and war dead because of modern sensibilities. Censorship is a double-edged sword—what is popular today can become unpopular and banned tomorrow. The First Amendment sought to protect 'the minority against the majority,' for precisely this reason.

NEW SUMMER RECORDS
FOR PC

In June and July 2015, in the Washington humidity, Jefferson's statue wept. French seismographs detected Voltaire spinning in his grave. These months were not good ones for free expression. The Confederate flag was just the start. Then came the Supreme Court ruling on gay marriage, and not long after, the media and cultural obsession with Cecil the lion. Walmart refused to bake a Confederate flag cake, but happily baked an ISIS one. Throw in some Trump-induced palpitations and some criticism from Cruz and Huckabee on the terrible Iran deal. It was a bad, bad show.

Let's start with "marriage equality."

THE POLITICALLY CORRECT GALE
OF GAY MARRIAGE

It is amazing how much, and how quickly, the world changes. I'd refer to the winds of change, but in this case it was more of gale.

In 2004, when I was still earning my stripes as a conservative political warrior at university, I recall we conservatives using the prospect of gay marriage successfully as a selling point for our student candidates (or at least a reason not to vote for the Left's candidate) on campus. It was a fringe issue, home to only the most feral and unattractive among the Left. It was my experience that non-political mainstream students, all millennials I might add, in great number, would react negatively to the idea.

It was no different in America. At the same time I was walking around the famous Quadrangle at the University of Sydney, Karl Rove was encouraging states to put gay marriage proposals on the ballot in a bid to energize the conservative base and assist President Bush's re-election. This is how toxic and culturally unpopular 'gay marriage' was.

Fast forward to June 2015.

In a 5-4 ruling, the Supreme Court of the United States, the world's most culturally conservative nation by any measurement, rules that the Constitution provides same-sex couples the right to marry, and allows gay marriage to become legal in all states.

President Obama blankets the White House in rainbow colors symbolizing lesbian, gay, bisexual, and transgender (LGBT) pride in Washington. Within a few days, 26 million people changed their Facebook pictures to include a rainbow flag to celebrate.

In America, Australia, and everywhere in the Western world, support for gay marriage is now a mainstream political position. It seems almost everyone is a 'rainbow person.' In fact, not supporting 'marriage equality' is now fringe. Having that position as a political candidate seeking office is an electoral liability.

The politics changed. The culture changed. But, why? And, how so quickly?

It became the fashion. Political correctness came to include gay marriage, and prevented any coordinated, cogent case to be made for the traditional definition. This was helped by a change in demographics, the emergence of social media, the increasing prominence of gay identity in popular culture, the unprecedented support of corporate America, and the continuing rise of women into positions of influence beyond their family homes.

Women are, by nature, more caring than men. They're more likely to pick up a stray kitten, for example. However, this wonderful human quality of compassion can sometimes be misdirected. In recent times we have seen more women gaining positions of economic and political prominence, not to mention positions of influence in the media and entertainment. Along with this rise has come the misdirected compassion mentioned above. In this case, it has been to do the right thing—help those on the margins—but doing the wrong way by trying to facilitate the argument for homosexual marriage.

As for the speed of change, gay marriage was much like the fall of Rome. It took a long time, but happened quickly. While the culture changed quickly, the groundwork had been underway for a long time. The path was set with feminism undermining what the original definition of marriage. Marriage needs to be defined in terms of what men and women are. That means it must be about the sexes and their relationships. That's not just physical, of course, but the physical is intrinsic to it.

When we stopped honoring what women really mean to society, we lowered them to be the same as men. When we did that we made the idea of womanhood—and hence motherhood—seem like something that needed to be overcome, instead of something that needed to be venerated. This perversion led to the confusion over the very nature of marriage, thereby opening the door to any number of perversions, the first of which is so-called 'marriage equality.'

CECIL THE LION

I like lions. I think they are magnificent creatures. (In fact, you will have observed I've used positive references to lions throughout this book).

With regard this whole incident, I didn't really like what happened, or how it happened, either. It left a bad taste in my mouth.

But I thought the outcry against the Minnesota dentist who killed the lion in Zimbabwe was astounding, disproportionate, devoid of perspective and a symbol of our moral decline. Not only was the outrage disproportionate, so, too, the media coverage.

Jimmy Kimmel cried for the lion. Mia Farrow tweeted the dentist's home address. He received death threats and disruption to his business. His Florida vacation home was vandalized. Major airlines banned big game trophies from their cargo. At a cost of one million dollars, the dead lion was honoured in an Empire State building light show. The United Nations General Assembly unanimously adopted its first-ever resolution aimed at combating illicit trafficking in wildlife as its sponsors expressed outrage at the killing. In just one day, a White House petition requesting immediate extradition of the dentist had sufficient numbers for the U.S. Fish and Wildlife service to begin an official recommendation.

Compare this to the action, or more correctly, inaction about the slaughter of Christians in the Middle East. They are being burned alive, hanged, beheaded, shot, and crucified. Their children are being murdered in the same way right before their eyes. But the stunning silence on Christians being told to convert to Islam or die is deafening. The silence and even the defense of Planned Parenthood are startling. While people banded together online to destroy a dentist who hunted a lion, they refuse to show the same energy, determination, collaboration or viciousness to destroy genuine evil, such as radical Islam, or those who harvest baby body parts. Cecil the lion got more press than the mass geno-cide of ethnic and religious minorities in Iraq, Syria, and Sudan.

Social media teaches us that there is a defect in our moral com-pass. The lack of perspective is shocking. It reveals a flaw in our humanity. The moral order has been turned upside down. Imagine how strong America would be if your Facebook friends had as much passion for the country, as they did for the lion! Imagine if average Americans were as thorough in their research and knowl-edge of their government's activity, as they were about facts re-lated to Cecil and other lions.

My friends, the world has changed, and not for the better. People value the life of a lion more than a human life. I welcome any kind of compassion, but there is something profoundly wrong with not caring as much about the harvesting of baby body parts by Planned Parenthood and the slaughter of Christians.

My advice? If the killing of Cecil the lion bothered you so much, take a trip to a children's hospital and wander around a bit. That should help you get over it.

MORAL OUTRAGE—
THE NEW COMMODITY

We must ask why our society gets outrages about the things it does. Why does the death of Cecil the lion cause more outrage than the slaughtering of thousands of Christians in the Middle East? Why did it cause more outrage than a story about Planned Parenthood butchering babies that was in the media that same week?

The answer is simpler than we realize. Moral outrage has become a commodity. And, like any commodity, before it is bought, its popularity is subject to an analysis of costs and benefits.

Let's start with the benefits. While there are other motivations, the primary benefit is the feeling of being a 'good' person. By feeling, and being seen to express, anger over 'evil' in the world, we distinguish ourselves from it. Evil is far away from us. In fact,

we're the opposite of evil. It follows that the more outraged we
are about 'evil,' the more 'good' we must be.

Now, let's talk about costs. It is a little more complicated, but
essentially revolves around burden. Outrage may require us to
make changes in our lives, take risks, accept blame, or to learn
and process unpleasant information. All of these things leave us
feeling burdened in some form. Using this model, we see decisions
on outrage remain in accordance with the Left's desire to deny,
and avoid confronting, real evil.

SO, WHY CECIL, AND NOT JIHADI JOHN?

Let's apply this cost/benefit analysis to the outrage over Cecil the
lion. It had an excellent cost/benefit ratio. It cost nothing, because
it had, literally, nothing to do with anyone. As a society, we:

- didn't need to learn anything
- risk anything
- accept any responsibility
- make any changes to our thinking or lifestyle.

The benefits, meanwhile, were excellent. People could position
themselves as lovers and defenders of animals (which they are free
to imagine from inside their air-conditioned apartments as cute,
fluffy, semi-anthropomorphic cartoon creatures). Not to mention,
'everyone' loves animals, so the bonus was that everyone was part
of an overwhelming collective.

On the other hand, outrage over radical Islam, the ongoing
conflict of the West of our time, has a very poor cost/benefit ratio.
Its cost is substantial. It requires us to:

- learn and process unpleasant information
- lay blame on our own society

- modify our behavior, and
- adopt a position perceived as unpopular

The benefit, if the outrage leads to defeating evil is not included, is nil. It brings:

- shame
- grief
- responsibility
- the stigma of being 'racist', and the risk of being an 'Islamophobe'

Put simply, getting outraged over Cecil the lion?
It's just better value.

ONE THING ABOUT THE DIGITAL AGE . . .

In the wake of the Cecil controversy, writer Heather Wilhelm noted how the digital age has brought along 'the thrill of discovering a new World's Most Despicable Person,' a game that leads the mobs to judge and shame. How true.

CORPORATE SOCIAL ACTIVISM

As we have seen in all the three instances examined in this chapter—the Confederate flag, gay marriage and Cecil the lion— big businesses now feel compelled to inject themselves in social issues of the day, not only adopting the fashionable position, but proceeding to act as the muscle for the politically correct mob.

The examples are becoming more and more frequent. For example, in August 2015, Target Corp., with no warning, announced it had removed gender labels from children's departments after customers complained about signs designating certain toys or clothing for girls.

This heralds a remarkable shift. Not too long ago, conservatives used to be able to rely on business. Traditionally, business leaders invariably would line up with our free-market principles, and a fairly traditionalist world view. But this assumption no longer holds true. The desire to keep pace with social currents (in other words, acquiescing to politically correct orthodoxy), has some CEOs behaving more like social justice warriors than anything else.

I believe in free markets, and these businesses are perfectly able to make any decision they want, but I think that their pandering to political correctness under pressure is utterly pathetic and the height of weakness. Corporate social activism is perhaps the most potent strand of political correctness yet, and it needs to become a front line of our battle if we are to rescue America. I think we should aggressively use the tactics of the Left—naming, shaming and boycotting—and the free market to make our displeasure known.

HEADING FOR A NUCLEAR IRAN

Guardians of political correctness and convention descended like locusts on Governor Mike Huckabee and Senator Ted Cruz, when the two, in separate instances, combined colorful language and plain speaking to make their displeasure for the Iran nuclear deal clear.

Cruz accused, "If this deal goes through, the Obama administration becomes the leading global financier of Islamic global terrorism, sending billions to jihadists who will use that money to murder Americans." This earned him the ire of Governor Mitt Romney, who tweeted ". . . *@SenTedCruz is way over the line on the Obama terrorism charge. Hurts the cause.*"

Meanwhile, Huckabee drew the personal wrath of President Obama when he said the pending deal "will take the Israelis and march them to the door of the oven." *"The particular comments of Mr. Huckabee are just part of a general pattern we've seen that would be considered ridiculous if it weren't so sad,"* Obama criticized, going on to lament "outrageous attacks" from Republican Presidential candidates that crossed the line of political decorum.

This all revolved around a discussion about a wildly imbalanced deal with potentially disastrous, cataclysmic, and civilization-altering consequences.

Who said political correctness wasn't a problem?

CLOSING THOUGHTS

Many know that William B. Travis, in his famous letter from the Alamo, wrote, "I shall never surrender or retreat." He wrote this knowing that, almost without question, his small army of Texans would be crushed by the massive Mexican army outside the walls. But he knew that liberty was worth fighting for.

Few know that Travis hastened to add, at the end of the letter, "P.S. The Lord is on our side."

17

RETAKING AMERICA

"Tyranny is our foe, whatever trappings or disguise it wears, whatever language it speaks, be it external or internal, we must forever be on our guard, ever mobilized, ever vigilant, always ready to spring at its throat. In all this, we march together. Not only do we march and strive shoulder to shoulder at this moment under the fire of the enemy on the fields of war or in the air, but also in those realms of thought which are consecrated to the rights and the dignity of man."

—SIR WINSTON CHURCHILL

In the movie *300*, depicting the famous Battle of Thermopylae in 480 BC, between the Spartans and Persians, there is a scene where the gallant King Leonidas I of Sparta meets King Xerxes of Persia.

Xerxes, 7 foot tall, stares down at King Leonidas, a mere 5 foot 7, aware of the Persian forces' vast numerical superiority, and patronisingly accuses him of "unwise" defiance "in the face of annihilation" telling him:

"You Greeks take pride in your logic. I suggest you employ it."

Leonidas responds:

"You have many slaves, Xerxes, but few warriors. It won't be long before they fear my spears more than your whips."

Later, when King Leonidas and his men have been given up by a Greek traitor, and the Persians surround them, and victory is impossible, he is told:

"Have your men lay down their spears and shields, and surrender."
"Molon labe," *Leonidas grins.*
[Come and get 'em.]

REMEMBER THE SPARTANS

I was only seven years old when I learned the story of the Trojan horse, and the role it played in ending the Trojan War. In fact, I remember vividly watching the film *Helen of Troy* on a weekend with my parents, and choosing it as my *"Show and Tell"* story one sunny afternoon in a classroom in first grade.

Since you couldn't pry a book out of my hands or quell my intellectual curiosity early on, it wasn't long after that I discovered the Battle of Thermopylae. It was at that point I truly fell in love with all things Spartan. I was drawn to their passion, open resistance, bold disobedience, moxie, and love of freedom. Here were men and women of principle prepared to die for what they believed in. When they fought for individual freedom, they did so strategically, wisely and tactically. Retreat and surrender weren't options; they just weren't in the Spartan dictionary. The "no ifs ands or buts" nature of the approach really appealed to me at a young age, and in a world increasingly characterized by a lack of mooring and prioritizing of convenience, it speaks to me even more now.

For me, Spartan defiance and passion is what is exactly what is needed in America now.

THE BATTLE OF THERMOPYLAE

For those who have forgotten their high school ancient history, let me refresh your memory. My friend, former Lt. Col. Allen West tells the story of The Battle of Thermopylae best:

> Persian King Xerxes sought to exact revenge against the Greeks for the previous defeat of his father Darius I at the Battle of Marathon. Upon the death of his Father, Xerxes continued preparations, and in the second invasion of Greece, he amassed an even greater army and navy.
>
> Leonidas pleaded with Sparta's Council of Elders, called Ephors, to let him march the Spartan army to meet the invading Persians. They denied that request because of an impending Spartan festival. Leonidas knew that stemming the invasion and breaking its initiative was important to the future of freedom and of Greece. He decided, within his right, to call up his personal guard of 300 men.
>
> Realizing the numerical superiority of the advancing Persians, he selected terrain that afforded him a battle advantage based upon Spartan tactics. He chose to make the blocking maneuver at a place called the "Hot Gates," or Thermopylae, a narrow pass with mountains on one side and the sea on the other.
>
> Word spread that the fierce fighters would march to Thermopylae. Troops from other Greek city-states joined Leonidas and his 300 Spartans, and their numbers grew to an estimated 7,000. It was still a far inferior force in numbers to the Persian horde. However, the Greeks arrived at the Hot Gates ahead of the Persians and began fortifying their position.
>
> Over three days, the Greeks exacted massive casualties against the Persians. It took a Greek traitor who showed the Persians a hidden mountain pass to the rear of the Thermopylae defense to initiate the fateful end for the Spartans.
>
> But under the Spartan code, the law of Lycurgus, there would be no retreat. As a matter of fact, Spartan mothers issued their

sons their shields with the command to "return bearing your shield or being borne upon it."

Some would say that Leonidas and his Spartans gained a Pyrrhic victory. That was hardly the case. Their brave sacrifice and delaying action bought valuable time for Greece. Subsequently, the country defeated the Persian navy at the Battle of Salamis—and with the entire Spartan Army rallied, Persia was defeated at the Battle of Platea a year later.

THE LESSON

There are many lessons to take from the Spartan's brave stand against the Persians. Chief among them, though, is the lesson that it only takes a few men to make a stand, for freedom to survive. Even if you're heavily outnumbered as the Greeks were here, you can fight on a narrow front to buy yourself time. Sometimes a tactical defeat serves a larger purpose. Sometimes a stalwart stand leads to strategic victory. We should always stand and fight on principle.

THE GOOD NEWS

I know what you're thinking. These Spartans sound like us. Yes, that's right. The Spartan spirit is the American spirit. Historically and traditionally, Americans have always fought on principle, forever prepared to sacrifice their life for freedom. Consider President Kennedy's positively Spartan words and sentiment:

> Let every nation know, whether it wishes us well or ill, that we shall pay any price, bear any burden, meet any hardship, support any friend, oppose any foe, in order to assure the survival and the success of liberty.

Americans have always been undaunted by odds, and often outnumbered. *"Come and take it"* remains a patriotic slogan in our country today, and was used in both the American and Texan revolutions. Spartan-like defiance is not in the DNA of modern Europeans, but it is in the American DNA: it comes naturally to us.

BUT THE BAD NEWS IS . . .

We are not who we used to be.

Our readiness to show courage in defending freedom has taken a hit. Our ability to reason morally has been shrunk. Many are too prepared to protect people's feelings over freedom of speech. The nation, led by the Left and the media elite, has developed a "character" problem, reducing the morality of its citizenry and introducing a readiness to lead from behind. More so now than ever before, excluding our military, Americans are less prepared to stand on principle. We are less willing to undertake something difficult, more disposed to allow others to do it when we feel it's just too hard. There is an entire generation that has been conditioned to not root for America in world affairs which has bought in to the masochistic mistruths hawked by the politically correct. The culture that exists today has done everything in its power to dilute, deride and defame Spartan-like sentiments and approaches.

WHAT IS AMERICA TO DO?

Political correctness must go.

It must disappear. It has to be absent, for American success and exceptionalism to exist. So, this all begs the questions: *what must America do? How do we retake America by crushing political correctness?*

Our answer: we must think and act like Spartans. Only then can we retake America.

King Leonidas was right. Just as Xerxes had many slaves, but few warriors, the same is true of our fight with political correctness. We have the warriors; they have the slaves. Just as there was a moment the Persians ended up more frightened of the spears of the Greeks than the whips of their own King, so will the increasingly large segment of the American people influenced by political correctness, once we complete our mission to retake America.

We will win, if we are prepared to assert the American ideal. We will win, if we are fearless. We will win, if we stand up for our principles, our law and our Constitution. This is true, regardless of the odds or numerical inferiority at first, because we know the long-term victory to be gained by our stand: the future of the American republic.

CLAWING BACK EVERY INCH

One of my favorite scenes in any movie is in *Any Given Sunday*, where Al Pacino plays Tony D'Amato, the coach of the fictional NFL team the Miami Sharks, and delivers an inspirational pre-game locker room speech to his players. He speaks about how both life and football are a game of inches, and explains that desire and passion determine any victory. I mention it here because it applies directly to our fight to reclaim the territory of American values away from political correctness. The reality is that we have ceded inch after inch, and still today seem prepared to submit some more. We're to blame. It's our lack of passion, awareness, and yes, sometimes, intended goodwill, that has gotten us into this situation. It plays straight into the politically-correct bullies' hands because they know that the key to dominion always lies in the first conciliating act of submission. That's why we should never have given an inch in the first place. Now, we need to purchase back those inches, at much greater expense than what we gave them away for. But, if we are to have life—if we are to retake America—we are going to have to be prepared to give everything we have for each inch. We're going to have to want it more than them.

SUBMIT, OR IGNORE—
NOT A WINNING STRATEGY

Here's the point. As conservatives, we never make the argument. We prefer to live the good life, and treat the Left as though it is benign, misguided and helpless. But in fact, we are benign, misguided, and currently helpless. The Left never stop making the argument. It calls us names, studies us intently, points to the 'suffering we've caused' and take the moral high ground. How do we respond? We're like a shaking son trying to explain himself and appease a clearly angry parent, apparently read to spank him. Or we decide to turn our noses up, and refuse to acknowledge the Left like a wilful teenager who takes pride in his ignorance. It's either "submit, or block out". Instead, we need to "fight and study".

When Pacino says: *In any fight, it is the guy who is willing to die who is going to win that inch.* He's talking about a will to win. Right now, and for a long time, in the culture war, we're not showing any will. We're not showing any fight. No hunger, determination or strength is on display. We regularly show an incredible readiness to change our ways. We habitually show a remarkable willingness to allow the Left to dictate the terms, nature and length of the discussion. Let me put it in a way that highlights the absurdity: political correctness is at war with America. They've invaded. Instead of pushing them back, we keep giving them terrain. Patriots are ceding ground to traitors. Since when has that been the American way? Or think about it in another way. If you know you have an enemy that wishes to do harm to you, your family and home, do you submit or ignore that enemy? Would you open the front door of your house, or choose to be blissfully unaware and decide to concentrate on hosting one of those pool parties you so dearly love? Of course, you don't. You fight the enemy, and you study its movements and habits, until you know it back-to-front so you can best inoculate yourself from that threat. Then why don't we as Americans do this to an enemy that wishes to harm us, and our home—our country?

Newsflash, people! The Left wants to destroy America more than we want to protect it. The Left wants to destroy civilization more than we want to defend it.

Where's our eye of the tiger?

The *Rocky* franchise is my favorite of all-time. Most think it is about boxing. But it's not really. It's more about life and America. It's patriotic, inspirational and educational. The lessons and motivation of all six installments have anchored me throughout my life. Much of it is applicable not only to individuals, but the American nation.

In *Rocky III*, world heavyweight champion Rocky wants to fight a hungry, determined title challenger, but his boxing trainer, Mickey, has great reservations. He explains to Rocky that before becoming champion, Rocky had an incredible intensity, an unwavering determination to overcome and a desire to win at all costs. However, according to Mickey, Rocky became like almost every other fighter—civilized, his will to win weakened by the spoils of success—no match for a challenger with an intense need to compete. For this reason, his first instinct is to suggest the champion retire.

Does America want to retire? Do you want America to retire? If not, then things need to change.

We can only win the culture war, and retake America, if we want to win more than they do. America is like Rocky, the undisputed boxing heavyweight champion of the world who demonstrated incredible and unparalleled hunger, discipline and heart to get there. But like Rocky, while he remains a remarkable fighter, America has lost its edge. It trains and fights relatively hard, but it doesn't have the 'eye of the tiger.' It has gotten so used to the good life; it lost the hunger necessary to overcome fearsome challengers. After winning the War of Independence, fighting through the Civil War, overcoming the Great Depression, closing two world wars, putting man on the moon, defeating the USSR, and acting as the catalyst for the fall of communism, America relaxed.

This is understandable, even an unavoidable reality, but we can never relax. If we do, freedom as we've known it for two centuries, will not endure. Unless we start descending on politically-correct injustice like avenging angels and continually banish the politically-correct from the office they hold, or intend to hold, American exceptionalism will be no more than a great bedtime story for our great-grandchildren.

America needs to regain its passion, intensity, and have an unmatched will to win the culture war, retake America and crush political correctness. We need to have the eye of the tiger and understand that politically correct tyrants are not immortal, and their agenda is not permanent. We can damage their agenda. We can beat them. We can change course. No excuses. No weakness. No fear.

RETAKING AMERICA—BY GIVING THEM A TASTE OF THEIR OWN MEDICINE

We retake America, and crush political correctness by doing what the Left does. *What?* I hear you ask. Yes, you heard right. We win by using the Left's, or politically correct's, own tactics against it. We do it by starting to make the argument, just like the Left does every second, of every minute, of every hour, of every day. We do it by fighting, not submitting. Studying, not ignoring. As my friend, Jamie Glazov, a survivor of a Soviet Union gulag is fond of saying, "You don't fight the culture war by canceling your cable subscription. You don't get off the field during a football game and think you're going to win it". The Left has been fighting and studying us for years, learning our weaknesses, and have exploited them to perfection. You can count on the Left to continue this tradition. The Left thinks we're predictable, stupid, and tailor-made for its strategy. They think we will just keep responding with facts and statistics and evidence, and that comforts the Left because it knows it's not enough. That is true. It's not enough to be right; we need to know how to win. *Who would have thought that there would ever be anything where we'd be the idealistic ones, and the Left, the pragmatists?* Well, in this fight our idealism is costing us. It's time to pair the evidence, facts and truth on our side with a strategy to win.

It's time to take the gloves off.

OPERATION RETAKE AMERICA: OUR STRATEGY

WINNING THE FIGHT

Here's my simple five point *Operation Retake America* strategy, including the use of Leftist tactics, to effectively crush political correctness:

1. **Reassert the American idea.** Give new life to patriotism and attention to American exceptionalism. Have Americans understand that the American idea and political correctness are incompatible and that their dreams are more unlikely to come to fruition in the presence of political correctness. Make them understand that they are the victims of this ideology.

2. **Study the enemy—don't tune out.** Watch *MSNBC*, read *The Huffington Post* and *Daily Kos*. Play and replay President Obama's speeches until you know them virtually by heart. I don't care whether you get 'sick' doing these things, and can't even stomach the thought. If you don't do it voluntarily now, soon you'll be forced to. Stop complaining, and do it, because it's your patriotic duty. Know every one of the politically-corrects talking points; observe every pivot they make when pressured. Learn to anticipate what's coming. Learn the words the enemy uses that seem nonthreatening, but are really daggers to the heart of the country. See how they turn situations to suit them.

3. **Reengage cultural institutions.** It's time to reclaim our schools, universities, and newsrooms, including Hollywood and popular music. We need an active campaign to infiltrate these seedbeds of the politically correct. Ordinary Americans must look at teaching and journalism as careers. In addition, average Americans need to write their own movie scripts, pen their own song lyrics, and create their own media organizations. If they can't do it themselves, then they should support somebody who can.

4. **Attack them, but be a happy warrior.** Don't play the nice guy, or be fooled into believing that the politically-correct agenda is simply misguided. It's not. It knows exactly what it's doing. Point to the suffering the Left has and continues to cause. Suggest that political correctness tolerates genital mutilation and honor killings of women. Expose its hypocrisy and illuminate its failings. But do it with a smile. Do it with humor. It's the way you'll get others to join our cause. Remember, the politically correct, unlike us, are a naturally miserable bunch, and what they stand for, makes them appear ugly (there are some exceptions). Don't mirror this behavior . . .

5. **Take the moral high ground, and call them names back.** Don't let the politically correct leave us gasping for air. Make the case for the moral superiority of our arguments. Accuse the Left of protecting the aggressors and punishing the victims. Charge these people with celebrating victimhood over heroism. Reproach them for attacking the bravest in our society—police and military. When they call you names, don't get frightened. Call them names back. Call them 'Sharia-lovers,' 'Constitution-haters,' 'Soviet-wannabees,' 'Dream dashers,' 'Polar bear advocates,' 'Civilization-skeptics,' 'American doubters,' and 'Opportunity Wreckers.'

EMPOWER THIS

"Empowerment" is one of those politically-correct buzzwords, tossed around like candy on a hot summer's day on a university campus or high-school gymnasium. The interesting thing is, though, that it is never used in conjunction with that which really needs boosting, that which potentially has deep, across-the-board benefits.

For the best example, how about we start empowering America again?

I believe in American empowerment, in a world consumed with empowering, because that is when the world is at its safest, strongest and most prosperous. It is needed to combat the bulging army of cultural dieticians, social workers, academics and inner-city feminists that are constantly telling Americans and the world how bad America is. It is necessary so that the 'pursuit of happiness' promise in the Declaration of Independence can be kept to ordinary, everyday Americans. It is necessary so people can once again have the opportunity to achieve the American Dream.

Let me close with Charlton Heston's remarks at Brandeis University some time ago:

> So I challenge you to take up the torch that freed exiles, founded religions, defeated tyrants and provokes an armed and roused rabble to break out of bondage and build this country.
>
> There is still some of them, in all of us.
>
> So don't give up just yet.
>
> We're not quite finished with their Revolution.

POSTSCRIPT: 2016

"The world is filled with concern, but also with hypocrisy. Hypocrisy on the part of people who see no evil and speak no evil to avoid becoming involved."

—MARCELLO PERA

L et me begin where I will end.

We have to win, and we will win.

Defeat is not in our creed; retreat is not in our vocabulary; weakness is not in our heart, and pessimism is positively un-American. Standing as the faithful guards of freedom, we will not weep, whine, gripe, blame, and sulk, for these actions do not aid liberty, but impede it. We will be happy warriors, prepared to take a setback in stride, undaunted, yet un-defensive.

But we will be loud, for stories of freedom are never quiet. In fact, they're deafening.

UNITED FLIGHT 93

It is tyranny that calls for silence. On September 11, 2001, the final words of hijacker Mohammad Atta to the passengers of American Airlines Flight 11 were:

"Be quiet and you'll be ok."

Just 109 minutes later, on United Flight 93 (the hero-filled flight that crashed in Shanksville, Pennsylvania), tyranny heard the defiant, firm, and loud voice of freedom: *"Let's roll."* In less than two hours, after this new form of terrorism—the most deadly yet—came into use, it was rendered obsolete by ordinary Americans turned freedom fighters.

No action is a better symbol for the way we should handle threats against our Constitution and our culture. We must defeat or neutralize our enemies and defend our liberty. No event demonstrates the connection between freedom and American exceptionalism better. On a day of unconscionably dark evil, here was a bright moment of incredible valor.

THE OBAMA LEGACY

Yet President Obama has let down those on United Flight 93 who went out fighting. He has let down the gallant Marines who spilt their blood, lost their limbs, and even paid the ultimate price, all for the great profit of America. He has failed freedom. He has faltered in preserving liberty. He has folded to tyranny.

He has done this because President Obama was America's first (full-on) politically-correct President. He walked political correctness right into the Oval Office, framed it, hung it on the wall, and used it as his inspiration. The President determinedly, unapologetically, and unfailingly represented every tenet of its creed. That's why he is hesitant, apologetic, and failing at everything an American President is supposed to be.

Rather than be a commander-in-chief, he has been a critic-in-chief. Rather than unite, he has divided. Rather than win wars by being present, he has lost them by being absent. Rather than say what he means and doing what he says, he has, in the words of Martin Luther King Jr, shown a high blood pressure of words but an anemia of deeds. Rather than concentrate on present realities, he focuses on past sins. Rather than finding the address of barbarism, he only wants to visit the sparsely populated neighborhoods of American bigotry. Rather than speaking the truth and de-bunking spent ideas, he traffics in them. Rather than shun this galloping era of secularism, he celebrates it. Instead of enjoying the benefits of huge sacrifices that Americans have made, he is giving America's power away in a fire-sale. He was prepared to bring back a known deserter at the expense of releasing Guanta-namo prisoners, but left behind four dead Americans in Benghazi and never avenged their deaths.

President Obama has shown reluctance to lead, a propensity to be a slave to the polls, kept election promises at the expense of doing what was right, and generally, has shown a sheepish naivety with deadly consequences. His failings have one root cause: he elevated a desire to be loved and popular, over being respected. In a period when America needed passionate, hot leadership, he chose cool detachment. At a time when American confidence and exceptionalism needed to be touted, he sought to deliberately di-minish it, in accordance with his ideological view of the world. As a result, he lessened our leadership prowess, dismantled our mil-itary, and dampened our excellence, innovation and position on the world stage. More than anything, he squandered our best tool: peace through strength. Everything that the President as a candi-date appeared to symbolize ended up having the reverse effect— whether as a racial healer or peace broker. Overall, America is respected less, weaker and more politically correct because of his Administration. The only exception to this type of behavior was the hunting down and killing of Osama bin Laden.

WHAT WE NEED AND WHAT WE DON'T NEED

The next President of the United States can't be afraid to lead. He or she needs to be a lion, not a pussycat. Freedom needs lions to defend it. A leader skilled in rhetoric is one thing, but Ameri-ca's greatest need right now is a leader skilled in leadership. Put another way, we need our own King Leonidas—a man of vision, passion, strategy who is prepared to fight for freedom in the most improbable and trying circumstances. The next President and Commander-in-Chief of the United States must be prepared to sacrifice himself for the greater cause of America.

Importantly, the next President cannot be the *Chief Bureaucrat of America*, hosting talkfests, driving "awareness campaigns," and holding inquiries, without achievement. He or she cannot elevate process and symbolism over good policy and effective action. This only offers confusion when clarity is needed.

I want the next President, Republican or Democrat, regardless of his or her ideology, to be a person of substance. I don't want to see this person automatically embracing a collection of soft-headed, bleeding heart causes. If you're a Democrat, be a real Democrat of substance. Don't just let your party serve as the National Complaints Bureau. Embrace class-based analysis in favor of identity politics. Genuinely pursue social justice rather than hugging every feel-good campaign. Look at socio-economic need, not sexuality, ethnicity, culture, and gender. Spend time with the impoverished, not your fellow media, ethnic, and feminist elites. Don't allow nanny state causes to drag away resources from people in genuine need. Don't rein in our ambitions or lower our horizons best represented by environmentalism; embrace the old Left's major ambitions for progress and to build a futuristic world. Be a true liberal, who believes in free expression, instead of a modern Leftist.

I won't vote for you, but I will respect you. For you will be standing for something; not sitting for politically-correct nothing.

SETTING THE TONE

Call me old-fashioned—an archaic conservative warrior whose style, values, and substance belong to a bygone era—but I believe there is some behavior beneath the Office of the President of the United States. The most powerful man in the world must run an Administration that is adult and mature, uninterested in self-obsession and grand announcements. This is not to say that the President has to be boring, or scripted or even modest. Sometimes it's not in America's interest for its President to be any of those things. But I do believe a certain degree of authority and dignity must be preserved.

For this reason, I believe the next President of the United States (and where relevant, his Office) should not:

- be on Twitter
- be on Facebook
- take selfies
- be interviewed by "YouTube stars"
- participate in "goofing off" videos
- speak in teen slang Internet acronyms and reference hashtags

I'm not being the fun police, and I recognize that many will consider some of these things to constitute clever political outreach. But to my mind, President Bill Clinton playing his saxophone on a late night show is very different than President Obama being interviewed by a woman whose claim to fame is that she once ate cereal out of a bathtub, and wears green lipstick. I believe the President should set the agenda and tone, and not be governed by the anarchic modern media with its thirst for drama and obsession with gesture.

Again, I'm not suggesting the President cannot be irreverent, or should be dull and lifeless. By now, you should understand that is the last thing I would advocate. But consider the example set by President George W. Bush. Unfortunately, I'm yet to have the privilege of meeting him, but I am convinced from everything I know and have heard, that he is a fun character and would be an incredible dinner companion. Yet, he never once compromised the dignity or gravitas of his Office the way President Obama has.

SETTING THE WORLD'S MORAL TONE

It's often forgotten, and uncomfortable for many to acknowledge these days, but President Obama has truly showcased that the President of the United States is still a moral beacon for the world. Whether by design or not, there is a correlation between the way other nations' political leaders and populations behave to the moral standard the President sets. In the seven years of the Obama Presidency, fourteen countries around the world decided to legalize gay marriage, and many others are now pursuing it. There was an undoubtable shift in, not only American, but also worldwide sentiment on this issue, and it was largely due to President Obama's position. The change would have been impossible if not for the President's behavior, demeanor, identity, tacit and ultimately, overt approval.

LIBERTARIAN APOLOGY TOUR

Imagine this news piece in the *Washington Herald* on June 4, 2017, about newly elected President Russell Peters:

WASHINGTON DC, May 4—President Russell Peters flew back into Washington last night to a gathering storm of criticism, following his week-long visit to the Middle East where he delivered his controversial address about American foreign policy.

The Commander-in-Chief was seen waving to photographers as he walked across the lawn from Marine One following a short flight from Andrews Air Force Base in Maryland.

The 45-minute speech in Riyadh was a direct appeal by the President to the Islamic world, attributing the rise and existence of Islamic fundamentalism in the region to American democracy, and pledging to not "repeat the mistakes of the past".

The "age of the cabal of neo-cons was over, the President declared, and promised that America would "no longer meddle in the Middle East, creating blowback."

The speech has angered many, including in the President's own party, who feel he is not taking the Islamists' ideology seriously, and apologizing for what he considers American failings in foreign policy.

"He's no different than a liberal," Republican Senator Stooze huffed. "He has the masochistic view of America and this mega-chauvinistic view of the world. According to him, we're responsible for everything—9-11, ISIS—what's next? It's like he's never picked up a history book. Has he never heard of Constantinople? What is it about their ambitions for a world caliphate he doesn't get? 1400-year war? Hello?"

The President will hold a much anticipated press conference later this week. His return coincides as he readies executive actions and legislative proposals to in a bid to fulfil many of his campaign promises.

Returning briefly to what America does not need. It is essential that the American people do not have another American apologist in the White House, however they are dressed up.

I think it is eminently dangerous for the American people to elect a President who considers the problems of the world to rest at the hands of America. This particular worldview is not exclusive to Democrats; in fact, it enjoys more consistent support among libertarians than it does even traditional Democrats. Furthermore, I would consider it deeply troubling if the American President did not believe a strong American presence worldwide wouldn't make the world a safer place.

As much as libertarians loathe President Obama, it is ironic that, they would likely engage in a very similar apology tour to the one conducted by the President in June of 2009. Neither the current President nor one like the one I described, understand the Islamist ideology, because if they did, they would take a very different stance. America has not evolved Islamist ideology any more than it did Nazism. But I tell you this. The Islamists have the potential to wreak just as much havoc if they are not stopped.

LIBERTARIAN GROUPTHINK

It's an unlikely couple.

You wouldn't think those following an ideology committed to liberty would tend to have a groupthink mentality, an integral part of political correctness. But those on college campuses do. Ann Coulter says it best:

> . . . these libertarian college kids— unlike libertarian adults like Richard Epstein and Gary Lawson for example— they are just consumed by groupthink. They're really like liberals this way. They remind me of those Howard Stern groupies who, you know, would obsessively call into radio shows, to TV shows or try to show up on TV . . . this is what these young— many of the young libertarians are like . . . they ought to put down their pro-pot signs and read some Richard Epstein— probably the leading libertarian in the country.. "It's not even liberals I hate so much," she said. "I hate groupthink. And the libertarians have it every bit as much as the college liberals I speak to.

Is it just me, or do others see the political correctness in individual libertarians? As one friend put it to me recently, "Have you noticed that they (libertarians and leftists) often look the same, dress the same, and present the same? And they tend to engage in similar social activity and love social media?" They are strange bedfellows, but the cultural similarities are undeniable. Libertarians are supposed to be the greatest individualists alive, but they seem to fit today's culture much more than conservatives. A belief in limited government and the individual over the collective is as American as apple pie. But so is cultural conservatism.

THE 2016 RACE

At the time of this writing, it appears there are almost a record number of candidates standing for the nomination of the Republican Party to be President. On the Democratic side, there is only one serious contender.

As outlined in the previous chapter, I believe a one or two-term Hillary Clinton Presidency would be utterly devastating for American cohesion and culture. I pray that America has learned its lesson. There is a world of difference between a symbol and the reality of being a chief executive. From her record, one can only conclude that she would be the second official political correctness President of the United States. Critically, I am not convinced a President Hillary Clinton can defeat Islamic State. After all, it was under her tenure as Secretary of State that the Islamic State blossomed and Iraq was abandoned. Additionally, I do not consider her to have the capacity to unify America, and I feel she would continue the Obama legacy of vindictiveness toward her Administration's opponents. While there is a temptation to expect her Presidency would be more aligned with that of her husband's tenure, I think that is an erroneous assumption. I feel there is a substantial difference between her politics and those of her husband. President Bill Clinton had politically-correct sympathies, but he was a not a political-correctness President. He believed in American exceptionalism, sought consensus, and was a pragmatist, prepared to sacrifice his liberal ambitions to find center ground. On the other hand, everything we know about Hillary Clinton suggests she is addicted to the politics of conflict, not co-operation.

Thankfully, though, I am unswervingly convinced that the next President of the United States will be a Republican. I believe that candidate will be a conservative not out of convenience, but out of deep conviction. I believe that person will make a great President who is capable of ending the waste, paying back the debt, limiting government power, axing political correctness, protecting the borders, preserving Judeo-Christian traditions, ending the culture of entitlement, cutting taxes, exercising fidelity to the Constitution, and keeping the peace through unquestioned military advantage.

Here's what else I believe:

- The next President will be invested in America, not identity politics. He or she will be a patriotism-urger, not identity-urger.
- At home, freedom of speech and religious liberty will be restored.
- Abroad, America will once more be feared and respected, freezing the sweat and chilling the bones of men who aspire to tyranny, even fleetingly.
- American self-belief will again prove itself to be the flame that refuses to be snuffed out.
- American exceptionalism will once more inject new life into the veins of civilization, undaunted by odds, unwearied by constant challenge, and unstained by the perpetual attack of its opponents.

I believe all of this because there is, and we have, no alternative.

Let's re-assert the American idea. Let's restore the American dream. Let's harness the American can-do spirit. Let's use Leftist tactics against political correctness. Let's study and fight the enemy comprehensively. Let's re-invigorate American values as an alternative to political correctness. Let's help, guide, and inspire Americans to join that movement. Let's convince our fellow citizens that for America to be America again, and for the world to be a safer and better place, the complete removal of political correctness from American society, top to bottom, is non-negotiable.

Let's begin it with the decision we make in 2016.

Then, and only then, will we retake America, by crushing political correctness, relegating it to the dustbin of history, rendering it no more than an obscure footnote in a dusty book on the lowest-shelf of a third-rate library—just where it belongs.

That is the day when America will be truly free again.

ACKNOWLEDGEMENTS

It was English writer John Heywood who elegantly observed: "Many hands make light work."

And so it was for this book.

Firstly, I must thank my mother and father for their unfailing support and love. To my great profit, I have always followed their advice.

From the moment it was possible, I have loved reading books. (Not so much, arithmetic, much to my father's eternal chagrin.) To now have two of my own written and published, I am deeply grateful and humbled.

Anthony Ziccardi acquired this book, and it was one of the best things that ever happened to me. Not only do I have in my corner one of the best and most experienced in the book business, but also an incredible friend and confidante.

Michael Wilson, Gavin Caruthers, and the entire team at Post Hill Press in Nashville and New York were outstanding.

Special mention also goes to Keith Urbahn and the Javelin team, as well as Duane Ward and Jordan Smallwood at the Premiere Speakers Bureau.

I'm grateful to Dennis Prager for writing the foreword. Dennis is one of the seminal thinkers of our times, bringing a compelling, brilliant and clear moral voice to the issues confronting the world. His expertise on American exceptionalism is unparalleled. I'm proud to call him a friend.

If I'm the protégé; John Andrews is the mentor. In my life, he leads the list of important men who reached down and took an interest in me when there was nothing in it for them. He is, in every sense "a gentleman, an officer, and a scholar." A former naval officer, President of the Colorado Senate, a speechwriter for President Nixon, an appointee of President Ronald Reagan and President George W. Bush, John is a leading national voice for liberty. Recently, I stumbled across a piece he wrote several years ago about his own mentor, Bill Buckley:

> I just seek opportunities to 'be someone's Bill Buckley,' in the sense of taking time to encourage that eager, questing youngster as he long ago encouraged me. Winning a million in the lottery is nothing compared to the rewards of this.

John Andrews is my Bill Buckley, and a model to me in life, family, faith, and career. Later in life, I will try to pay his generosity forward, in his honor.

Many of my friends are family.

Maybeth Nunn and Linda Stratton, of Texas; Jack Temple and Becky Gerritson, of Alabama; and John and Sandra Parrott, of Illinois, are six of the greatest people I have ever met, and I love them dearly.

Eldad Yaron and Sam Theodosopoulos are my New York brothers. Charlie Kirk has been an amazing friend, support and inspiration. He is America's future.

Others include: radio titan Hugh Hewitt, Allen Estrin, Col. Allen West, Ed Feulner, Col. Oliver North, Sanjay Gidwani, Shawn Tully, Jodi Watson, Vernon Easttep, Paul Rieger, Vince Primo, Tim Blake, John Rogitz, Jared Vallorani, Jack Fowler, Dana Perino,

Warren Smith, Ben Weingarten, Cam Edwards, Doug Brunt, Phillip Meehan, Robert Krueger, Caleb Bonham, Keri Brehm, Megan Brown, John Vobis, Carol Elmore, Dick Morris, Lance Kennedy, and the Murrells.

My brothers in Australia are always there for a laugh, dinner, and a few beers: Evan, Angelo, Michael, James, Nick and Pete.

You all radiate energy in an entirely too arid and godless society.

My advice to readers is to live your life for your eulogy, not your resume. In your lifetime you should always, in Shakespeare's words, "bestride our narrow world like a colossus." Always dream, always believe, and be relentless, even in the face of continual failure. Everything takes time, but nothing is impossible. Activate your faith, not your fear. Even on your most unproductive day, do one thing, no matter how small, toward your dream. Be inspired by a dream, and powered by belief. Never allow yourself to be a punching bag. Embrace risk. When preparing to fight for what you want, "Keep in a crouch, and lead with your right." Creativity always beats out intelligence. If you've got both, you're very dangerous.

I never had the honor of serving in the military, but I applaud the commitment and sacrifices of our men in uniform. I thank the people of America for their continued support of my work, and for making all my own dreams possible. I, and now FLAG, will always be a voice for you, defending, cajoling and uplifting, as needed.

And above all, thanks to my Lord and Savior, Jesus Christ.

WORKS CONSULTED

AUTHOR'S NOTE

Churchill, Winston S. *Churchill: The Power of Words.* Edited by Martin Gilbert. Boston: Da Capo Press, 2012: 330.

INTRODUCTION

Real Southern Men. *"God. Family. Football. A Twanglish Lesson."* Accessed January 10, 2013. http://real-southern.com/2013/01/10/god-family-football-a-twanglish-lesson/.

Chapter 1: AMERICA and PC—HEAD TO HEAD

Reagan, Ronald. *The Public Papers of the Presidents of the United States: The Public Papers of President Ronald W. Reagan,* Ronald Reagan Presidential Library, 1986.

The Edmund Burke Institute. *"Edmund Burke: Conservative Statesman Par Excellence."* Accessed 2006. http://www.edmundburkeinstitute.org/edmundburke.htm

The Huffington Post. *"Bill Maher And Ben Affleck Have A Fierce Debate Over Radical Islam."* Last modified January 7, 2014. http://www.huffingtonpost.com/2014/10/04/bill-maher-ben-affleck-debate_n_5931832.html

Chapter 2: RED, WHITE AND BLUE

ESPN 30 For 30. *"Survive and Advance."* Last modified April 6, 2015. http://espn.go.com/30for30/film?page=survive%20and%20advance

Columbia University. *"Alexis de Tocqueville."* http://www.columbia.edu/cu/tat/core/tocqueville.htm

Capitalism Magazine. *"Margaret Thatcher: In Her Own Words."* Accessed April 10, 2013. http://capitalismmagazine.com/2013/04/thatcher-the-lady-who-was-not-for-turning/.

National Churchill Museum. *"Week Ahead: Let's Hope Churchill Was Wrong About Americans."* Accessed October 7, 2013. https://

www.nationalchurchillmuseum.org/10-07-13-lets-hope-churchill-was-wrong-about-americans.html.

Google. *"The American Crisis."* Accessed 2006. https://books.google.com.au/books/about/The_American_Crisis.html?id=ZTyatPBYG0cC

Chapter 3: UNDERSTANDING THE ENEMY

Oxford Dictionaries. *"John Milton: living at this hour?"* Accessed 2015. http://blog.oxforddictionaries.com/2012/12/john-milton-living-at-this-hour/

Atkinson, Philip. *A Study Of Our Decline.* Lulu.com, 2007.

The Christian Broadcasting Network. *"Presidential Proverbs: The Ten 'Cannots' of Abe Lincoln."* Accessed 2015. http://www.cbn.com/spirituallife/BibleStudyAndTheology/Discipleship/lincoln_cannots.aspx

Newsweek. *"The 12 Year Itch."* Accessed March 30, 2003. http://www.newsweek.com/12-year-itch-132309

Newsweek. *"State of the Union speech, Sotu, President George W. Bush, International Reactions."* Accessed January 29, 2002. http://www.newsweek.com/state-union-speech-sotu-president-george-w-bush-international-reactions-143651

Real Clear Politics. *"State Dept's Harf: "We Can Not Kill Our Way Out Of This War," Must Address Root Causes Like Joblessness."* Accessed February 17, 2015. http://www.realclearpolitics.com/video/2015/02/17/state_dept_spokesperson_we_can_not_kill_our_way_out_of_this_war_must_address_root_causes_like_joblessness.html

"State Dept's Harf: "We Can Not Kill Our Way Out Of This War," Must Address Root Causes Like Joblessness." http://www.realclearpolitics.com/video/2015/02/17/harf_on_jobs_for_terrorists_comment_argument_may_be_too_nuanced_for_some_bush_said_it_too.html

Real Clear Politics. *"The Left Hates Conservatives."* Accessed July 27, 2010. http://www.realclearpolitics.com/articles/2010/07/27/the_left_hates_conservatives_106478.html

Obama, President Barack. *"National Security Strategy."* February 2015. https://www.whitehouse.gov/sites/default/files/docs/2015_national_security_strategy.pdf

Family Security Matters. *"The Tyranny of Political Correctness."* Accessed May 17, 2007. http://www.freerepublic.com/focus/f-news/1835136/posts

CNN. *"5 things to know about the celebrity nude photo hacking scandal."* Accessed October 12, 2014. http://edition.cnn.com/2014/09/02/showbiz/hacked-nude-photos-five-things/

Daily Mail. *"Why chivalry may not always be what it seems: Men who hold doors open and smile may actually be sexist, study claims."* Accessed March 10, 2015. http://www.dailymail.co.uk/sciencetech/article-2988310/How-smile-reveals-man-s-SEXIST-Beliefs-women-betrayed-facial-expressions-claims-study.html

National Review. *"Microaggression."* Accessed February 3, 2014. http://
www.nationalreview.com/article/370078/microaggression-alec-torres
Joint Committee on Printing Congress (U.S.). "Memorial Services in
the Congress of the United States and Tributes in Eulogy of Ronald
Reagan, Late a President of the United States." 2005: 215. https://
books.google.com.au/books?id=L-Oup8TM63MC&pg=PA215&lpg=
PA215&dq=ronald+reagan+Of+the+four+wars+in+my+lifetime,
+none+came+about+because+the+U.S.+was+too+strong.%27&-
source=bl&ots=8mRZ0TT1m-&sig=94lxrqRj_2atVDqWrH-vo-
3f4UO0&hl=en&sa=X&ei=_4ViVeqOG-a2mQXi0IHgCA&ved=0C-
DQQ6AEwBA#v=onepage&q=ronald%20reagan%20Of%20the
%20four%20wars%20in%20my%20lifetime%2C%20none%20
came%20about%20because%20the%20U.S.%20was%20too%20
strong.'&f=false

Chapter 4: MISSING COJONES

Churchill, Winston S. *The Gathering Storm.* New York: Mariner Books,
1986: 15.
History Commons. "Context of '1967: US President: US Is an 'Elephant,'
Greece and Cyprus Are 'Fleas' that 'May Just Get Whacked.' " Accessed September 1, 2009. http://www.historycommons.org/context.
jsp?item=a1967johnsonflea#a1967johnsonflea
Youtube.com. *"Harvard Address"* (video). Accessed April 12, 2013.
https://www.youtube.com/watch?v=WuVG8SnxxCM
New York Times. *"More Africans Enter U.S. Than in Days of Slavery."*
Accessed February 21, 2005. http://www.nytimes.com/2005/02/21/
nyregion/more-africans-enter-us-than-in-days-of-slavery.html

Chapter 5: EMBOLDENING THE ENEMY

The Wall Street Journal. *"Margaret Thatcher's best quotes."* Last updated
April 8, 2013. http://www.wsj.com/articles/SB1000142412788732405
0304578410460056812192
The Washington Times. *"Editorial: Another 'smidgen of corruption' at the
Internal Revenue Service."* Accessed June 25, 2014. http://www.wash-
ingtontimes.com/news/2014/jun/25/editorial-new-scandal-at-the-irs/
History.com. *"1942: Roosevelt ushers in Japanese-American internment."* http://www.history.com/this-day-in-history/
roosevelt-ushers-in-
japanese-american-internment
National Archives of Australia. *"Wartime internment camps in Australia."*
http://naa.gov.au/collection/snapshots/internment-camps/index.aspx
Time. *"Growing Up Patton."* Accessed March 26, 2012. http://nation.
time.com/2012/03/26/growing-up-patton/

The Patton Society. *"The Famous Patton Speech."* http://www.pattonhq. com/speech.html

Fox News. *"Marines delay female fitness plan after half fail pull-up test."* Accessed January 2, 2014. http://www.foxnews.com/politics/2014/01/02/ marines-delay-female-fitness-plan-after-half-fail-pullup-test/

The New York Times. *"Obama Ends 'Don't Ask, Don't Tell' Policy."* Accessed July 22, 2011. http://www.nytimes.com/2011/07/23/us/23military.html

USA TODAY. *"Army eases ban on transgender soldiers."* Accessed March 7, 2015. http://www.usatoday.com/story/news/nation/2015/03/06/ transgender-troops-chelsea-manning/24512731/

The New York Times. *"Pentagon Plans to Shrink Army to Pre-World War II Level."* Accessed February 23, 2014. http://www.nytimes. com/2014/02/24/us/politics/pentagon-plans-to-shrink-army-to-pre-world-war-ii-level.html?_r=0

The Inquisitr News. *"U.S. Military Training Course Calls the Bible, Constitution Sexist."* Accessed April 17, 2015. http://www.inquisitr.com/2020159/ u-s-military-training-course-calls-the-bible-constitution-sexist/

Judicial Watch. *"New Army Manual Orders Soldiers Not To Criticize Taliban."* Accessed December 11, 2012. http://www.judicialwatch.org/blog/2012/12/ new-army-manual-orders-soldiers-not-to-criticize-taliban/#respond

The Washington Times. *"Pentagon training course says modern sexism rooted in Bible, Constitution."* Accessed April 14, 2015. http://www. washingtontimes.com/news/2015/apr/14/pentagon-training-course-says-modern-sexism-rooted/

ABC News. *"Grownups Pay Big Bucks to Attend NYC 'Adult Preschool.'"* Accessed March 17, 2015. http://abcnews.go.com/Lifestyle/ grownups-pay-big-bucks-attend-nyc-adult-preschool/story?id= 29701836

New York Daily News. *"Eva Mendes says sweatpants comment was a 'bad joke' as boyfriend Ryan Gosling defends her via Twitter."* Accessed March 20, 2015. http://www.nydailynews.com/entertainment/ gossip/eva-mendes-sweatpants-comment-bad-joke-article-1.2156735

Ronald Reagan Presidential Library & Museum. *"A Time For Choosing (The Speech—October 27, 1964)."* http://www.reagan.utexas.edu/archives/reference/timechoosing.html

Institute For Strategic Leadership. *"Leadership Quotes."* http://www. leadership.ac.nz/resources/quotes/

The Sydney Morning Herald. *" 'I suspect Phelps': Chinese official hits back Ye Shiwen speculation."* Accessed July 31, 2012. http://www.smh. com.au/olympics/news-london-2012/i-suspect-phelps-chinese-official-hits-back-over-ye-shiwen-speculation-20120731-23c6d.html

Politico. *"Giuliani: Obama doesn't love America."* Accessed February 18, 2015. (http://www.politico.com/story/2015/02/rudy-giuliani-president-obama-doesnt-love-america-115309.html

Chapter 6: DEFILING OF CITIZENSHIP AND HUMANITY

D'Souza, Dinesh. *Ronald Reagan: How an Ordinary Man Became an Extraordinary Leader.* New York: Touchstone, 1997.

TheodoreRoosevelt.com. *"Theodore Roosevelt Quotes."* http://theodore-roosevelt.com/theodore-roosevelt-quotes/

WhiteHouseMuseum.org. *"Theodore Roosevelt Renovation: 1902."* http://www.whitehousemuseum.org/special/renovation-1902.htm

New York Post. *"A complete list of every president's favorite drink."* Accessed October 14, 2014. http://nypost.com/2014/10/18/what-every-president-drank/

Tyson Talk. *"Quotes by Cus D'Amato."* http://www.tysontalk.com/Media/tysonian_quotes_idea/CusQuotes.html

Los Angeles Times. *"Gov. Brown doesn't want California to use this word for immigrants."* Accessed August 10, 2015. http://www.latimes.com/local/political/la-me-pc-gov-jerry-brown-signs-bills-to-help-immigrants-20150810-story.html

Church of the Good Shepherd. *"More Serious Than a Heart Attack."* August 18, 2014. http://goodshepherdbermudarun.org/more-serious-than-a-heart-attack

Chapter 7: PLASTIC PEOPLE

Penguin Books Australia. *"Lady Windermere's Fan."* http://www.penguin.com.au/products/9780141197937/lady-windermere-s-fan

Youtube.com. *"Nick Adams—Fox News—The War on Men"* (video). Accessed February 4, 2014. https://www.youtube.com/watch?v=8YG7KTMyOnw

Daily Mail. *"Richard Littlejohn: Too white. Too male. And too damned British. No wonder the Beeb wants shot of Clarkson."* Last updated March 12, 2015. http://www.dailymail.co.uk/debate/article-2990777/RICHARD-LITTLEJOHN-white-male-damned-British-No-wonder-Beeb-wants-shot-Clarkson.html

ABC News. *"What separates a death in Iraq from one in Boston."* Accessed April 17, 2013. http://www.abc.net.au/news/2013-04-18/green-what-separates-a-death-in-iraq-from-one-in-boston/4635252 (

The Washington Post. *"President Obama endorses mandatory voting."* Accessed March 19, 2015. http://www.washingtonpost.com/news/volokh-conspiracy/wp/2015/03/19/president-obama-endorses-mandatory-voting/

Stanfords. *"Stephen Fry in America—The Introduction."* Accessed September 24, 2008. http://www.stanfords.co.uk/blog/stephen-fry-in-america-the-introduction/

Live Leak. *"Charlton Heston: Political Correctness And Common Sense"* (video). Accessed January 28, 2013. http://www.liveleak.com/view?i=ba9_1359417987&comments=1

CNN. *"Charlton Heston Speech Highlights Second Day of NRA Convention."* Accessed May 20, 2000. http://edition.cnn.com/TRANSCRIPTS/0005/20/cst.12.html

The Verge. *"Mozilla CEO resigns amind controversy over donation to anti-gay proposition."* Accessed April 3, 2014. http://www.theverge.com/2014/4/3/5578984/mozilla-ceo-resigns-amid-controversy-over-donation-to-anti-gay

National Review. *"Exclusive: Rice Withdraws from Rutgers Commencement."* Accessed May 3, 2014. http://www.nationalreview.com/corner/377165/exclusive-rice-withdraws-rutgers-commencement-nro-staff

Associated Press. *"Businesses, performers boycott Indiana because of new law."* Accessed April 2, 2015. http://www.washingtontimes.com/news/2015/apr/2/businesses-performers-boycott-indiana-because-of-n/

UShistory.org. *"53a. McCarthyism."* http://www.ushistory.org/us/53a.asp

Chapter 8: CONTROL, ALTER, DELETE

NYU Journalism. *"Lecture: Brian Williams."* http://journalism.nyu.edu/publishing/archives/bullpen/brian_williams/lecture_brian_w/

Anadolu Agency. *"Charlie Hebdo: Thousands tweet hashtag to back Muslims."* Accessed August 1, 2015. http://www.aa.com.tr/en/world/447242--charlie-hebdo-thousands-tweet-hashtag-to-back-muslims

National Review. *"Islamophobia is a Myth."* Accessed January 9, 2015. http://www.nationalreview.com/article/411371/islamophobia-myth-brendan-oneill

The Telegraph. *"Stop your whingeing: why the Left are such bad losers."* Accessed May 12, 2015. http://www.telegraph.co.uk/news/politics/labour/11597436/Stop-your-whinging-why-the-Left-are-such-bad-losers.html

The Dish. *"The Left's Intensifying War on Liberalism."* Accessed January 27, 2015. http://dish.andrewsullivan.com/2015/01/27/the-lefts-intensifying-war-on-liberalism/

Nick Adams. *"Wristband society"* —my definition, a reference to the emergence of a trend in the last decade where people wear charity wristbands of different colors and designs for every cause imaginable.

The Guardian. *"President Obama gives the Queen an iPod."* Accessed April 2, 2009. http://www.theguardian.com/music/2009/apr/02/barack-obama-presents-queen-ipod

Oxford Modern Australian Dictionary. "Larrikin" —an Australian slang term meaning "a mischievous young person, an uncultivated, rowdy but good hearted person", or "a person who acts with apparent disregard for social or political conventions."

The Churchill Centre. *"Famous Quotations and Stories."* http://www.winstonchurchill.org/resources/quotations/famous-quotations-and-stories

Chapter 9: PANSY POLITICIANS

The Sydney Morning Herald. *"Mild Mike Baird the right man for the moment."* Accessed March 29, 2015. http://www.smh.com.au/comment/mild-mike-baird-the-right-man-for-the-moment-20150328-1m9jtk.html

The National Security Archive. *"A Study of Lunar Research Flights, Volume I."* http://oai.dtic.mil/oai/oai?verb=getRecord&metadataPrefix=html&identifier=AD0425380

CNN. *"U.S. had plans to nuke the moon."* Accessed November 28, 2012. http://security.blogs.cnn.com/2012/11/28/u-s-had-plans-to-nuke-the-moon/

Daily Mail. *"Revealed: How the U.S. planned to blow up the MOON with a nuclear bomb to win Cold War bragging rights over Soviet Union."* Accessed November 25, 2012. http://www.dailymail.co.uk/news/article-2238242/Cold-War-era-U-S-plan-bomb-moon-nuclear-bomb-revealed.html

Washington Examiner. *"President Obama's biggest British gaffes."* Accessed July 27, 2012. http://www.washingtonexaminer.com/president-obamas-biggest-british-gaffes/article/2503321

Macmillan Dictionary. *"Churchillian."* http://www.macmillandictionary.com/dictionary/british/churchillian

The White House. *"Remarks by the President at the Summit on Countering Violent Extremism."* Accessed February 19, 2015. https://www.whitehouse.gov/the-press-office/2015/02/19/remarks-president-summit-countering-violent-extremism-february-19-2015

The Daily Beast. *"Nidal Hasan's Murders Termed 'Workplace Violence' by U.S."* Accessed August 6, 2013. http://www.thedailybeast.com/articles/2013/08/06/nidal-hasan-s-murders-termed-workplace-violence-by-u-s.html

The Washington Times. *"Obama outrages by calling 4 Jewish victims of Paris terror 'a bunch of folks' shot randomly."* Accessed February 10, 2015. http://www.washingtontimes.com/news/2015/feb/10/obama-outrages-by-calling-4-jewish-victims-of-pari/

USA TODAY. *"Obama's anti-American crusade comments: Column."* Accessed February 10, 2015. http://www.usatoday.com/story/opinion/2015/02/10/president-obama-prayer-breakfast-crusades-comment-column/23148065/

The White House. *"News Conference by President Obama."* Accessed April 4, 2009. https://www.whitehouse.gov/the-press-office/news-conference-president-obama-4042009

The Washington Times. *"Obama criticizes 'less-than-loving' Christians."* Accessed April 7, 2015. http://www.washingtontimes.com/news/2015/apr/7/obama-criticizes-less-than-loving-christians-at-ea/?page=all

Prager, Dennis. *Still The Best Hope: Why the World Needs American Values to Triumph.* New York, HarperCollins, 2012: 77.

Prager, Dennis. *Still The Best Hope: Why the World Needs American Values to Triumph.* New York, HarperCollins, 2012: 177.

Prager, Dennis. *Still The Best Hope: Why the World Needs American Values to Triumph.* New York, HarperCollins, 2012: 333.

Prager, Dennis. *Still The Best Hope: Why the World Needs American Values to Triumph.* New York, HarperCollins, 2012: 337.

The Sydney Morning Herald. *"Prime Minister Tony Abbott's full national security statement."* Accessed February 23, 2015. http://www.smh.com.au/federal-politics/political-news/prime-minister-tony-abbotts-full-national-security-statement-20150223-13m2xu.html

Churchillcentral.com. "Quotes." https://www.churchillcentral.com/quotes

The Churchill Centre. *"Famous Quotations and Stories."* http://www.winstonchurchill.org/resources/quotations/famous-quotations-and-stories

Chapter 10: THE AMERICAN DREAM V
THE PC NIGHTMARE

Politico. *"Susana Martinez RNC speech."* Accessed August 29, 2012. http://www.politico.com/news/stories/0812/80421.html#ixzz3ZGUqOPap

Vatican Publishing House. *"ADDRESS OF POPE FRANCIS TO THE EUROPEAN PARLIAMENT."* Accessed November 25, 2014. http://w2.vatican.va/content/francesco/en/speeches/2014/november/documents/papa-francesco_20141125_strasburgo-parlamento-europeo.html

The Denver Post. *"Anti-Americans among us."* Accessed March 4, 2007. http://www.denverpost.com/opinion/ci_5335348

Prager, Dennis. *Still The Best Hope: Why the World Needs American Values to Triumph.* New York, HarperCollins, 2012: 176.

The Wall Street Journal. *"Risk-Averse Culture Infects U.S. Workers, Entrepreneurs."* http://www.wsj.com/articles/SB10001424127887324031404578481162903760052

Chapter 11: ENID BLYTON

PBS. *"Primary Resources: The Man With The Muck Rake, 1906."* http://www.pbs.org/wgbh/americanexperience/features/primary-resources/tr-muckrake/

The Guardian. *"The enduring appeal of Enid Blyton."* Accessed March 23, 2012. http://www.theguardian.com/lifeandstyle/2012/mar/24/enid-blyton-famous-five-70-anniversary

New Statesman. *"Entrepreneurship in Gibraltar: a pioneering spirit."* Accessed January 27, 2015http://www.newstatesman.com/node/144675

Gov.uk. *"The Stephen Lawrence Inquiry."* Accessed February 1999. https://www.gov.uk/government/uploads/system/uploads/attachment_data/file/277111/4262.pdf

BBC. *"Race: The Macpherson report."* Accessed May 7, 2001. http://news.bbc.co.uk/news/vote2001/hi/english/main_issues/sections/facts/newsid_1190000/1190971.stm

The Telegraph. *"BBC banned Enid Blyton for 30 years."* Accessed November 15, 2009. http://www.telegraph.co.uk/culture/books/booknews/6573855/BBC-banned-Enid-Blyton-for-30-years.html

Sp!ked. *"This bullying of Blyton is jolly trying."* Accessed August 17, 2010. http://www.spiked-online.com/newsite/article/9431#.VUxEavmqpBc

Spark Notes. *"Bessie's beginnings."* http://www.sparknotes.com/biography/bessiesmith/section1.rhtml

Daily Mail. *"Row faster, George! The PC meddlers are chasing us!"* Accessed June 26, 2006. http://www.dailymail.co.uk/news/article-392400/Row-faster-George-The-PC-meddlers-chasing-us.html

The Telegraph. *"Town torn over celebrations of Enid Blyton's 'racist' work."* Accessed February 14, 2013. http://www.telegraph.co.uk/culture/books/booknews/9870065/Town-torn-over-celebrations-of-Enid-Blytons-racist-work.html

Youtube.com. *"Enid Blyton's children's books condemned by some as racist"* (video). April 9, 2013. Accessed https://www.youtube.com/watch?v=Z49Rd476mro

Hot Culture. *"Controversy over Blyton Exhibit."* Accessed March 17, 2015. https://hotculturekent.wordpress.com/2015/03/17/controversy-over-blyton-exhibit/

Daily Mail. *"Hate mail for 'racist' Enid Blyton shop owner who started to stock golliwogs."* Accessed October 30, 2008. http://www.dailymail.co.uk/news/article-1081815/Hate-mail-racist-Enid-Blyton-shop-owner-started-stock-golliwogs.html

Daily Mail. "Row faster, George! The PC meddlers are chasing us!" Accessed June 26, 2006. http://www.dailymail.co.uk/news/article-392400/Row-faster-George-The-PC-meddlers-chasing-us.html

Elsewhere. *"BIGGLES shot down: But not by the Boche this time."* Accessed July 23, 2010. http://www.elsewhere.co.nz/writingelsewhere/2020/biggles-shot-down-but-not-by-the-boche-this-time/

Chapter 12: PERSONAL STORIES

The Christian Science Monitor. *"Ben Carson cancels at Johns Hopkins: the perils of commencement speakers."* http://www.csmonitor.com/USA/Politics/2013/0411/Ben-Carson-cancels-at-Johns-Hopkins-the-perils-of-commencement-speakers-video

Imdb.com. *"Top Gun quotes."* http://www.imdb.com/title/tt0092099/quotes

The University of Sydney Library. *Mein Kampf* titles. http://opac.library.usyd.edu.au/search/t?SEARCH=mein+kampf&sortdropdown=-&searchscope=4

The University of Sydney Library. Mao Tse-tung quotes. http://opac.library.usyd.edu.au/search~S4/?searchtype=t&searcharg=quotations+from+chairman+mao&searchscope=4&sortdropdown=-&SORT=D&extended=0&SUBMIT=Search&searchlimits=&searchorigarg=tthe+communist+manifesto

The University of Sydney Library. *The Communist Manifesto.* http://opac.library.usyd.edu.au/search~S4/?searchtype=t&searcharg=the+communist+manifesto&searchscope=4&sortdropdown=-&SORT=D&extended=0&SUBMIT=Search&searchlimits=&searchorigarg=tmein+kampf

Feulner, Edwin and Tracy, Brian. *The American Spirit: Celebrating the Virtues and Values that Make Us Great.* Nashville: Thomas Nelson, 2012: 26.

Chapter 13: GETTING SCHOOLED

Jewish World Review. *"Summer de-programming."* Accessed June 23, 2004. http://www.jewishworldreview.com/cols/sowell062304.asp

BDCwire. *"A third-grader who was disappointed by Disneyland's stereotyping decided to speak out."* http://www.bdcwire.com/a-third-grader-who-was-disappointed-by-disneylands-stereotyping-decided-to-speak-out/

Brain Pickings. *"Two Nine-Year-Olds' Magnificent Open Letter to Disney About Racial and Gender Stereotypes."* http://www.brainpickings.org/2015/08/03/dexter-disney/

Inquisitr. *"Jerry Seinfeld: Political Correctness Ruining Comedy."* Accessed June 5, 2015. http://www.inquisitr.com/2148675/jerry-seinfeld-political-correctness-ruining-comedy/

DennisPrager.com. *"Florida Atlantic University: Another Left-Wing Seminary."* Accessed March 26, 2013. http://www.dennisprager.com/florida-atlantic-university-another-left-wing-seminary/

Time. *"Kareem Abdul-Jabbar: How to Tell if You're a Racist Like Donald Sterling."* Accessed May 5, 2014. http://time.com/87024/kareem-abdul-jabbar-why-donald-sterling-does-not-think-he-is-racist/

Huffington Post. *"Howard Zinn Dead, Author of 'People's History Of The United States' Died at 87."* http://www.huffingtonpost.com/2010/01/27/howard-zinn-dead-author-o_n_439350.html Youtube

.com. *"Clip_Good Will Hunting 1997 zinn"* (video). Accessed January 10, 2010. https://www.youtube.com/watch?v=_2cSB70ZjuM

Youtube.com. *"The Sopranos 'Christopher Columbus-Milo-shevic"* (video). Accessed August 18, 2010. www.youtube.com/watch?v=HOn8DXb0inM

New Republic. *"Howard Zinn's influential mutilations of American history."* Accessed March 19, 2013. http://www.newrepublic.com/article/112574/howard-zinns-influential-mutilations-american-history

Campus Reform. *"Bias-Free Language Guide claims the word 'American' is 'problematic.' "* http://www.campusreform.org/?ID=6697

Chapter 14: EXAMPLES EVERYWHERE

Los Angeles Times. *"Remember political correctness? It's back, frothing at the mouth and at hurricane force."* Accessed February 2, 2015. http://www.latimes.com/opinion/op-ed/la-oe-daum-pc-political-correctness-chait-20150203-column.html

Churchill, Winston S. *The River War Vol. II.* London: Longmans, Green & Co., 1899:248-250.

Daily Mail. *"Arrested for quoting Winston Churchill: European election candidate accused of religious and racial harassment after he repeats wartime prime minister's words on Islam during campaign speech."* Accessed April 28, 2014. http://www.dailymail.co.uk/news/article-2614834/Arrested-quoting-Winston-Churchill-European-election-candidate-accused-religious-racial-harassment-repeats-wartime-prime-ministers-words-Islam-campaign-speech.html

BBC. *"Euro candidate Paul Weston arrested over Islam remarks."* Accessed April 28, 2014. http://www.bbc.com/news/uk-england-hampshire-27186573

The Wall Street Journal. *"In defense of Pamela Geller."* Accessed May 11, 2015. http://www.wsj.com/articles/in-defense-of-pamela-geller-1431386626 Salon. Bill Maher: *"Islam's 'the only religion that acts like the mafia, that will f**king kill you if you say the wrong thing.' "* Accessed October 4, 2014. http://www.salon.com/2014/10/04/bill_maher_islams_the_only_religion_that_acts_like_the_mafia_that_will_fking_kill_you_if_you_say_the_wrong_thing/

Founders Online. *"American Commissioners to John Jay, 28 March 1976."* http://founders.archives.gov/documents/Jefferson/01-09-02-0315

The Daily Caller. *"Numbers Show Most Baltimore Cops Are Minorities."* Accessed May 14, 2015. http://dailycaller.com/2015/05/14/most-baltimore-cops-are-minorities/

Bureau of Justice Statistics. *"Homicide Trends in the United States , 1980-2008."* Accessed November 2011. http://www.bjs.gov/content/pub/pdf/htus8008.pdf

FBI. *"Crime in the United States 2013."* https://www.fbi.gov/
about-us/cjis/ucr/crime-in-the-u.s/2013/crime-in-the-u.s.-2013/
offenses-known-to-law-enforcement/expanded-homicide/ex-
panded_homicide_data_table_6_murder_race_and_sex_of_vicitm_by_
race_and_sex_of_offender_2013.xls

The Baltimore Sun. *"Baltimore police union: Cops more afraid of
going to jail than getting shot."* Accessed May 28, 2015. http://www.
baltimoresun.com/news/maryland/crime/blog/bs-md-ci-fop-statement-
20150528-story.html,

CBS Baltimore. *"Baltimore Gets Bloodier As Arrests Drop Post-
Freddie Gray."* Accessed May 28, 2015. http://baltimore.cbslocal.
com/2015/05/28/baltimore-residents-fearful-amid-rash-of-homicides/

Huffington Post. *"Murders Rise As Arrests Plunge In Baltimore."* Accessed May 28, 2015. http://www.huffingtonpost.com/2015/05/28/
baltimore-murders_n_7463918.html

CNN. *"O'Malley apologizes for saying 'all lives matter' at liberal conference."* Accessed July 19, 2015. http://edition.cnn.com/2015/07/18/
politics/martin-omalley-all-lives-matter/

The White House. *"Remarks by the First Lady at Tuskegee University Commencement Address."* Accessed May 9, 2015.
https://www.whitehouse.gov/the-press-office/2015/05/09/
remarks-first-lady-tuskegee-university-commencement-address

Bloomberg. "Obama Says Hedge Fund Mangers Are 'Society's Lottery Winners.' " Accessed May 12, 2015. http://
www.bloomberg.com/politics/articles/2015-05-12/
obama-sees-opening-for-both-parties-to-attack-poverty-in-u-s—

The Washington Post. *"U.S. Patent Office cancels Redskins trademark
registration, says name is disparaging."* Accessed June 18, 2014. http://
www.washingtonpost.com/local/us-patent-office-cancels-redskins-
trademark-registration-says-name-is-disparaging/2014/06/18/
e7737bb8-f6ee-11e3-8aa9-dad2ec039789_story.html

The Sacramento Bee. *"California lawmakers vote to urge Washington
Redskins name change."* Accessed August 18, 2014. http://www.sacbee.
com/news/politics-government/capitol-alert/article2607015.html

Chapter 15: HILLARY FEMINISM

New York Times. *"Robertson Letter Attacks Feminists."* Accessed August
26, 1992. http://www.nytimes.com/1992/08/26/us/robertson-letter-at-
tacks-feminists.html

The Washington Post. *"Feminists want us to define these ugly sexual
encounters as rape. Don't let them."* Accessed May 20, 2015. http://
www.washingtonpost.com/posteverything/wp/2015/05/20/feminists-
want-us-to-define-these-ugly-sexual-encounters-as-rape-dont-let-them/

Youtube.com. *"Prime Minister's Speech at the Women for Gillard*

Launch" (video). Accessed June 11, 2013. https://www.youtube.com/ watch?t=47&v=IUtOzlz-AZo

Youtube.com. "Gillard fires another shot in misogyny debate" (video). Accessed June 11, 2013. https://www.youtube.com/ watch?v=BS5Mw6KL_FA

News.com.au. *"Hillary Clinton condemns 'outrageous' sexism experienced by Julia Gillard in new book Hard Choices."* Accessed June 10, 2014. http://www.news.com.au/entertainment/ books-magazines/hillary-clinton-condemns-outrageous-sexism-experienced-by-julia-gillard-in-new-book-hard-choices/ story-fna50uae-1226949350709

Youtube.com. *"Gillard—Vote Hillary!—To End ~~Religious Genocide~~, Misogyny?"* (video). https://www.youtube.com/watch?v=5pRu7A8Ycus

Herald Sun. *"Gillard's secret women's strategy."* Accessed September 28, 2013. http://blogs.news.com.au/heraldsun/andrewbolt/index.php/ heraldsun/comments/gillards_secret_womens_strategy/

Chapter 16: The Terms of Our Surrender

BrainyQuote. *"Voltaire Quotes."* http://www.brainyquote.com/quotes/ quotes/v/voltaire109645.html

Youtube.com. *"West Point Blank with Allen West: Pyrrhic Victory or Thermopylae? Fighting to Defend Obamacare."* (video). Accessed September 25, 2013. https://www.youtube.com/watch?v=rf6rcP-BOzY

Watchdog Wire. *"Allen West: America Needs Men With The Courage To Take A Stand."* Accessed September 27, 2013. http://watchdogwire.com/florida/2013/09/27/ allen-west-america-needs-men-with-the-courage-to-take-a-stand/

The Hill. *"Confederate flag sales spike as Amazon announces ban."* Accessed June 23, 2015. http://thehill.com/blogs/blog-briefing-room/ news/245862-amazon-becomes-latest-retailer-to-ban-confederate-flag

The Hill. *"Ebay to ban Confederate flag listings."* Accessed June 23, 2015. http://thehill.com/policy/ technology/245849-ebay-to-ban-confederate-flag-listings

The Hill. *"Walmart, Sears to stop selling Confederate flag merchandise."* Accessed June 23, 2015. http://thehill.com/blogs/blog-briefing-room/ news/245804-walmart-sears-to-stop-selling-confederate-flag

TechCrunch. *"Apple Bans Games And Apps Featuring The Confederte Flag [Update: Some Games Being Restored]."* Accessed June 25, 2015. http://techcrunch.com/2015/06/25/apple-bans-games-and-apps-featuring-the-confederate-flag/#.94hqwi:LZjg

CBS News. *"Warner Bros. to stop 'Dukes of Hazzard' General Lee toys with Confederate flag."* Accessed June 24, 2015. http://www.cbsnews.com/news/warner-bros-to-stop-dukes-of-hazzard-general-lee-toys-with-confederate-flag/

Daily Mail. *"Should Gone with the Wind be banned? Anger at confederate symbols turns on classic movie and book."* Accessed June 26, 2015. http://www.dailymail.co.uk/news/article-3140256/Should-Gone-Wind-banned-Anger-confederate-symbols-turns-classic-movie-writer-tweeting-original-book-line-line-gets-shunned.html

Fox 4 KDFW. *"Civil rights group wants Birdville's Richland HS to drop Rebel mascot name."* Accessed July 10, 2015. http://www.fox4news.com/story/29521331/fort-worth-sclc-president-seeks-to-eliminate-confederate-traditions-from-public-schools

The Washington Post. *"Unraveling the threads of hatred, sewn into a Confederate icon."* Accessed June 20, 2015. https://www.washingtonpost.com/opinions/unraveling-the-threads-of-hatred-sewn-into-a-confederate-icon/2015/06/20/aa6a73f4-1775-11e5-9518-f9e0a8959f32_story.html

WFAA 8 ABC. *" 'Shame' written across Robert E. Lee statue in Dallas."* Accessed July 10, 2015. http://www.wfaa.com/story/news/local/dallas-county/2015/07/10/shame-vandal-vandalism-robert-e-lee-dallas-lee-park/29966959/

Live 5 News. *"John C. Calhoun statue vandalized in downtown Charleston."* Accessed June 23, 2015. http://www.live5news.com/story/29386563/john-c-calhoun-statue-vandalized-in-downtown-charleston

Huffington Post. *"CNN Host Asks If Jefferson Memorial Is Equal With Confederate Flag."* Accessed June 24, 2015. http://www.huffingtonpost.com/2015/06/24/conferderate-flag-jefferson_n_7656316.html

Fox News. *"Connecticut Dems strip Jefferson, Jackson names from fundraising dinner."* Accessed July 23, 2015. http://www.foxnews.com/politics/2015/07/23/connecticut-democrats-remove-jefferson-and-jackson-from-fundraising-dinner/

The Tennessean. *"Blockage sought of I-65 Nathan Bedford Forrest statue."* Accessed June 23, 2015. http://www.tennessean.com/story/insession/2015/06/22/blockage-sought- of- i-65-nathan-bedford-forrest-statue/29128551/

iCasualties.org. *"Operation Enduring Freeom: U.S. Wounded Totals."* http://icasualties.org/OEF/USCasualtiesByState.aspx

Mannkal Economic Education Foundation: *"Quotes."* http://www.mannkal.org/quotes.php

WND.com. *"What Confederate Battle Flag Truly Stands For."* Accessed June 25, 2015. http://www.wnd.com/2015/06/what-confederate-flag-truly-stands-for/#62Y5CygfMJxZd953.99

The New York Times. *"Robert C. Byrd, a Pillar of the Senate, Dies at 92."* Accessed June 28, 2010. http://www.nytimes.com/2010/06/29/us/politics/29byrd.html

NBC News. *"Landmark: Supreme Court Rules Same-Sex Marriage Legal Nationwide."* Accessed June 26, 2015. http://www.nbcnews.com/news/us-news/do-not-pub-same-sex-marraige-legal-nationwide-supreme-court-n375551

BBC News. *"Zimbabwe's 'iconic' lion Cecil killed by hunter."* Accessed July 27, 2015. http://www.bbc.com/news/world-africa-33674087

ABC News. *"Walmart Apologizes for Making ISIS Cake for Man Denied Confederate Flag Design."* Accessed June 29, 2015. http://abcnews.go.com/Business/walmart-apologizes-making-isis-cake-man-denied-confederate/story?id=32103721

Politico. *"Trump Schools the Republican Establishment."* Accessed July 28, 2015. http://www.politico.com/magazine/story/2015/07/trump-republican-establishment-120713.html#.VcMZM6aqpBc

Real Clear Politics. *"Lead Iran Deal Negotiator Responds To Ted Cruz: 'We All Understand We're In A Presidential Silly Season.' "* Accessed July 30, 2015. http://www.realclearpolitics.com/video/2015/07/30/lead_iran_deal_negotiator_responds_to_cruz_we_all_understand_were_in_a_presidential_silly_season.html

The Washington Post. http://www.washingtonpost.com/politics/huckabee-iran-nuclear-deal-will-march-israelis-to-the-door-of-the-oven/2015/07/26/bc963910-33bc-11e5-94ce-834ad8f5c50e_story.html

The New York Times. *" Moral Values' Carried Bush, Rove Says."* Accessed November 10, 2014. http://www.nytimes.com/2004/11/10/politics/campaign/10rove.html

NBC News. *"Landmark: Supreme Court Rules Same-Sex Marriage Legal Nationwide."* Accessed June 26, 2015.http://www.nbcnews.com/news/us-news/do-not-pub-same-sex-marraige-legal-nationwide-supreme-court-n375551 CNN. *"White House shines rainbow colors to hail same-sex marriage ruling."* Accessed June 30, 2015. http://edition.cnn.com/2015/06/26/politics/white-house-rainbow-marriage/

The Washington Post. *"More than 26 million people have changed their Facebook picture to a rainbow flag. Here's why that matters."* Accessed June 29, 2015. https://www.washingtonpost.com/news/the-intersect/wp/2015/06/29/more-than-26-million-people-have-changed-their-facebook-picture-to-a-rainbow-flag-heres-why-that-matters/

Newsweek. *"How Corporate America Propelled Same-Sex Marriage."* Accessed June 30, 2015. http://www.newsweek.com/2015/07/10/shift-corporate-america-social-issues-become-good-business-348458.html

The Sydney Morning Herald. *"Cecil the lion: Jimmy Kimmel breaks down on air as he condemns animal's killing."* Accessed July 30, 2015. http://www.smh.com.au/entertainment/tv-and-radio/cecil-the-lion-jimmy-kimmel-breaks-down-on-air-as-he-condemns-animals-killing-20150730-ginejd.html

Daily Mail. *"EXCLUSIVE: Dentist who killed Cecil the lion hires armed security and installs covert cameras after death threats and vandalism at the homes crammed with evidence of his hunting obsession."* Accessed August 5, 2015. http://www.dailymail.co.uk/news/article-3186081/Dentist-killed-Cecil-lion-hires-armed-security-installs-covert-cameras-death-threats-vandalism-homes-crammed-evidence-hunting-obsession.html

Time. *"Dentist Who Killed Cecil the Lion Writes Letter Apologizing to His Patients."* Accessed July 29, 2015. http://time.com/3977018/cecil-lion-walter-palmer-letter/

The Guardian. *" 'Lion killer': Walter Palmer's Florida vacation home vandalized."* Accessed August 5, 2015. http://www.theguardian.com/environment/2015/aug/05/walter-palmer-florida-home-vandalized-cecil-the-lion

The Washington Times. *"Empire State Building's $1M Cecil the lion display outrages 'Black Lives Matter' supporters."* Accessed August 4, 2015. http://www.washingtontimes.com/news/2015/aug/4/empire-state-buildings-1m-cecil-the-lion-display-o/

Reuters. *"U.N. tackles illicit wildlife poaching amid Cecil the lion uproar."* Accessed July 30 2015. http://www.reuters.com/article/2015/07/30/us-un-wildlife-poaching-idUSKCN0Q429X20150730

CNN. *"White House petition to extradite lion-killing dentist Walter Palmer reaches threshold for response."* Accessed July 31, 2015. http://edition.cnn.com/2015/07/30/politics/white-house-cecil-the-lion-petition/

Daily Mail. *"Planned Parenthood's top doctor caught on undercover video discussing the sale of aborted fetus organs to potential buyers—including how much each body part is worth."* Last updated July 15, 2015. http://www.dailymail.co.uk/news/article-3161040/Planned-Parenthood-s-doctor-caught-undercover-video-discussing-sale-aborted-fetus-organs-potential-buyers-including-body-worth.html

Bloomberg. *"Target Removes Gender Labels From Kids Sections After Complaints."* Accessed august 7, 2015. http://www.bloomberg.com/news/articles/2015-08-07/target-removes-gender-labels-from-kids-sections-after-complaints

Real Clear Politics. *"Lead Iran Deal Negotiator Responds To Ted Cruz: "We All Understand We're In A Presidential Silly Season."* Accessed July 30, 2015. http://www.realclearpolitics.com/video/2015/07/30/lead_iran_deal_negotiator_responds_to_cruz_we_all_understand_were_in_a_presidential_silly_season.html

The Washington Post. http://www.washingtonpost.com/politics/huckabee-iran-nuclear-deal-will-march-israelis-to-the-door-of-the-oven/2015/07/26/bc963910-33bc-11e5-94ce-834ad8f5c50e_story.html

The New York Times. *"Obama Criticizes Huckabee, Trump, Cruz and Other Republicans."* Accessed July 27, 2015. http://www

.nytimes.com/2015/07/28/us/politics/obama-criticizes-hucka-
bee-trump-cruz-and-other-republicans.html?_r=0
Texas A&M University. *"William Barret Travis' Letter from the Alamo."*
http://www.tamu.edu/faculty/ccbn/dewitt/adp/history/bios/travis/trav-
text.html#breakdown

Chapter 17: RETAKING AMERICA

The Churchill Centre. *"The Gift of a Common Tongue."* Accessed
September 6, 1943. http://www.winstonchurchill.org/resources/
speeches/1941-1945-war-leader/the-price-of-greatness-is-responsi-
bility Youtube.com. "Thermopylae—300—Leonidas Vrs. Xerxes"
(video). Accessed March 20, 2010. https://www.youtube.com/
watch?v=zvILGIIVsMU
Youtube.com. "WEST POINT BLANK w/ ALLEN WEST: Pyrrhic Victory
or Thermopylae? Fighting to Defund Obamacare" (video). Accessed
September 25, 2013. https://www.youtube.com/watch?v=rf6rcP-BOzY
John F. Kennedy Presidential Library and Museum. "President Kennedy's Inaugural Address, January 20, 1961." http://www.jfklibrary.
org/Research/Research-Aids/Ready-Reference/JFK-Quotations/Inaugu-
ral-Address.aspx
Drew's Script-O-Rama. *"Rocky 3 Script—Dialogue Transcript."* http://
www.script-o-rama.com/movie_scripts/r/rocky-3-script-transcript-iii.
html
Live Leak. *"Charlton Heston—Political Correctness And Common
Sense"* (video). Accessed January 28, 2013. http://www.liveleak.com/
view?i=ba9_1359417987&comments=1

POSTSCRIPT

Churchill, Winston S. *Churchill: The Power of Words.* Edited by Martin
Gilbert. Boston: Da Capo Press, 2012.
Freedom to Marry. *"The Freedom to Marry Internationally."* http://www.
freedomtomarry.org/landscape/entry/c/international
Pew Research Center. *"Changing Attitudes on Gay Marriage."* Accessed July 29, 2015. http://www.pewforum.org/2014/09/24/
graphics-slideshow-changing-attitudes-on-gay-marriage/
The Daily Caller. *"Ann Ccoulter: Libertarian college students 'like
liberals,' consumed by 'groupthink.' "* Accessed March 19, 2013.
http://dailycaller.com/2013/03/19/ann-coulter-libertarian-college-stu-
dents-like-liberals-consumed-by-groupthink/

ABOUT THE AUTHOR

Nick Adams is the Founder and Executive Director of FLAG, *The Foundation for Liberty and American Greatness* (www.flagusa.org). He is an internationally renowned speaker, lecturer, author and commentator. He is best known for his work in the field of American exceptionalism and is credited with fueling a resurgence in the idea worldwide. He is a Fellow of Colorado Christian University. He has spoken throughout America, Germany, South Korea, and the United Kingdom. He contributes to numerous media organizations and has received several state awards. Adams holds degrees in Media and Communications, Government and International Relations, Germanic Studies, and Education from the University of Sydney. In 2005, at the age of twenty one, he was elected as the youngest deputy mayor in Australian history, a record he still holds to this day.